The Economics of Power

Habent sua fata libelli

Volume XXIV
of
Sixteenth Century Essays & Studies
Charles G. Nauert, Jr., General Editor

ISBN 0-940474-25-5

Composed by NMSU typographer Gwen Blotevogel,
Kirksville, Missouri
Cover design by Teresa Wheeler, NMSU Designer
Printed by Edwards Brothers, Ann Arbor, Michigan
Text is set in New Century 10/12

The Economics of Power: The Private Finances of the House of Foix-Navarre-Albret during the Religious Wars

S. Amanda Eurich
Volume XXIV
Sixteenth Century Essays & Studies

This book has been brought to publication with the
generous support of
Northeast Missouri State University

Library of Congress Cataloging-in Publication Data

Eurich, S. Amanda, 1956–

The Economics of Power : The private finances of the house of Foix-Navarre-Albret during the religious wars / S. Amanda Eurich.
    p.   cm. — (Sixteenth century essays & studies ; v. 24)
Includes bibliographical references and index.
ISBN 0-940474-25-5 (alk. paper)
    1. Finance, Public—France—History—16th century. 2. Income—France—History—16th century. 3. Revenue—France—History—16th century. 4. Albret family.   I.Title.   II. Series.
HJ1079.E95 1993
339.2'2' 094409031—dc20   93–6176
                                                                                        CIP

    Copyright© 1994 by Sixteenth Century Journal Publishers, Inc., Kirksville, Missouri. All rights reserved. No part of this work may be reproduced or transmitted in any format by any means, electronic or mechanical, including photocopying and recording, or by any information storage or retrieval system, without permission in writing from the publisher. Printed in the United States of America.
    The paper used in this publication meets the minimum requirements of the American Standard for Permanence of Paper for Printed Library Materials Z39.48, 1984.

Contents

List of Tables vii

Genealogy of the House of Foix-Navarre-Albret ix

Abbreviations x

Acknowledgments xi

Perspectives xiii

Landed Revenues 1
    I.   Seigneurial Administration and Innovation 5
    II.   Leasing Policies 8
    III. The Wars of Religion, Leasing Policies and Rebates 19
    IV. Rebates 29
    V.   Rents in Kind and Sales of Produce 35
    VI. Conclusion 43

The Fruits of Office and the Bounty of Kings 44
    I.   In Pursuit of Royalty 46
    II.   Jeanne d'Albret and Antoine de Bourbon 60
    III. Henri de Navarre 62
    IV. Catherine de Bourbon 69
    V.   Conclusion 76

The Economy of Patronage 78
    I.   Household Structure 81
    II.   The Politics of Numbers 85
    III. The Wars of Religion 89
    IV. The Cost of War Patronage 99
    V.   The Lure of Office 101
    VI. Conclusion 123

Dietary Conceits and Purveyorship Contracts 124
  I.   The Albrets at Table 127
  II. The Purveyorship System... 144
  III. The Evolution of Purveyorship Contracts
       during the Religious Wars.. 150
  IV. Wine and other Bacchanalian Pleasures.......................... 157
  V.   Conclusion 162

The Burden of Status 164
  I.   Adorning the Body 166
  II. Palaces and Gardens.. 178
  III. The Use of Space and Furnishing 187
  IV. Cultural Values 189
  V.   Conclusion 193

Financing the Faith.. 194
  I.   Military Finance... 195
  II. A Reluctant Beginning.. 196
  III. The St. Bartholomew's Day Massacre
       and Its Aftermath 203
  IV. Conclusion 217

Conclusion... 219

Glossary of Measurements... 223

Bibliography 225

Index 239

Tables

1.1	Rent Receipts from the Duchy of Périgord	12
1.2	Rental Receipts from Fézenzaguet, 1562-1566	14
1.3	Annual Landed Revenues for Armagnac, 1555–1579	21
1.4	Percentage Changes in Armagnac Revenues, 1555–1579	22
1.5	Impact of Wars of Religion on Armagnac Land Revenues	24
1.6	Rental Receipts from Fézenzaguet, 1569-1595	26
1.7	Rent Rebates in the County of Armagnac	34
1.8	Revenues from Wheat in the Duchy of Albret	36
1.9	Revenue from Woodlands in the County of Armagnac	40
2.1	Sources of Income, Henri d'Albret, 1546	58
2.2	Sources of Income, Henri de Navarre, 1582	68
2.3	Catherine De Bourbon's Treasury Receipts 1579–1598	72
3.1	Annual Household Expenses, Henri d'Albret, 1518	104
3.2	Salaries in the Households of Henri d'Albret and Henri de Navarre 1518–1587	108
3.3	Jeanne d'Albret's and Catherine de Bourbon's Households 1559–1598	110

3.4 Wages, Gifts, and Pensions,
     Catherine De Bourbon's Household 113

3.5 Wages Adjusted to Include Gifts and Pensions 122

4.1 *Marchés de Pourvoirie* in Meat and
     Fish 1538–1595 130

4.2 Patterns of Bread Consumption 135

4.3 Consumption Patterns in the Household
     of Foix-Navarre-Albret: Feasting and Normal Meals 137

4.4 Expenditures on Food and Drink—
     Servant vs. Seigneurial Repasts 141

4.5a Summer Food Costs in the Ordinary
     Accounts: 1571–1589 142

4.5b Winter Food Costs in the Ordinary
     Accounts: 1571–1589 142

4.6 Accounts of Treasurers of the Royal Household 143

4.7 *Marchés de Pourvoirie* House of
     Foix-Navarre-Albret: 1571–1589 158

4.8 Wines Furnished to the King of Navarre, 1582 160

5   Extraordinary Expenditures in the
     Treasurer's Accounts 169

6   Military Expenses Drawn from
     Navarre's Personal Treasury 1579-1587 209

Genealogy

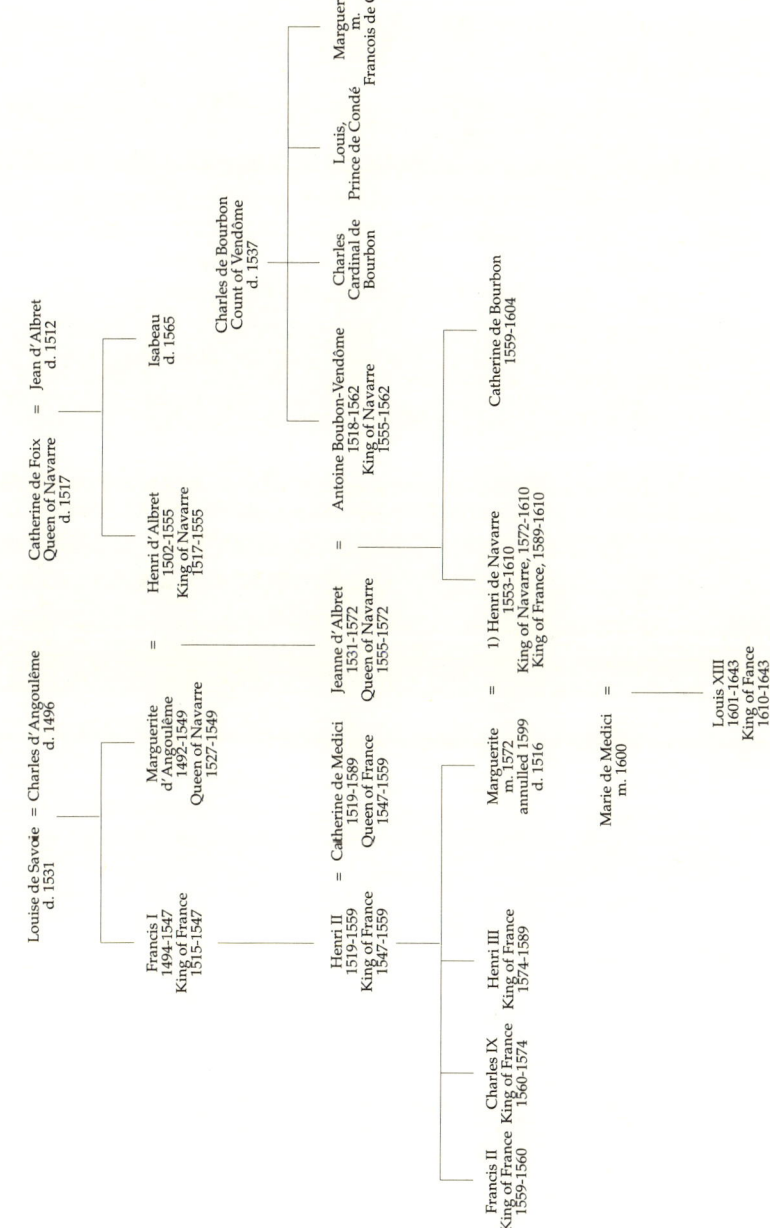

Abbreviations

Manuscript Sources

AD	Archives Départementales de...
AD-PA	Archives Départementales des Pyrénées-Atlantiques
AN	Archives Nationales
BM	Bibliothèque Mazarine
BN	Bibliothèque Nationale
FF	Fonds Français
MC	Minutier Central des notaires de Paris

Frequently Cited Published Sources

Actes de François Ier	*Catalogue des actes de François Ier*, Académie des sciences morales et politiques, 10 vols., Paris, 1887–1908
IAD	Inventaire sommaire des Archives Départementales...
Lettres Henri IV	*Recueil des lettres missives de Henri IV*, ed. Berger de Xivrey and J. Gaudet, 9 vols., Paris, 1872–83.

Acknowledgments

The publication of this book gives me the opportunity to thank the many people who have helped along the way. I owe an intellectual debt to a number of scholars who read the manuscript at various stages. Charles Le Guin first awakened my interest in French social history while I was still an undergraduate and created such a compelling atmosphere of inquiry and discovery in his classes and out that I resolved to become a practicing historian. Susan Karant-Nunn encouraged my interest in the Reformation and set a standard of scholarship and publication that I hope someday to emulate. Both Charles and Susan have followed my progress through the profession and deserve credit for seeing this manuscript through to publication.

As a graduate student, I was fortunate to work with J. Russell Major, who was unfailingly patient with me through the long period of creation. He was the best kind of graduate adviser, constantly pushing me to think more clearly and write more boldly while protecting my interests and praising my work when he thought it deserved it. Russell's high standards have produced a number of students of early modern France who also read the manuscript at various stages and offered suggestions for improving it: among them Donna Bohanan, Mack Holt, and Al Hamscher deserve a special note of thanks. I am also grateful to Robert A. Smith and James Melton who offered suggestions on the earliest versions of the manuscript. The late George Rothrock, Raymond Mentzer, Susan Karant-Nunn, Ron Love, Sharon Kettering, and David Buisseret also read and identified problems in the manuscript, which I have attempted to correct.

A number of colleagues at Western Washington University have helped with revisions. Carol Janson and Elizabeth Mancke discussed and proofread the entire manuscript and helped me with some last-minute changes. Their presence at Western has significantly heightened the level of intellectual discussion and the standards of academic sociability for which I am very grateful. A grant from the Bureau for

Faculty Research at Western allowed me to do additional research for chapters 3 and 5. Harriet Wender, Gabriel Mayers, and Melissa Ramming also provided crucial help in preparing this manuscript for publication.

One of the pleasures of researching this book in France was making new friendships, many of which have endured and deepened over the years. I have incurred a debt of gratitude to these friends and colleagues that I cannot adequately repay here, but it gives me great pleasure to acknowledge them anyway. Pierre and Jacqueline Beneteau, Daniel and Laurence Dubois, Henric and Anne-Marie Dorogi, Agnès Métrot, and Henriette Menou sustained me in various ways during my visits to France and taught me the value of food and friendship. I have benefited again and again from the courtesy and competence of the staffs at the Archives Départementales of the Pyrénées-Atlantiques, of the Ariège, of the Haute-Garonne, and of the Meurthe-et-Moselle. Jacques Staes, Anne-Catherine Marin, Mme Lassus, and Daniel Roger in the archives in Pau, where I did most of my research, merit a special mention for their willingness to service my often excessive requests. In Paris, I thank Catherine Grodecki, who has helped innumerable scholars decipher the mysteries of the Minutier Central, and the staffs of the Bibliothèque Nationale and Archives Nationales. My greatest debt of gratitude by far, however, is to Grégoria Pontgelard, whose generosity to researchers is legendary among those who have worked in Pau; her gifts of food, lodging, and friendship match sixteenth-century traditions of generosity both in kind and degree.

Finally, I want to thank my family. My parents, Gerald and Dixie Eurich, and my sister, Sara Beeson, have endured all my anxious years of research and writing, providing practical assistance as well as emotional sustenance when needed. They all proofread and typed various parts of the original dissertation. Sara gave up a week of her European grand tour and helped me copy estate records in the archives. I could never have done this without their loving help, and it is to them that this book is dedicated.

Perspectives

In sixteenth-century France no noble dynasty could claim a more pivotal and enduring role in national politics and court life than the house of Foix-Navarre-Albret. By virtue of shrewd marriage alliances, extensive landholdings, and vast clientage networks, the Albrets wielded enormous political and social influence and by the third quarter of the sixteenth century enjoyed an annual income second only to the royal house of Valois. Histories and biographies of the house of Foix-Navarre-Albret abound. Indeed, in the last hundred years a significant biography of every ruling member of the Albret family in the sixteenth century has been published. In the late nineteenth century, for example, Achille Luchaire wrote his classic monograph on Alain le Grand, the scion of the house of Albret during the late fifteenth and early sixteenth centuries. With enviable thoroughness, Luchaire plumbed the departmental archives in the Béarnais capital of Pau in order to render a clear portrait of one of the last great feudatory lords of France on the eve of the Renaissance.[1]

Notable, too, is Charles Dartigue-Peyrou's study of Henri d'Albret, the grandson of the wily Alain, and his administrative innovations in his viscounty of Béarn.[2] And in 1968, Nancy Lyman Roelker published her much hailed biography of Henri's contentious daughter, Jeanne d'Albret, who played a signal role in the French Reformation and the establishment of the Huguenot party. With her admitted interest in the political and religious influence of noblewomen in early modern France, Roelker focuses on Jeanne as a political creature.[3] Finally, the biographies and histories that have been written about Henri de

---

[1]A. Luchaire, *Alain le Grand, sire d'Albret* (Paris: Hachette, 1877), 52–53.
[2]Charles Dartigue-Peyrou, *La Vicomté de Béarn sous le règne d'Henri d'Albret, 1517–1555* (Paris: Belles Lettres, 1934).
[3]Nancy Lyman Roelker, *Queen of Navarre, Jeanne d'Albret, 1528–1572* (Cambridge: Harvard University Press, 1968).

Navarre, later Henri IV of France, are far too numerous to mention. Generations of academic scholars and popular writers have lavished volumes on this red-bearded Gascon, revered for his open handed generosity, amorous ways, apparent *joie de vivre*, and *politique* spirit. Janine Garrisson, a fine historian of Protestant France, has produced the most recent offering on the first Bourbon king—a good solid biography. Among other more narrowly focused works on Henri are the masterpieces by the grand doyen of early modern French history, Roland Mousnier: *The Assassination of Henri IV* and *The Sale of Offices under Henri IV and Louis XIII*.[4]

This present study owes much to the work of these well-established and respected scholars. Nevertheless, these fine studies have contributed very little to our understanding of the evolution of the family's fortunes over the entire course of the sixteenth century, a period of crisis for the French aristocracy as a whole and the house of Foix-Navarre-Albret in particular. For almost three decades now, the "crisis of the aristocracy" thesis has enlivened the pages of academic journals and scholarly monographs; its proponents argue that the wars, inflation, new men, and new methods of the sixteenth and seventeenth centuries decisively challenged the stability of many noble dynasties and noble fortunes throughout Europe. Lawrence Stone's seminal work, *The Crisis of the Aristocracy in England, 1558–1641*, set the stage in the 1960s for the discussion of a general, supranational political, cultural, and economic crisis, engendered by the emergence of the capitalist economy and bureaucratic state which threatened the traditional powers and resources controlled by the nobility. For Stone, the archaic structure of English leaseholds, the prodigious consumption patterns of the great nobility, and the mania for investing in building projects and bad business schemes ruined aristocratic fortunes generally in England and paved the way for the emergence of the new bourgeois elite, capable of more effectively exploiting the developing capitalist economy.[5]

---

[4]Janine Garrisson, *Henry IV* (Paris: Editions de Seuil, 1984); Roland Mousnier, *La Vénalité des offices sous Henri IV et Louis XIII* (Paris: Presses Universitaires de France, 1934); idem, *L'Assassinat d'Henri IV: 4 mai 1610* (Paris: Gallimard, 1964).

[5]Lawrence Stone, *The Crisis of the Aristocracy, 1558–1641* (Oxford: Oxford University Press, 1965) has become the most famous study in this vein for the English side; for a discussion of the impact of the "crisis thesis" on historical studies, see Charles Jago, "The 'Crisis of the Aristocracy' in Seventeenth-Century Castile," *Past and Present*, 84 (1979):60–90; Davis Bitton, *The French Nobility in Crisis, 1560–1640* (Stanford: Stanford University Press, 1969); J. H. Elliott, *Imperial Spain, 1469–1716* (New York: Penguin, 1963); Helen Nader, "Noble Income in Sixteenth-Century Castile: The Case of the Marquises of Mondéjar, 1480–1580," *Economic History Review*, 2d ser., 30 (1977):411–428.

For historians of France the "crisis" has achieved great significance as the first stage in the slow political and economic decline of the French nobility and the Old Regime which would in turn provoke the destruction of both during the French Revolution. There is little question that literary evidence, deeply imbued with a "long tradition of aristocratic complaint," points at the very least to the growing psychological malaise among sixteenth-century French nobles.[6] Most recent studies, however, have emphasized that the empirical evidence suggests the flexibility of leaseholds and rent structures in France, the general resilience of nobles' landed revenues, and the general success of French nobles in dealing with, even pioneering, nascent capitalist techniques of exploitation.[7] Even more recently historians have demonstrated the degree to which nobles reshaped their cultural identities to respond to growing pressures from the emerging bureaucratic state, worked closely with the new bureaucratic elite, and continued to play a prominent role in provincial and court politics.[8]

As close as we appear to be to a new synthesis which emphasizes the continuing political and economic vitality of the French nobility during the Old Regime, the complexity of the issues under debate continues to enliven the discussion initiated by Stone, and perhaps prefigured in French studies done over three decades ago. The decline of court favors and royal pensions described by Lucien Romier almost eighty years ago still remains one of the standard explanations for the

---

[6] Jonathan Dewald, *Pont-St-Pierre, 1398–1789: Lordship, Community, and Capitalism in Early Modern France* (Berkeley: University of California Press, 1987), 2.

[7] Louis Merle, *Le Métairie et l'évolution agraire de la Gâtine poitevine de la fin de Moyen Age à la Révolution* (Paris: S.E.V.P.E.N., 1958); J. M. Constant, "Gestion et revenus d'un grand domaine aux XVIe et XVIIe siècles d'après les comptes de la baronnie d'Auneau," *Revue d'histoire économique et sociale*, 50 (1972):165–202; James Wood, *The Nobility of the Election of Bayeux, 1463–1666: Continuity Through Change* (Princeton: Princeton University Press, 1980); J. Russell Major, "Noble Income, Inflation and the Wars of Religion in France," *American Historical Review* 86(1981):21–48; Robert Forster, *The Nobility of Toulouse in the Eighteenth Century: A Social and Economic Study* (Baltimore: Johns Hopkins University Press, 1960); and Dewald, *Pont-St-Pierre*.

[8] Ellery Schalk, *From Valor to Pedigree: Ideas of Nobility in France in the Sixteenth and Seventeenth Centuries* (Princeton: Princeton University Press, 1986); idem, "Clientage, Elites, and Absolutism in Seventeenth-Century France," *French Historical Studies* 14(1986):442–446; and Kristen B. Neuschel, *Word of Honor: Interpreting Noble Culture in Sixteenth-Century France* (Ithaca: Cornell University Press, 1989); Daniel Dessert, *Argent, pouvoir, et société au Grand Siècle* (Paris: Fayard, 1984); William Beik, *Absolutism and Society in Seventeenth-Century France: State Power and Provincial Aristocracy in Languedoc* (Cambridge: Cambridge University Press, 1985); Arlette Jouanna, *Le Devoir de révolte: La noblesse française et la gestation de l'état moderne, 1559–1661* (Paris: Fayard, 1989).

outbreak of civil and religious unrest in France.[9] Recently, it has also been argued that it was extravagant expenditure and debt which pushed members of the *haute noblesse* into the thirty-year conflict with the Crown known as the Religious Wars.[10]

A good deal of the history of the financial fortunes of the house of Foix-Navarre-Albret supports the contention of many recent studies that the French nobility retained its dominance over rural life, royal pensions and political offices, and provincial clientage networks. In an era of allegedly declining resources and income, the Albrets enjoyed a marked increase in their revenues from land, royal offices, and pensions, which often kept pace with rampant inflation. By the same token, increasing revenues provided them with the resources to enhance their image both at court and in the provinces. However, the Albrets' political and economic success also brought new responsibilities which taxed even further their full treasury. In the last decades of the sixteenth century, Henri de Navarre's rise to power and his involvement in the Huguenot party put almost unbearable pressures on the family wealth. In many respects, the Albrets' story highlights and illuminates the complexity of the debate over the "crisis of the aristocracy."

The silence that, until now, has reigned over the issue of the family's fortunes during the sixteenth century is impressive, indeed daunting, particularly because extensive documentation exists. Accounts of the family's revenues and expenditures are housed in the Archives-Départementales des Pyrénées-Atlantiques in Pau, the administrative seat of the family's power, and related documents are scattered throughout departmental archives in southwestern France and in the major libraries and repositories of Paris. Indeed, thanks to the administrative acumen of Henri d'Albret, who established a Chambre des comptes in Pau in 1520 and another in Nérac in 1527 to audit the accounts of the financial officials in his numerous domains, literally hundreds of accounts still exist which document the evolution of the family fortunes over the sixteenth century. With the exception of some documents destroyed in a fire in 1908, more than four thousand cartons and *cahiers* containing records germane to this study are listed in Raymond's 1863 inventory of the Pau archives.[11]

---

[9]Lucien Romier, *Les Origines politiques des guerres de religion*, 2 vols. (Paris: Perrin, 1913–14); Robert Harding, *Anatomy of a Power Elite: The Provincial Governors of Early Modern France* (New Haven and London: Yale University Press, 1978), 48–51, 139–141.

[10]Denis Crouzet, "Recherches sur la crise de l'aristocracie en France au XVI siècle: les dettes de la maison de Nevers," *Histoire, Economie et Société*, 1(1982):7–50.

[11]P. Raymond, ed. *Inventaire sommaire des archives départementales antérieures à 1790: Basses-Pyrénées*, sér. B, (Paris, 1863).

Why, then, have these accounts only been mined in a piecemeal fashion? Cited frequently in biographies, histories, even in rather obscure tangential studies, this rich repository of information about the fortunes of one of the most powerful families in early modern France has generally been ignored by social historians. In 1981, J. Russell Major called attention to these documents in his seminal article on noble income and inflation during the Wars of Religion in France. Basing many of his findings on a cursory perusal of some of these accounts, he suggested that these documents could sustain detailed study.[12] But he also described some of the pitfalls of dealing with these documents which, I suspect, have deterred many a scholar. The most imposing problem is, quite simply, the very confusing manner in which sixteenth-century accounts were kept. Both estate and household accounts were compiled on the system of "charge and discharge," an ancient form of account with the object of establishing the liability of the accounting official and not of presenting actual income and expenditure.[13] Thus, the treasurers recorded only the money that passed through their hands. Money transferred to other accounts was listed as expense; and money transferred in was listed as receipts. The margin for error on the historian's part, particularly during the tumultuous period of the Wars of Religion, should be readily apparent.

Bearing in mind such caveats, however, it is possible to ascertain the deliveries of rent and revenues into the household and to trace in detail the Albrets' expenditures, thanks, in large part, to the sweep and variety of records which were reviewed annually by the Albrets' auditors in the Chambres des comptes in Pau and Nérac. The mere creation of the Chambres des comptes not only centralized the administration of the Albrets' domains; it also encouraged more refined and extensive record keeping among even low-level estate managers and household stewards. The greatest store of documents concerning the Albrets' fortunes in the sixteenth century are the accounts of the domanial treasurers, which reflect the tremendous importance of land as the source of both the nobility's territorial and economic power. But the Chambres des comptes also housed the records of special domanial commissioners

---

[12]Major, "Noble Income," passim.

[13]The difficulties of working with household accounts are corroborated by historians. For a discussion of the intricacies of noble finance and accounting systems in early modern Europe, see A. C. Littleton, *Accounting Evolution to 1900* (New York: Russell & Russell, 1966); N. Denholm-Young, *Seignorial Administration in England* (London: Barnes & Noble, 1937); M. E. James, ed., *The Estate Accounts of the Earls of Northumberland, 1562–1637*, vol. 163 (Durham: Surtees Society, 1955), i–xiv; William Weary, "Royal Policy and Patronage in Renaissance France: The Monarchy and the House of La Trémoille" (Ph.D diss., Yale University, 1972), 51–56, 74–84.

sent to lease domanial land or reform the administration of domanial forests and other precious natural resources. Household officials were also encouraged to keep meticulous accounts, and they duly recorded their expenditures in monthly or quarterly accounts which came under the purview of the Chambres des comptes. Fortunately, the greatest number of surviving records and the most continuous record series date from the last quarter of the sixteenth century and the Religious Wars. Nothing could be more fortuitous for the purposes of this study since these are precisely the decades which posed the greatest challenges to the financial fortunes of the French aristocracy according to recent historiography.

Until now, historians have had only a very general notion of how and where powerful noble clans, such as the Albrets, the Guises, the Nevers, and the Bourbons, both secured and spent their wealth. There are few collections of family records and accounts as compact and detailed as those of the house of Foix-Navarre-Albret. To circumvent this dearth, studies have emerged which have made innovative use of notarial records. Denis Crouzet's discussion of the Nevers family and their cycles of indebtedness is one such study; Joseph Bergin's fascinating reconstruction of the various components of Cardinal Richelieu's wealth is another.[14] But Bergin has stressed that "notarial records are an inadequate replacement for accounts." As he explains, "income from different sources [can only] be treated as *ordres de grandeur*, or approximations to the reality; expenditures, whether on the household, works of art, building projects, patronage and pensions can only be guessed at, and even then only in a highly unsatisfactory way."[15] Household accounts, on the other hand, make it possible to explore the intimate relationship between income and expenditure which is at the very center of the "crisis of the aristocracy" debate. How did the great nobles balance the competing demands placed upon their fortunes?

The members of the house of Foix-Navarre-Albret represent the very cream of the French aristocracy, tied by birth and by marriage to the royal house of France. Their story, it is true, will tell us little about the fate of the entire nobility in the sixteenth century. But it does have much to say about the way in which those few great and influential families in France accumulated wealth and used it to maintain their positions of considerable power during a period of flux and change.

---

[14]Denis Crouzet, "Recherches sur la crise," 7–49; Joseph Bergin, *Cardinal Richelieu: The Pursuit of Power and Wealth* (New Haven and London: Yale University Press, 1985).

[15]Bergin, *Cardinal Richelieu*, 10.

One

Landed Revenues

Like most great nobles during the Ancien Régime, the Albrets derived their principal revenues as well as their fundamental territorial powers from land and the seigneurial privileges attached to it. By 1517, Henri d'Albret could claim lordship over a complex mosaic of principalities, fiefs, and seigneuries which stretched northward from the Pyrenees to the Garonne River and eastward from the Atlantic to the city of Toulouse. The revenues which he garnered from these estates clearly established the house of Foix-Navarre-Albret as one of the richest noble dynasties in all of Renaissance France, second only to the royal house of Valois.

In political terms, the truncated kingdom of Basse-Navarre was Henri d'Albret's most valued domain, the basis of his royal pretensions at court in France, Spain, and Italy. In financial terms, however, the revenues that Henri and his successors drew from Basse-Navarre paled in comparison to the income which could be claimed from many of his other estates. Tolls, mills, judicial fines, and a dozen or so seigneuries comprised the full extent of Henri's domanial revenues in Navarre, which rarely surpassed 5,000 livres in any given year. By the time the local Navarrese treasurer subtracted his expenses, the domanial revenues turned over to the Albrets' general treasurer usually accounted for no more than 1 percent of their annual revenues in toto.[1]

---

[1] The Albrets periodically received *ex gratia* donations from the estates of Navarre, but the actual amounts varied enormously. In 1568, for example, nobles in Navarre, in rebellion against Jeanne d'Albret's Reformed policies, made no donation to the treasury; seven years later, the estate made a lavish present of 15,021 livres to Henri de Navarre. See AD-PA, B1415, B1417. These donations, mercurial as they were, were not figured into domanial revenues, and do not figure into this assessment of Navarre's landed revenues. For the accounts of the general treasurer, see AD-PA, B143, B146, B148, B150, B159, B163.

2 • The Economics of Power

By contrast, the viscounty of Béarn, over which the counts of Foix had claimed sovereign rule since the middle of the eleventh century, generated revenues in the tens of thousands of livres and was, in many respects, the centerpiece around which the Albrets' landed fortunes were built. By the early sixteenth century, the Pyrenean viscounty could boast over one hundred thousand inhabitants, most of whom were keenly aware of the cultural, political, and linguistic traditions which distinguished Béarn from Henri d'Albret's other remaining domains, all French fiefs ultimately subject to the authority of the Valois monarchy. By virtue of his *sobiranetat*, or sovereignty, over Béarn, Henri d'Albret enjoyed a number of royal privileges from which he derived lucrative revenues, including the right to coin money and the right to request donations from the estates of Béarn.[2] These privileges, together with revenues from tolls, judicial fines, mills, and verdant domanial lands, guaranteed Béarn a central economic and political position in the Albrets' landed fortunes.

From Béarn, Henri's inheritance spread east to three other Pyrenean principalities, the counties of Foix, Bigorre, and Lautrec. Henri and his successors claimed an array of seigneurial privileges over these domains, including mining rights guaranteed by grants from the kings of France. From his father Jean d'Albret, Henri extended the claims of the house of Foix-Navarre-Albret northward to the Garonne River, over which he levied tolls. The barony of Albret, elevated to a duchy in 1520, the viscounties of Tursan and Gabardan, and the counties of Périgord and Limoges substantially increased Henri's territorial powers and landed revenues, while creating a ring of buffer provinces around the viscounty of Béarn.

---

[2] For the revenues the Albrets received from farming their right to coin money, see P. Raymond, "Extraits des registres de la Chambre des comptes de Pau (XVI-XVIII siècles) d'après un manuscript appartenant au baron de Laussat," *Bulletin de la société des sciences, lettres, et arts de Pau* 1 (1872):124, 141, 256; also J.-Andrien Blanchet, *Histoire monétaire du Béarn* (Paris, 1893), 9-11. It is difficult to calculate how much money the Albrets received annually from the estates of Béarn because their *procès-verbaux* do not record every gift. The receipts of the general treasurer suggest annual gifts between 15,000 and 20,000 livres were common, and generally increased to 25,000 to 30,000 livres during the reign of Henri de Navarre. See AD-PA, B143, B146, B148, B150, B155, B159, B163. In their capacity as *grands seigneurs* and governors, the Albrets, like many of their peers, also received periodic *ex gratia* gratifications from estates in their French fiefs of Foix and Bigorre, but these were subject to royal approval and by the 1540s were seriously curtailed by royal commissioners, thus increasing both the financial and symbolic importance of the Béarnais donation. On this issue, see Mark Greengrass, "Property and Politics in Sixteenth-Century France: The Landed Fortune of Constable Anne de Montmorency," *French History* 2 (1988):380-382. The impact of these gifts on the Albrets' fortunes will be discussed more fully in chap. 6.

Finally, Henri's marriage to Marguerite d'Angoulême, sister of Francis I, in 1527 assured future generations of Albrets almost total dominance over southwestern France. By virtue of her first marriage to Charles d'Alençon, Marguerite could lay claim to the counties of Armagnac, Rodez, and the viscounty of Fézenzaguet, which under ordinary circumstances should have escheated to the royal domain upon her remarriage. In a magnanimous gesture, however, Francis I awarded the vast and enormously lucrative patrimony of the august counts of Armagnac to Marguerite, which she brought to her second marriage as part of her dowry, nearly doubling the landed revenues of the house of Foix-Navarre-Albret in the process.[3] The marriage of Henri and Marguerite's daughter, Jeanne d'Albret, to the dashing Antoine de Bourbon, duc de Vendômois, and first prince of the blood, in 1548 grafted some of the most important Bourbon holdings in Picardy, Artois, Flanders, and the Ile-de France onto the Albrets' estates and added around 71,000 livres annually to their treasuries in the north (see map, p. 4).[4]

The geographic range and complexity of Henri d'Albret's estates, as well as his peripatetic lifestyle, shaped to a large extent the manner in which his landholdings were managed by the 1530s. In common with many of his noble contemporaries, Henri preferred to farm out his estates, leasing the domain, seigneurial offices, and even his seigneurial privileges in return for a guaranteed income. As a result, the Albrets became *rentier* landlords, who increasingly left the daily business of managing their estates to local stewards and household officers.[5] These men in turn presided over the scores of domanial treasurers, castle guards, forest guards, lawyers, judges, and notaries necessary to collect rents, authorize leases, and enforce the Albrets' privileges and prerogatives in the countryside. Did this indirect system of administration and exploitation threaten the Albrets' customary seigneurial control over rural society and the rural economy? Did it compromise the enormous profits that lay waiting for the landowner capable of directly exploiting the sixteenth-century surge in population and prices? Until recently, historians have emphasized the inherent

---

[3]Charles Dartigue-Peyrou, *Vicomté*, 245–53.
[4]The only surviving record of these Bourbon holdings is found in the Archives-Nationales, KK278. Kristen Neuschel, *Word of Honor*, 136–59 has analyzed this record extensively.
[5]For lists of the men who served in the Albret household and on their estates, see the family accounts housed in the Archives Départmentales, Pyrénées-Atlantiques, sér. B.

4 • The Economics of Power

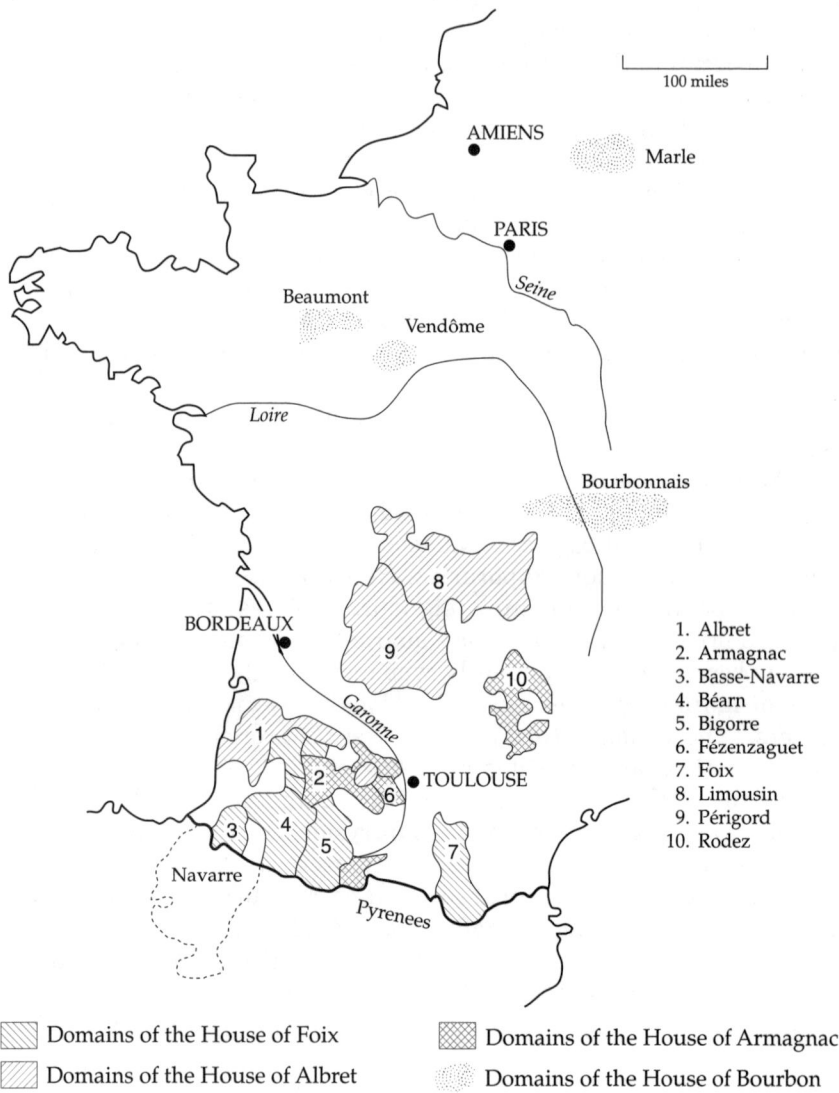

DOMAINS OF THE HOUSE OF FOIX-NAVARRE-ALBRET

1. Albret
2. Armagnac
3. Basse-Navarre
4. Béarn
5. Bigorre
6. Fézenzaguet
7. Foix
8. Limousin
9. Périgord
10. Rodez

Domains of the House of Foix
Domains of the House of Albret
Domains of the House of Armagnac
Domains of the House of Bourbon

Sources: Roelker, *Queen of Navarre*, and Buissert, *Henry IV*

and long-term dangers in *rentier* landlordship in an era of nascent capitalism.⁶ The image of boorish aristocrats, more concerned with immediate pleasures than long-term profits tied to fixed rents, however, is being challenged by recent studies which have demonstrated the extent to which many nobles attempted to adapt to the developing capitalist economy with varying degrees of success.⁷ Does the history of the Albrets and their estates suggest the continuing vitality of the nobility or its slow demise? Did the Albrets respond with any degree of flexibility and ingenuity to the enormous changes and difficulties which were part of economic life in the sixteenth century? How did they manage in the second half of the sixteenth century when the triple threat of demographic growth, inflation, and religious warfare challenged the traditional privileges they exercised over land and the revenues they drew from it?

I. Seigneurial Administration and Innovation

Any consideration of the Albrets' efforts to manage their estates must begin with the administrative reforms and innovations of Henri d'Albret, who very early in his tenure displayed a flair for management and organization. Borrowing a practice he had observed at court, the young viscount of Béarn established his own Chambre des comptes in 1520 to audit the accounts of the financial officials in his numerous domains. In 1527, after his marriage to Marguerite and in order to facilitate the enormous task of keeping track of all domanial treasuries and accounts, Henri reduced the jurisdiction of the Chambre at Pau

---

⁶See, for example, Robert Boutruche, *La Crise d'une société: Seigneurs et paysans du Bordelais pendant les Guerres de Cent Ans* (Paris: Belles Lettres, 1947); Guy Bois, *The Crisis of Feudalism: Economy and Society in Eastern Normandy c. 1300–1550* (Cambridge: Cambridge University Press, 1984); Emmanuel Le Roy Ladurie, *Les paysans de Languedoc*, 2 vols. (Paris: S.E.V.P.E.N., 1966); idem, "Les Masses profondes: La Paysannerie" in F. Braudel and E. Labrousse, eds., *Histoire économique et sociale de la France*, 1 (Paris: Presses Universitaires de France, 1977):523–29. See also the lively discussion of the particular vagaries of French lordship and capitalist development in T. H. Aston and C. H. E. Philpin, eds. *The Brenner Debate: Agrarian Class Structure and Economic Development in Pre-Industrial Europe* (Cambridge: Cambridge University Press, 1985).

⁷See, for example, Jean-Marie Constant, *Nobles et paysans en Beauce aux XVIe et XVIIe siècles* (Lille: Champion, 1981); idem, "Gestion et revenus d'un grand domaine aux XVIe et XVIIe siècles d'après les comptes de la baronnie d'Auneau," *Revue d'histoire économique et sociale* 50 (1972):165–202; Wood, *The Nobility of the Election of Bayeux*; Dewald, *Pont-St-Pierre*; J. Russell Major, "Noble Income", 21–48; and Greengrass, "Property and Politics," 372–77, 382–96.

and created a second Chambre des comptes at Nérac, in the duchy of Albret, with jurisdiction over his easternmost territories: Albret, Armagnac, Périgord, Limousin, Rouergue, Fézenzaguet, Foix, Nébouzan, Lautrec, and Villemur.[8] Every year, usually after Toussaints, the members of the Chambres des comptes gathered together to verify painstakingly the records of the general treasurer of the household against the accounts of the domanial treasurers.[9] They cross-checked every entry against royal discharges not yet remitted or recorded, fiscal decrees issued by Albret himself, and signed receipts (*quittances*), noting in the margins of these accounts when and by what means the treasurers had discharged themselves of their responsibilities. Indeed, the auditors' remarks sometimes ran into the treasurers' texts in an attempt to clarify the status of every receipt and expenditure. In some accounts, running totals in Arabic numerals were kept at the bottom of each page.[10] At the beginning of the calendar year, the work was presented to Henri's privy council for approval. Through such a system, then, Henri d'Albret was able to keep tight control over his fortunes.

Henri's administrative reforms and the precise bookkeeping of his auditors made viable his persistent attempts to enforce centuries-old seigneurial rights, collect rents in arrears, and reclaim fortunes lost by the passage of time and inattentive management. In 1534, charging that his predecessors had allowed the family possessions to "fall into disorder and diminution, and that several subjects, noble and non-noble, had seized land, woodlands, pastures, and vacant fiefs, always without paying rent, *cens*, tributes or other rights," Henri ordered Pierre de Biaix, a member of his privy council, to conduct an exhaustive survey of his domains in Béarn.[11] Four years later, Henri ordered his auditors to implement a similar survey (*dénombrement*) of his domains in Tursan, Marsan, Gabardan, Armagnac, and Bigorre.[12] Massive lists were compiled delineating every rent, *cens*, or fief belonging to the house of Foix-Navarre-Albret. Once the list was complete, Henri commissioned members of his council to use it to reassert claims on "lands found to be usurped," to "constrain tenants to pay arrears" by the sei-

---

[8] P. Raymond, ed., *Inventaire sommaire des archives départémentales antérieures à 1790: Basses-Pyrénées,* sér. B., (Paris, 1863), 11. (Hereafter *IAD, Basses Pyrénées*).
[9] See AD-PA, B6, B8, B140, B146, B155, etc.
[10] For example, the auditor's calculations appear in Arabic numerals in the Foix accounts, AD-PA, B1076.
[11] AD-PA, B2078.
[12] Some of these survive, but I have not examined them. See AD-PA, B2082–2084.

zure of their property if necessary, and, most important, to rent anew "lands which are found to be vacant."[13]

In many respects Henri's obsession with seigneurial privileges, no matter how minor, reflects the political and cultural meaning with which such rights were invested by nobles and their peasant tenants. Beyond their obvious economic value, seigneurial monopolies (or charges for their use) on mills, winepresses, and ovens, seigneurial ownership of certain pastures, streams, and woodlands, the seigneurial right to collect dues (*lods et ventes*) when property changed hands, and finally the right to administer justice, all demonstrated in the most pervasive fashion the seigneur's control of the most basic necessities and activities of daily life. Given such conditions, no rent or seigneurial due was too small to be collected. In Béarn, for example, commissioners reclaimed Albret's right to rent the Igon and Montestruc mills, both of which yielded sixteen *conques* of wheat in rent annually.[14] In the marketplace, these rents in kind could rarely have brought more than fifteen livres and represented less than 1 percent of Henri's total revenues in the viscounty.[15] Other mills and numerous domanial vineyards were also reentered on the rent rolls. As a result of the *redressement* of petty properties and rights in Béarn, satisfied agents could report in 1539 that "the vicomtal domain increased by 2,000 écus [6,000 livres] without doing an injustice to anyone."[16]

The success of the 1534 and 1538 surveys encouraged Henri to conduct a census of some of his northern properties. From 1540 to 1544 commissioners were active in the duchy of Périgord and the viscounty of Limousin, policing Albret interests and compiling lists of errant fiefholders.[17] In 1546, the commissioners extended their investigations to include the small Pyrenean county of Nébouzan.[18] Henri's ambitions did not stop with his attempts to recover long-lapsed rights, leases, and rents. He showed an entrepreneurial turn in 1541 when he obtained the rare privilege—in France at least—of pocketing all royal revenues from mining activities in the province of Guyenne for a twenty-year period.[19] Henri moved quickly and ordered surveys to investigate the

[13] Henri d'Albret's charge to Jean de LaVie for the reformation of Tartas in the county of Bigorre, AD-PA, B1492. For the *dénombrement* of Bigorre, see AD-PA, B999–B1009.

[14] Dartigue-Peyrou, *Vicomté*, 250.

[15] This calculation is based on figures taken from the treasurer's accounts of rents paid in kind in the kingdom of Navarre, AD-PA, B1420-B1435.

[16] AD-PA, B246.

[17] AD-PA, B2100, B2104, B2107.

[18] AD-PA, B2115.

[19] Académie des sciences morales et politiques. *Catalogue des actes de François Ier*, 10 vols. (Paris, 1887–1908), 3:312.

profitability of silver mining in his county of Foix.[20] That nothing ultimately came from this burst of activity suggests that Henri found that the chances of success were poor.[21]

II. Leasing Policies

As we have seen, Henri d'Albret, like many *grands seigneurs*, preferred to lease his domains rather than assume the time-consuming and financially risky responsibilities of direct management. Yet he was far from being a passive participant in the booming economy of the sixteenth century. Albret agents entered the marketplaces and public squares of southwestern France ready to exploit to their master's advantage the economic opportunities offered by sixteenth century population growth and inflation. In his monumental reconstruction of the rural landscape of Languedoc, Emmanuel Le Roy Ladurie has argued that the sixteenth century promised tremendous profits to the farmer with a little initiative and a little land. Real wages were declining and prices, especially for agricultural products, were rising, largely because of the demographic explosion which was one of the salient features of the century. "Whether landowner or tenant," claims Le Roy Ladurie, "the active farmer stood to gain."[22] The working landowner pocketed an ever-increasing surplus as he sold his goods in a flourishing market and doled out low wages to his field hands and farmworkers; likewise, the tenant farmer enjoyed growing profits while paying "rents that did not increase." According to the economic register established by this pioneering French historian, "The sixteenth century ranked the simple working or tenant farmer in the first place, followed by the working landlord or gentleman farmer second, then the rentier landlord third, and finally the big loser of the century the hired farm worker."[23]

However, the same conditions which made direct farming such a profitable enterprise also made the land on which farming occurred an increasingly valuable commodity and could favor even *rentier* landlords who paid particular attention to rapidly changing values in the land market. With the help of loyal and efficient officers and agents

---

[20]AD-PA, B1101.

[21]See Lawrence Stone, *The Crisis of the Aristocracy* (Oxford: Oxford University Press, 1965), 338–55, for a discussion of the risky mining activities of English landowners during the sixteenth century.

[22]Emmanuel Le Roy Ladurie, *Les paysans de Languedoc* (Paris: S.E.V.P.E.N., 1966), 297.

[23]Ibid., 300.

Henri d'Albret leased his estates with skill and cunning, characteristics supposed to be the preserve of the bourgeois and peasant farmer-entrepreneur. As a result, the auction records and domanial accounts kept by Henri's agents show few signs of tenant farmers who "paid rents that did not increase."[24] Indeed J. Russell Major's work on domanial revenues in the viscounty of Béarn, the symbolic heartland of the Albrets' estates, clearly demonstrates that land rents could and did increase dramatically in relatively healthy and protected local economies, shielded from the continuous depradations of war.[25] Surrounded on three sides by territories and French fiefs also held by the Albrets, the viscounty of Béarn was invaded only once during the entire course of the Religious Wars, in 1569 by French troops. Moreover, local custom prohibited the Albrets from alienating any of their Béarnais domain for much the same reason that French monarchs could not easily alienate their royal domains, which represented in both legal and symbolic terms the inviolable patrimony of the kingdom. Thus, in Béarn landed revenues increased over the course of the sixteenth century, surpassing even rapidly rising grain and wine prices in Toulouse and Paris (see figure 1.1, page 10). The tremendous symbolic importance that both the Albrets and their subjects attached to the inviolable sovereignty of Béarn assured that domanial revenues there would continue to rise.

While the paucity of continuous domanial accounts for many of the Albrets' other estates renders any assessment of their entire holdings problematic, it is possible to trace rent structures longitudinally in three other critical *pays* belonging to them: Périgord, the key to the Albrets' dominance of *la France profonde*; Armagnac, their vast inheritance from the crown; and Fézenzaguet, at the gateway to the markets of Languedoc. Each of these regions presented a different set of problems and opportunities to the Albrets and their estate managers, which in turn shaped the way in which the landholdings in each were manipulated and marketed to produce the highest returns. Périgord's distance from the geographic and symbolic center of the Albrets' domains in Béarn encouraged less expense on protection and a greater level of land alienation to raise money during the Religious Wars. By contrast, the lucrative markets of Toulouse near Armagnac encouraged stewards to control the county much more directly, especially in light of the extensive forest resources of the county. Finally, the manipulation of Fézenzaguet revenues demonstrates the attention to detail in even the

---

[24] For Le Roy Ladurie's discussion of the felicitous positions of the tenant farmer, see *Les paysans de Languedoc*, 122–25.

[25] Major, "Noble Income," 21–48.

Figure 1.1 Domanial Receipts from the Viscounty of Béarn and Price Indices

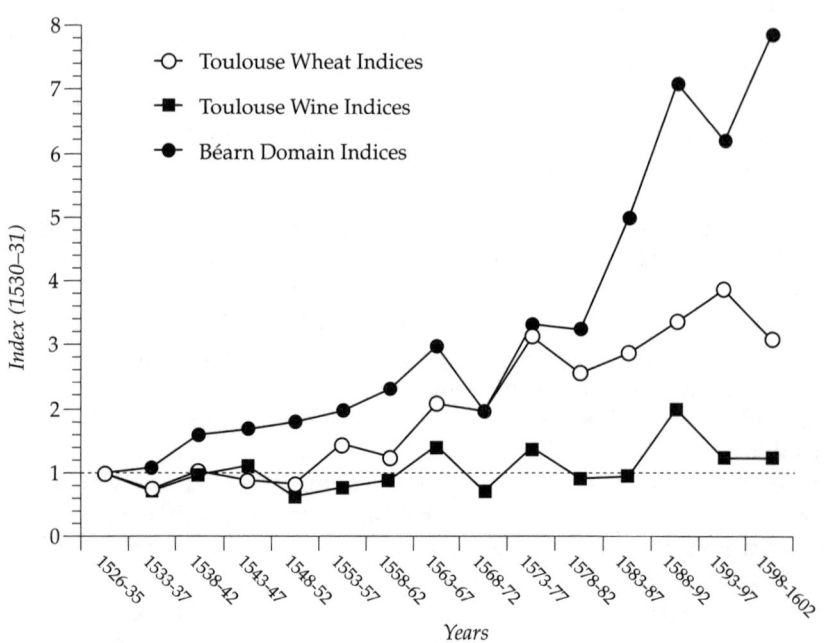

Sources: J. Russel Major, "Noble Income, Inflation and the Wars of Religion in France," *American Historical Review* 86 (1981): 34.
Price indices are based on Micheline Baulant and Jean Meuvret, *Prix des céréales extraits de la mercuriale de Paris, 1520–1698,* 1 (Paris, 1964): 243, and Georges Frêche and Geneviève Frêche, *Les Prix des grains, des vins, et des légumes à Toulouse, 1486–1868* (Paris, 1967), 85–87.

smallest of viscounties. Together these three regions reveal the complex economy of noble landholding in the sixteenth century, as well as the symbolism which nobles attached to their lands, which in turn shaped their administration of landed revenues.[26]

Henri d'Albret's agents deserve a large share of the credit for rising revenues, which they nudged upward by devising leasing practices which took advantage of the peasants' hunger for land. First, they leased the domains for very short terms. Except for mills, which were normally leased for six years, and tolls, which were usually granted for one year, all domanial lands and privileges were leased for a period of three years. These short leases distinguished the Albrets from their Parisian and Poitevin counterparts, who rented their lands for nine and seven years respectively, and permitted the Albrets to take full advantage of the rising demand for land and the overall upward trend in prices.[27] The kind of fluctuation possible in just a three-year period could be staggering. In Périgord land prices leaped upwards by 42 percent from 1550 to 1553, though increases were not uniform among the eighteen properties auctioned.[28] The seigneuries of Chalus and Corbassy, which were leased on one contract, attracted 976 livres a year in the 1550 auctions. Three years later they commanded 1200 livres a year, an increase of 23 percent. The rents on Chalusset increased from 425 livres to 1485 livres, and the rents on Montpaon leapt from 10 livres to a staggering 1980 livres (see table 1.1). In Fézenzaguet total rental receipts from the 1562 auction to the 1565 auction increased 54 percent, ranging from a decrease of 11 percent (for the tiny seigneurie of Cirac) to a 122 percent increase for the combined properties of Brunhenx and Urdenx (see table 1.2).

The manner in which Henri d'Albret's special agents—usually select members of the Chambres des comptes and local noblemen—auctioned leaseholds also encouraged rent increases. Early in the sixteenth century, they selected large cities and trade centers as auction sites, perhaps in order to attract the largest crowds. In 1530, for example, trumpeters summoned potential lessees for the domain in the little viscounty of Lautrec to the fortified city of Carcassonne.[29] By mid-century, however, the Albrets realized that it might better serve their

---

[26] See Neuschel's discussion of the significance of landed property in the Bourbon family, including Antoine de Bourbon's properties in Marle and La Fère, in *Word of Honor*, 147, 159.
[27] For Paris see Jean Jacquart, *La Crise rurale en l'Ile de France, 1550–1670* (Paris: A. Colin, 1974), 27; for Poitou, see Louis Merle, *La Métaire*, 161–75.
[28] AD-PA, B1827, B1832.
[29] AD-PA, B1714, as cited in Major, "Noble Income," 27.

12 • The Economics of Power

Table 1.1 Rent Receipts from the Duchy of Périgord (in *livres tournois*)

Jurisdiction	1551-2	1553-4	1573-4	1575-6	1583-4	1593-4	1600-1
Montignac	1273	1293	2228	1363	2028	n/a[a]	n/a[a]
Limoges	n/a[b]	250	855	1050	1440	226	240
Geniès	739	726	[800][d]	891	1190	900	498
Ans	604	675	1594	834	1234	1100	699
Auberoche	390	410	755	602	405	395	219
Massère	20[b]	[10,000][b]	195[b]	—[b]	1425	600	n/a[a]
Chalusset	425	1485	1150	1021	823	665[j]	600
Thiniers	n/a[a]	n/a[a]	510	350	372	210	285
Montron	640	620	650	550	500	366	399
Ségur	726	739	770[e]	[25,000][e]	387[e]	172[e]	100[e]
Péyzac	993	1014	[60,000][f]	—[f]	—[f]	1528	948
Chalus/Corbassy	976	1200	[50,000][g]	—[g]	—[g]	850	600
Exideuil	1039	985	2732	1532	[50,000][a]	—[k]	—[k]

(continued next page)

Table 1.1 (continued)

Larche	362	307	492	257	[6,000]^l	—^{l}	—^{l}
Lisle	180	25	n/a^h	n/a^h	n/a^h	n/a^h	n/a^h
Montpaon	10	1980	n/a^i	n/a^i	n/a^i	n/a^i	[100,000]^o
Périgeux	n/a^a	170	417	1058	204	n/a^a	[6,000]^p
Ayen	n/a^a	n/a^a	1255	1058	1354	[20,000]^n	—^{n}
Total	8377	11879	13573	9508	11362	7012	4398
Total Reciepts	8418	—^{c}	16761	10564	40358	52694	7569

AD-PA Source, respectively by year: B1827, B1837, B1862, B 1898, B 1898, B1898, B1918.

^{a}Not listed in the account.
^{b}Part of the domain was alienated to Saint-Geniès for 10,000 livres.
^{c}An auction account; receipts are not totaled.
^{d}Granted to Count Montgomery (Saint-Geniès) for his brilliant campaign in Béarn against the Baron Terride in 1569.
^{e}Parts of the domain were alienated in 1558 and 1564 for 10,000 livres and 15,000 livres respectively.
^{f}Alienated in 1556 to the Bishop of Poitiers for 60,000 livres.
^{g}Alienated for 50,000 livres.
^{h}Alienated to Jehan de La Porte; price not given in the account.
^{i}Alienated to Dame de Longua; price not given in the account.
^{j}The treasurer noted in his account that several *estières* of woodland were sold for sums totaling 13,938 livres, but no summation of these receipts is added into the general total.
^{k}Alienated in perpetuity for 50,000 livres, March 26, 1582.
^{l}Alienated (with rights of repurchase) to the Dame de Noailles, for 60,000 livres.
^{m}Receipts include 40,000 livres from the sale of "the forests the most subject to ruin."
^{n}Alienated in perpetuity for 20,000 livres.
^{o}Realienated to Sr de Rohan for 10 years at 100,000 livres, July 24, 1559, B1917.
^{p}Alienated for 6,000 livres, B1917.

Table 1.2 Rental Receipts from Fézenzaguet, 1562-1566 (in *livres tournois*)

Jurisdiction	1562–63	1565–66	Percentage change
Mauvesin	357	400	12%
Montfort	186	265	42%
Ceran	145	260	79%
Puycasquier	214	280	31%
Tourget	185	290	57%
Brunhenx & Urdenx	185	410	122%
Bayonette	35	70	100%
Pys	112	205	87%
Cirac	4.5	4	-11%
Torrenx	60	81	35%
Tarbic	20	20.5	3%
Saint Cric	13.5	15.5	15%
Terres château	—	30	
TOTAL	1517	2331	54%

financial interests to hold several auctions within the viscounty itself, so that a greater number of local farmers and peasants, many without the time or means to travel far from their fields, could bid as well on the properties and thereby increase rents. In 1549, agents divided the viscounty into eleven parts and sent heralds to announce their impending arrival in one or another segment of the domain.[30] The new approach

---

[30] Ibid.

apparently worked and was quickly implemented in other regions. Agents leasing Albret properties in Périgord four years later held fifteen on-site auctions in the duchy.[31]

Clearly seasoned observers of human behavior, agents for the house of Foix-Navarre-Albret knew well how to exploit the proverbial peasant hunger for land and could stretch out the bidding process for hours—sometimes days—until a satisfactory price was reached. Typically, the approach of agents to an auction site was announced well in advance to give potential lessees time to plot with other land-hungry locals anxious to share a plot of land. A trumpeter crisscrossed the countryside, declaring the news to every village and hamlet in close range of the auction, while the commissioned agents followed a day or two behind their herald. Auctions opened promptly at eight in the morning, and agents sometimes entertained bids in the public square all day—with the customary two-hour break for lunch that is still observed in much of provincial France—before they closed the bidding. The following morning they collected a sizable down payment from the lessees as a sign of good faith, and surveyed the surrounding fields and forests for signs of neglect before proceeding to the next auction site. The whole process could take from three to four weeks in just one county.[32]

The three noblemen commissioned to lease Henri d'Albret's domain in Périgord in 1553 demonstrated a keen awareness of market impulses and regional land values. Their first auctions in Périgord were rather perfunctory affairs. In Larche, where bidding was sluggish, the agents closed the auction after only one day, convinced that they had received the highest bid possible for the relatively mediocre property. Properties in Montignac only brought offers that amounted to a 2 percent increase over the previous lease. In Ans, however, rents from the castellany increased from 604 livres to 675 livres yearly, in spite of reports that the castle and prisons were virtually in ruins and incapable of holding lawbreakers and brigands (see table 1.1).

When the agents reached the busy marketplace of Montpaon, however, they paused to rest. At hand were the profitable properties surrounding this well-established trading center, and the noblemen, anxious to secure the highest price possible, sent their trumpeter all the way to Libourne, Coutras, Saint-Foy, and Puynormand to elicit bid-

---

[31]AD-PA, B1832.

[32]The auction process in Périgord, for example, took from June 3 to June 23 in 1553, AD-PA, B1832; and in the viscounty of Fézenzaguet in 1595 from May 19 to May 30, AD-PA, B1622.

ders. Two days later DePlancaux and his two colleagues stood before a small group of prospective tenants and decided to delay the auction a half day in the hopes of drawing a larger crowd. Even so, bids were neither fast nor furious when the auction finally opened at two o'clock on the afternoon of June 21. After two tedious hours of bidding, offers finally reached 1,880 livres, but the agents deemed this sum too far below the real market value of the land to accept it. Therefore, they continued the auction the next morning until, "after many overtures and bids," the domain of Montpaon was delivered into the hands of Jean and Antoine Chaussade, merchants from nearby Mussidan, for 1,980 livres per annum, an increase of 1970 livres over the previous lease (see table 1.1).[33]

Rent rolls and auction accounts show that the competition for land was frequently fierce by midcentury. Moreover, the Albrets' agents increased the competitive edge even further by subdividing their domains into small parcels within reach not only of merchants like the Chaussades, but also of small proprietors and peasants. In 1550, for example, the fifty-eight seigneuries, viscounties, and properties which made up the family holdings in the duchy of Albret were further subdivided into over four hundred leasable parts.[34] In Armagnac, bidders could choose among eighty-nine properties and offices.[35] The domain in the viscounty of Fézenzaguet was divided into more than a dozen parcels before it was leased. Seigneurial fines, privileges, and domains were leased together (*en bloc*), and properties were combined only when they could be rented no other way.[36] During the Wars of Religion, agents sometimes had no other choice but to combine two or three devastated properties to make an enticing package. Under such conditions, for example, the properties of Puycasquier and Torrenx were briefly combined and leased together in Fézenzaguet from 1569 to 1572 because no one would bid for the ruined properties separately. Three years later, however, agents divided the properties again and leased them separately.[37]

---

[33]AD-PA, B1827, B1832.
[34]AD-PA, B1500.
[35]AD-PA, B1588.
[36]The properties of Saint-Cric, Montbrun, Betpoy, and Encausse in Fézenzaguet were so small that they were always leased together; even so, they rarely drew two-figure bids. Agents also leased the domains in the minor seigneury of Rivière-Basse in the county of Armagnac with properties in Maubourget to bring up rents.
[37]AD-PA, B1588, B1595.

In the 1560s, the impact of the rationalization policies of previous decades became even more readily apparent. The small viscounty of Fézenzaguet provides an excellent example of the Albrets' agents' efforts to maximize profits through the shrewd manipulation of demographic forces and an emerging market economy, even when only a few hundred livres were at stake. Overshadowed by the neighboring county of Armagnac to the west, which regularly generated revenues in the tens of thousands, the small viscounty of Fézenzaguet rarely produced revenues over 3,000 livres during the entire sixteenth century. Despite its size and consistently modest revenues, the viscounty of Fézenzaguet offered almost unparalleled opportunity to increase rents. The Albrets' on-site agents recognized that the combination of population density and fertile arable lands put almost irresistible pressures on rents, which they intensified by auctioning domanial lands and seigneurial privileges pertaining there for three-year periods. While short-term leases routinely brought prospective tenants to the auctions in great numbers until the late 1580s and 1590s, the competition for Fézenzaguet properties and privileges drove many out of the market once the bidding started. The subdivision of properties perpetrated by the Albrets suggests a market system favorable to small, independent producers/farmers, but leasing records suggest otherwise. By the 1560s, two, but more often three or four people, had to join forces and pool resources in order to make a successful bid. Even then, lessees were often unable to hold onto their leaseholds for more than three years at a time. When leaseholds were auctioned in 1565 in Fézenzaguet, only one group managed to renew their lease from three years earlier. The rest found themselves outbid by newcomers.

The constantly changing roster of lessees recorded in the domanial accounts tells the grim story of failed hopes and expectations. Between 1565 and 1610 only a dozen aspiring lessees—among literally scores who tried—were able to establish their dominant control over a particular leasehold. Bernard Faget, a tavern owner from Mauvesin, latched onto the property of Garbic in 1586 and renewed his lease every term for the next twenty years.[38] More common, however, even among the successful, were those farmers like Jean DaGusan who moved from plot to plot, and thereby managed to clear enough money to remain active in the land market for a decade. In 1583, for example, DaGusan first appeared on the rent rolls along with two other hopeful farmers with whom he leased the property of Torrenx. When the lease expired in 1586 he and his comrades lost out to two other farmers. But the ever

---

[38] AD-PA, B1607, B1622, B1651, B1672, B1686.

resourceful DaGusan scrambled for his bit of land and managed to put together a successful offer to lease Brunhenx along with six other farmers. With another seven he leased the lucrative seigneury of Céran.[39] Men like DaGusan and Faget plotted and connived to get their *pied à terre* as they made their way in the feisty world of tenant farming. Other men, such as DaGusan's first partners in 1583, simply faded from view after one bid for property and prosperity, but played an important role in keeping the land market buoyed and prices high.

Short-term leases made investment in land a risky proposition for many small farmers and proprietors. Short-term leases, however, also made it easier for the Albrets to monitor the tenants who were farming their lands and the officials who were ostensibly guarding their woods, overseeing their prisons, and captaining their castles. The triennial auctions served as a pretext to conduct informal surveys of seigneurial forests, castles, and prisons. Commissioners spent at least part of their time assaying damages on domanial properties, charging the culprits where they could be found, ordering and sometimes funding requisite repairs. Triennial investigations—however informal or brief they might be—insured that no case of egregious negligence could go on too long before being reported to officials. And where such negligence represented a threat to property values or rents, commissioners were quick to take steps to arrest it.

Our men in Périgord, for example, made inquiries wherever they went in 1553 and gave members of the local notables both the means and the authority to carry out castle repairs and pursue thieves. In Bouil, fourteen livres were awarded to one De la Faye, "who promised to use the said sum to repair the tower of the local château damaged during a violent windstorm." Charges were heard that thieves were divesting the domanial forests of trees and guards were called to account. The commission found a castle also in ruins at Ans, "lacking a roof and also doors." The poor captain explained that he only received fourteen livres in wages and had "no fines, nor any other perquisites with which to make the necessary repairs." At Ségur, the commissioners authorized the sale of old crossbeams and other wood found in the dilapidated castle to "rebuild, cover and maintain the prison there." Indeed, wherever they found a castle poorly maintained, the commissioners ordered repairs because a crumbling castle meant no prisons and, accordingly, a diminution of seigneurial revenues from criminal prosecutions.[40]

---

[39]AD-PA, B1604, B1607.
[40]AD-PA, B1832.

As a result of such shrewd leasing practices, Henri d'Albret's legacy to his only daughter and heir, Jeanne d'Albret, was a full treasury and well-administered domains. By 1557–58 Jeanne's general treasurer recorded revenues from her estates worth 127,315 livres.[41] These had climbed five years later to 171,850 livres.[42] Total annual receipts before local treasurers deducted their expenses probably amounted to more. By virtue of Henri's efforts, Jeanne enjoyed revenues equal to those of the greatest royal favorite, the first in a long line of royal *mignons*, Anne de Montmorency, Constable de France, who cunningly used his position to enrich himself and expand his family patrimony. As a result, by 1563–64 he could claim 148,600 livres from his dozens of estates, scattered throughout thirteen *pays* and provinces. Jeanne also enjoyed greater revenues than her brother-in-law, duc of Clèves, reported to be the wealthiest "foreign" duke in France in the sixteenth century. In 1551 Nevers received 105,000 livres from his estates, a figure which probably dropped to below 100,000 livres by 1560 because of his extensive alienation of property.[43] Had not the Wars of Religion intervened and occasioned the widespread alienation of properties in Périgord and Armagnac, increases in Jeanne's revenues might have continued to the end of the century.

III. The Wars of Religion, Leasing Policies, and Rebates

The Wars of Religion forced the Albrets' agents to reassess and modify the leasing policies which had permitted them to so effectively exploit demographic pressures and growing hunger for land during the first half of the sixteenth century. Between 1562 and 1598, nine fullscale wars, innumerable localized skirmishes, and the brigandage and random violence that followed in the wake of each war seriously threatened the Albrets' economic control as well as their political authority over their domains in southwestern France. At the same time, their open support of the Calvinist cause after 1568 placed an almost relentless burden on their personal finances, which in turn increased the pressure on local agents and domanial treasurers to maintain the general upward trend in landed revenues realized in almost every one of the Albrets' domains in the 1550s and early 1560s. The tension between cultivating tenant interest in lands increasingly devastated by war and raising revenues to meet the growing demands on the Albrets' general treasury pushed local agents to adopt more flexible

---

[41] AD-PA, B143
[42] AD-PA, B146
[43] Greengrass, "Property and Politics," 376–77.

leasing practices to respond to the rapid changes in the land market occasioned by war. During times of severe crisis they attempted to facilitate the capital formation necessary for a strong land market by pursuing more lenient collection policies. Secondly, they periodically shortened leases to allay concerns about the continuing value and profitability of properties in war torn regions. Agents also played on religious sympathies, cultural distinctiveness, and the geographic orientation of tenants when devising a response to the sagging market for land.

Nowhere was the cumulative impact of warfare on the market for land and the seigneurial privileges attached to it more obvious than in the county of Armagnac, which was invaded repeatedly by royalist troops and subjected twice to the degradation of military occupation after the outbreak of the first of the Religious Wars in France in 1562. Almost immediately, hostilities between Catholics and Protestants erupted in Armagnac, even though Jeanne d'Albret herself carefully modeled a guarded neutrality to her subjects until 1568. Within weeks, royal troops under the command of Blaise de Monluc, who had three years earlier pledged himself to the Albrets' service, attempted to lay waste the Albret territories. Amazingly, the devastation created by troop movements and the prolonged siege and capture of the city of Lectoure by Catholics did not affect the ability of domanial treasurers to collect revenues. In fact, leases actually increased in nine out of the eleven fiefs into which Armagnac was divided, and the treasurer recorded a 7 percent increase in the 1562 revenues over rents garnered in 1558–59 before the war (see table 1.3).

Revenues, however, were not so resilent when royal troops commanded by the Baron of Terride swept through both Armagnac and Bigorre seven years later, under orders from Charles IX to seize all of Jeanne d'Albret's lands in retaliation for her declaration of support for the Calvinist cause. While Terride was more interested in Jeanne's lands in Béarn, which he invaded, occupied, and mercilessly taxed during the five months he held sway over the independent viscounty, the financial and psychological impact of troop movements through Armagnac in 1569 was also devastating. Leaseholders lost confidence in a land market which had been flattened twice, with little warning, in the course of eight years. Farmers who had leased seigneurial rights rather than the land itself were equally concerned about the potential challenge Terride's occupation and Charles IX's charge of *lèse majesté* presented to Jeanne d'Albret's seigneurial authority. In the face of such problems, land values in Armagnac plummeted; and between 1569 and 1572, the treasurer of Armagnac collected as much in revenue in three years as he normally had collected in one year before the invasion (see

Table 1.3 Annual Landed Revenues for Armagnac, 1555–1579 (in *livres tournois*)

Jurisdiction	1555–6[a]	1558–9	1562–3	1569–72[d]	est. annual revenue	1575–6	1578-9
Lectoure	2385	2470	2666	2606	869	2850	2783
Aurillac[b]	2840	1817	2769	2950	983	1887	2985
Lomaigne	1300	1200	1241	1500	500	1516	1674
Bruilhois[c]	2100	1507	1533	1785	595	1218	837
Fezensac	2305	2275	2676	3500	1167	4535	4511
Pardiac	3093	2703	3135	3692	1231	3800	3899
Eauzan	800	852	862	1110	370	505	1019
Rivière-Basse	435	468	481	610	203	675	683
Astaffort	122	124	75	100	33	161	165
Touron	310	333	375	380	127	610	639
L'Ile Jourdain	5103	5611	4931	5504	1835	6163	5052
TOTAL	20793	19360	20744	23737	7913	23920	24247

AD-PA Source, respectively by year: B2135, B1581, B1584, B1588, B1591, B1594

[a] The fiscal year ran from one St. John the Baptist day until the next.
[b] Also included in the receipts were 12 *pipes* of wine, used to pay the county syndic's salary.
[c] Alienated in 1569 to raise money for war expenses; rights of justice and tolls remained.
[d] Figures represent amount for which the domains were leased for a three-year period beginning in 1569, rather than an annual rent.

table 1.3). To bolster the sagging market, agents scrambled for a strategy to restore confidence in the land market and in the lordship of Jeanne d'Albret. They adopted a more lenient collection policy which stretched out rent payments over a three-year period instead of the normal fiscal year. Treasurers' accounts suggest that this policy of benevolence did indeed facilitate a rapid recovery of the land market in Armagnac by giving leaseholders the necessary time to rebuild the reservoir of investment capital necessary to enter the marketplace in the first place, while at the same time allowing the Albrets to demonstrate their liberality and generosity toward their impecunious subjects. By 1575–76 revenues in Armagnac had recovered and surpassed prewar figures, increasing a total of 202 percent over the drastic drop in 1569–72 (see tables 1.3 and 1.4).

Table 1.4 Percentage Changes in Armagnac Revenues, 1555–1579
(in *livres tournois*)

Jurisdiction	1555–6 to 1578–9	1562–3 to 1569–72	1569–72 to 1575–76
Lectoure	17%	-67%	228%
Aurillac	5%	-64%	92%
Lomaigne	29%	-60%	203%
Bruilhois	-60%	-61%	105%
Fezensac	96%	-56%	289%
Pardiac	26%	-61%	209%
Eauzan	27%	-57%	36%
Rivière-Basse	57%	-58%	232%
Astaffort	35%	-56%	383%
Touron	106%	-66%	382%
L'Ile Jourdain	-1%	-63%	236%
TOTAL	17%	-62%	202%

The resumption of hostilities in 1572 after the Saint-Bartholomew's Day Massacre, then again in 1576, 1577, and 1579, jeopardized efforts to increase revenues in Armagnac between late 1570s and early 1580s, but the internal pressure on leaseholds kept overall revenues relatively stable in Armagnac until 1585 when religious passions flared again and southwestern France collapsed into another decade of violence and devastation. During the 1570s and 1580s, according to treasurers' accounts, certain areas in Armagnac knew little relief from the passage of troops and the havoc they wreaked on the land.[44] But while the presence of troops in one area in Armagnac drove down the price of land, the resulting scarcity intensified rental pressure in other areas spared the indignities and depradations of war. For example, landed revenues around L'Ile Jourdain declined 18 percent between 1575–76 and 1578–79, a further 2 percent between 1578–79 and 1583–84, and a devastating 75 percent between 1583–84 and 1588–89. In Eauzan and Astaffort revenues declined 51 and 55 percent, respectively, between 1578–79 and 1583–84. But other larger properties, including Lectoure, Aurillac, Bruilhois, and Pardiac, experienced rises in rents ranging from 11 to 25 percent between 1578–79 and 1583–84. Despite warfare in Armagnac in the late 1570s and early1580s, rental receipts declined only 1 percent (see table 1.5).

The chequered pattern revealed by tracing percentage changes in land revenues in Armagnac reflects tenants' mad scramble for viable leaseholds from season to season, which buoyed up landed revenues even in troubled areas until the late 1580s. By 1587–88 such a scramble for land became increasingly untenable in many areas as the military crisis persisted with little end in sight and farmers were no longer able to cope financially or psychologically. Thus, when commissioners offered properties for lease in the beleaguered county of Armagnac in 1587, they faced subdued crowds. Seigneury after seigneury went unleased because no one would bid. In a few cases, bids were so small that commissioners even elected not to accept them.[45] Rents which had long been stagnant now declined precipitously. In l588–89, for example, treasurers recorded only 8,268 livres in rent—a 66 percent drop in revenues from previous years. In many ways, the crisis of 1587–89 was similar to the crisis experienced in 1568, except that recovery was much more attenuated (see table 1.5).[46]

By 1595, the first real year of peace in the region for over a decade, the crisis in Armagnac had become so serious that Henri de Navarre tried to lure wary tenants back to the land by offering shorter leases. In the spring of 1595 he issued a decree commanding his agents to lease lands in the particularly hard-hit counties of Armagnac and Fézenzaguet "for only the first year of the triennium."[47] Farmers in Armagnac

---

[44]AD-PA, B1594, B1600, B1608.
[45]AD-PA, B1606.
[46]AD-PA, B1606, B1608, B1610.
[47]AD-PA, B1622.

Table 1.5 Impact of Wars of Religion on Armagnac Land Revenues (in *livres tournois*)

Jurisdiction	1575-6	1578-9	% Change	1583-4	% Change	1588-9	% Change	1595-6	% Change	1600-1	% Change
Lectoure	2850	2783	-2%	3478	25%	645	-81%	2197	241%	2586	17%
Aurillac	1887	2985	58%	3345	12%	576	-83%	2010	249%	2715	35%
Lomaigne	1516	1674	10%	1545	-8%	267	-83%	1258	371%	985	-22%
Bruilhois	1218	837	-31%	1045	25%	393	-62%	732	86%	853	17%
Fezensac	4535	4511	-1%	4106	-9%	2223	-46%	4681	111%	3870	-17%
Pardiac	3800	3899	3%	4346	11%	1512	-65%	2209	46%	2169	-2%
Eauzan	505	1019	102%	501	-51%	648	29%	500	-23%	510	2%
Rivière-Basse	675	683	1%	588	-14%	246	-58%	300	22%	348	16%
Astaffort	161	165	2%	74[a]	-55%	84	14%	195	132%	462	137%
Touron	610	639	5%	—[b]	—[b]	450	—[b]	388	-14%	—[b]	—[b]
L'Ile Jourdain	6163	5052	-18%	4941	-2%	1224	-75%	4997	308%	4950	-1%
TOTAL	23920	24247	1%	23969	-1%	8268	-66%	19467	135%	19448	0%

AD-PA Source, respectively by year: B1591, B1594, B1600, B1608, B1621, B1652

[a] Represents collection of monies due to the Astoffort account from previous years. The seigneury was given to one of Navarre's captains of war to farm as a reward for services rendered.
[b] Sold.
[c] See table 1.3 for Armagnac rental receipts from the 1550s and 1560s.

responded by bidding for leaseholds more vociferously and competitively than they had since the reorganization of the Holy League in 1585. Rents were still comparatively low—they did not even match those offered in the 1570s—but the dramatic upswing from the depression of 1587, 1588, and 1589 must have been encouraging (see table 1.5).

In the viscounty of Fézenzaguet, the farmers' response was more checkered. The commissioners noted that they opened the auction in Mauvesin in 1595 to "a great number of people," many of whom proved to be aggressive bidders. The properties of Torrenx, Pys, Mauvesin, Bayonette, and the combined seigneuries of Brunhenx and Urdenx all attracted some lively competition among prospective tenants gathered in the public square. When the bidding closed on these favored domains, they had been leased for prices which were 11 to 39 percent higher than the 1587 contracts. But in other cases—notably Montfort, Céran, Tourget, Tarbic, and Saint Cric—bids did not even meet the base price, and rents declined (see table 1.6). Notary Antoine Verses, for example, was the sole offrant for the once lucrative seigneury of Tourget. His initial bid of 70 écus did not even clear the stated opening prices of 132 écus 70 sols. To tempt others present to bid, the commissioners offered to include the right to levy entry fines on fiefholders (*lods et ventes*), although previous leases had stipulated that the Albrets reserved that right for themselves. Even so, Verses remained the only party interested in the property, and so Tourget was delivered into his hands—along with *lods et ventes*—for a mere 70 écus.[48] In total, 1595 rental receipts from Fézenzaguet declined 2 percent over 1587–88 receipts (see table 1.6).

The anxious commissioners in Fézenzaguet chose more than once to close down auctions for a few days in hopes that more potential tenants would come forward. After the first day of auctioning, a herald was sent to all the cantons of Mauvesin to announce that the commissioners would continue to entertain bids the following morning. In fact, the auction did not open again for three days, and when bids still remained sluggish, the officials decided to proceed to L'Ile Jourdain to begin leasing the domain in the county of Armagnac. They returned briefly to Mauvesin a week later to close the auction definitively. They were compelled—after much deliberation—to lease the notary rights in Mauvesin below the opening price and offer the right to collect rents in arrears to the sole offrant, Pierre Bosquery, for a paltry two écus.[49]

[48]Ibid.
[49]Ibid.

Table 1.6 Rental Receipts from Fézenzaguet, 1569-1595 (in *livres tournois*)

Jurisdiction	1569-72	1579-80	Percentage Change	1584-5	Percentage Change	1587-8	Percentage Change	1595	Percentage Change
Mauvesin	545	767	41%	836	9%	426	-49%	582	37%
Montfort	350	300	-14%	342	14%	300	-12%	202	-33%
Céran	170	120	-29%	186	55%	189	2%	108	-43%
Puycasquier	105	264	151%	309	17%	357	16%	360	1%
Tourget	345	390	13%	411	5%	420	2%	241	-43%
Brunhenx & Urdenx	365	336	-8%	450	34%	441	-2%	513	16%
Bayonette	35	36	3%	54	50%	54	0%	75	39%
Pys	185	175	-5%	234	34%	252	8%	280	11%
Cirac	12	12	0%	9	-25%	9	0%		
Torrenx		99		114	15%	144	26%	200	39%
Tarbic	17	24	41%	12	-50%	33	175%	10	-70%
Saint Cric	18	12	-33%	15	0%	15	0%	9	-40%
Terres Château	30	—	—	—	—	—	—	—	—
TOTAL	2177	2535	16%	2972	17%	2640	-11%	2580	2%

Navarre and members of the Chambre des comptes clearly viewed the one-year lease as a temporary expedient responding to difficult times. Similar decrees were promulgated for the viscounty of Nébouzan in 1597 and 1598.[50] In the barony of Aspet, where receipts were usually appended to those of Nébouzan, the domain was leased out yearly from 1595 to 1598.[51] And in Rodez Albret agents offered the domain for two-year leases in 1597.[52] But nowhere did these shorter leases permanently supplant the standard Albret three-year lease. The administrative challenges of auctioning off lands and rights every twelve months was enough to deter Navarre from implementing the one-year lease as a permanent policy. Auctions could take, as we have seen, several days to several weeks in just one jurisdiction, and members of the Chambre des comptes hardly had the time to spend months each year journeying through the countryside in search of lessees. Even in 1595, officials in the Chambre des comptes at Nérac promptly appointed delegates to execute the onerous task of leasing domains in Armagnac. LaValade and Mazelières and the others commissioned by Navarre for the job complained that they were far too busy to conduct the auctions "particularly as it is the will of his Majesty to make them for the first year of the triennium only."[53] Clearly, in their minds the one-year lease was but a stopgap measure.

There were other concessions to tenant farmers during the crisis-ridden decades of the 1580s and 1590s. Contract after contract still required lessees to pay a sizable down payment (*caution*) before taking possession of the land as a measure of their ability to fulfill the terms of the lease, but agents increasingly turned a blind eye toward this formality or were slow to enforce it.[54] Estate officials sometimes chose to risk renting to an eager but insolvent farmer rather than not to rent at all. In the Pyrenean county of Bigorre, for example, agents warned bidders before the auction of 1575 that they had until noon the next day to close the deal by paying their *caution*.[55] Failure to do so would mean immediate forfeiture of the lease. By 1591, however, the agents could not afford to be so strict. Plague had ripped through Rebastenx and other Bigourdan villages in 1590, only to be followed less than a year later by the unholy revelry of League troops under the direction of the

---

[50] AD-PA, B1355, B1356.
[51] Ibid.
[52] AD-PA, B1955.
[53] AD-PA, B1622.
[54] See, for example, the general requirements set forth in the auction accounts for the county of Bigorre, AD-PA, B1013.
[55] Ibid.

Marquis de Villars.[56] In spite of rather generous rebates granted by officials to many ruined farmers in 1590 and 1591, people were still cash-poor when leases became available in the summer of 1591. Farmers had defaulted on their leases in great numbers; others had just barely survived. Hence, willing bidders were few in 1591 and agents decided to grant a number of leases without demanding the requisite down payment. They did not, of course, dispense with it entirely, but agreed to defer payment until the impecunious tenants could pay up.

And did the risk pay off? Treasurers' records show that all but one of the farmers, who died before he was able to pay, eventually fulfilled the conditions of their leases.[57] Elsewhere Albret agents were also more than willing to alter time-honored proscriptions, rules, and regulations in order to reinvigorate the sagging market for land. Old prohibitions against estate and household officials leasing lands were dropped or discreetly forgotten.[58] When Nicholas de Gariepuy bid for and won the right to lease the *greffe* in Mauvesin in 1586, no one bothered to point out that *maître* Gariepuy drew a salary of 50 livres from the domanial treasury in Fézenzaguet as viscounty judge.[59] Similarly, Raymond Despes, conservator for the Albret estates in Armagnac, managed to consolidate his hold over the Fézenzaguet seigneuries of Brunhenx and Céran with little opposition in 1600 and 1604.[60]

The changing social configuration of the men who leased the Albret lands during the reign of Henri IV also bears witness to the crisis which gripped the countryside in the last stages of the Religious Wars during which many nobles and Huguenot war captains pushed poor peasant-proprietors off the land and out of their leaseholds. In spite of the Albrets' efforts to make their leaseholds as attractive as possible to the small entrepreneur or peasant farmer, it became increasingly difficult in the 1590s to counteract the effect of decades of random religious violence and warfare. In regions directly in the path of marauding armies, even the most enterprising entrepreneur found it increasingly difficult to meet the terms of leases, and harder still to turn a profit. Declining yields and rising debts eventually took their toll on some fragile peasant patrimonies, while nobles, many of whom had profited from the legal as well as the extralegal fortunes of war, were in a position to

---

[56] AD-PA, B1023.
[57] AD-PA, B965.
[58] See this proscription in the Bigorre account, AD-PA, B1013.
[59] AD-PA, B1607.
[60] For Despes' position in the county of Armagnac, see AD-PA, B1588, B1598, B1626; for his lease in Fézenzaguet see B1672, B1651.

take advantage of the peasants' plight. The military demobilization which took place at the end of the wars may have furthered this process as well. In some areas where peasant landholding had been preponderant, it is possible to detect a small but growing number of noble leaseholders. In Fézenzaguet, names with noble epithets or the telltale toponym appear with increasing regularity on the domanial accounts after 1595, supplanting surnames of peasant farmers.[61] Nobles, such as Raymond Despes and Charles de Saint Lizier, assumed the leaseholds of the profitable seigneuries of Tourget, Brunhenx, Céran, and Saint-Cric between 1600 and 1608, and many a clever *capitaine de ville* was welcomed onto the leasing rosters during the same period.[62] In Armagnac, noble Pierre LaTaste dashed the hopes of many an aspiring peasant when he leased the entire county of L'Ile Jourdain (all rights included) for a whopping 1,435 livres in 1600.[63]

In the end, what can we say about the Albrets' leasing policies? First, they were subject to constant demographic pressure and price fluctuations which usually permitted the Albrets to make the most of the growing peasant demand for land. The modifications enacted at midcentury, as we have seen, were specifically geared toward small proprietors and artisans, who bid with much enthusiasm for their plots of land. During the Wars of Religion, the willingness to risk change permitted the Albrets to lease lands which otherwise might have lain fallow. Second, the Albrets' policy of short-term leases gave them considerable control over their lands (they could and did monitor tenants' use of their land) and over their revenues (they could take advantage of the general rise in prices). Henri d'Albret and his progeny were not slaves to custom, except when it was to their advantage to be so.

IV. Rebates

That the Albret domains, in general, continued to be leased at higher and higher rates until the late 1580s and 1590s when farmers found themselves caught in a paroxysm of violence and pestilence seems clear from the domanial accounts. Farmers in the beleaguered viscounty of Fézenzaguet, as we have seen, leased land at ever-

---

[61]AD-PA, B1642, B1651, B1668, B1686.
[62]Ibid.
[63]AD-PA, B1652. What happened in Fézenzaguet and Armagnac was echoed in many regions throughout France in the later decades of the Religious Wars. For Poitou, where 60 percent of the peasants abandoned their leaseholds between 1570 and 1590, see Merle, *Le Métaire*, 3–66, 178–79; for Burgundy, see P. de Saint-Jacob, "Mutations économiques et sociales dans les campagnes bourguignonnes à la fin du XVIe siècle," *Études rurales* 1 (1961–62):34–39.

increasing rates until the last decade of the century. Receipts rose from 1,517 livres in 1562–63 to 2,331 livres in 1565–66, more modestly to 2,535 livres in 1579–80, and finally to 2,972 livres in 1584–85 (see tables 1.2 and 1.6). Thus, after nearly two decades of civil war, farmers were still leasing land at rates far above those paid at the beginning of the wars in 1562–63. In 1587, the land market in Fézenzaguet lost some of its buoyancy and rental receipts fell to 2,640 livres. Nevertheless, leasehold rates still increased in six out of thirteen fiefs into which the viscounty was divided (see table 1.6). In Bigorre, leaseholds in 1574–75 were sometimes two to three times higher than those of 1538–39 and in 1595–96 leases on those properties spared the ravages of war had doubled again.[64] Undoubtedly, the biggest gains were made in the cradle of the family's power, the viscounty of Béarn. There, receipts quintupled between 1530 and 1595. Indeed, the only exception to this general upward trend in rents and receipts occurred in 1569, when the Baron Terride, under orders from Charles IX, invaded the little viscounty and despoiled the Albrets' estates and treasuries. Within a few years of Terride's invasions, however, domanial receipts were once again on the rise, outstripping records set earlier in the century. By 1575–76, vigilant estate officials had managed to collect 42,500 écus for the Albrets. By the end of the century, revenues from Béarn routinely surpassed 100,000 écus.[65]

In some of their territories, the Albrets compromised their returns from the domain by alienating large, attractive properties in order to turn a quick profit. The short-term benefits of alienation were particularly compelling during the Religious Wars, as we will see in chapter 6. In Béarn, customary law prohibited the Albrets from selling or alienating any part of their domain, which may also explain the sure and steady rise in domanial receipts throughout the sixteenth century. But few of the Albrets' other territories were protected by similar strictures. Receipts in the duchies of Périgord and Albret and the country of Armagnac, for example, were periodically depressed by alienation, most of which were made to noblemen or noblewomen, who alone could afford to pay the enormous sums a large seigneury could command (see table 1.1 notes). The Albrets were careful to reserve their right to redeem the lands they alienated (*rachat perpétuel*). Nonetheless, large-scale alienation often skewed receipts and obscured general secular trends. Treasury receipts could be spectacular for the year in which the alienation

---

[64]AD-PA, E378, B1013, B965.
[65]For a discussion of these receipts, see Major, "Noble Income," 27–35.

took place, only to fall off dramatically in the following years until the alienated domain was redeemed.

Perhaps the best example of the effect of such alienation on domanial revenues is the duchy of Périgord, where the Albrets alienated a number of properties between 1566 and 1600 in order to finance the Huguenot war effort and pay off their old debts. Leaseholds doubled on most Périgourdan properties between 1551–52 and 1583–84, but domanial receipts only partially reflected what amounted to a phenomenal boom in property values. Receipts showed a 62 percent increase from 8,377 livres in 1551–52 to 13,573 livres in 1573–74 and dropped off sharply to 9,508 livres in 1575–76, the latter drop in large part due to the Albrets' extensive alienations. While receipts from rents rallied slightly in 1583–84 to a respectable 11,362 livres, that figure conveys little sense of what was happening in marketplaces all over Périgord when estate officials put land up for rent. Even more misleading, of course, were the total treasury receipts, which soared to 40,000 and 50,000 livres in years when lucrative seigneuries were alienated, then plummeted in succeeding years. To judge by the aggregate figures, land values were extremely unstable in wartime Périgord, but individual rent returns tell a different story. Where seigneuries remained intact and in the Albrets' possession, they commanded ever more lucrative rents (see table 1.1).

Rising rents, however, tell only half the story. During the Wars of Religion, estate expenditures also rose rapidly, and domanial treasurers saw their cash reserves dwindle as they paid out ever-increasing sums to the judges, notaries, and accountants who braved highways thick with thieves and enemy troops to collect rents and oversee leaseholds.[66] Imbert Venier's personal record—a sixty-six-page *"cayer des frais"*—of his efforts as a special envoy to recover receipts from the family holdings in Nébouzan, Marson, Bigorre, and Foix in 1574 offers the most telling testimony of the increasing cost of carrying out even the most routine estate business. Accompanied by a sergeant-at-arms, and several soldiers, Venier traveled through the war-torn counties of Bigorre and Nébouzan in September of 1574 to retrieve 2,493 livres in a dozen different currencies from the domanial treasuries at a cost of 87 livres. Three months later Venier returned to Nébouzan to collect another 21,863 livres for the Chambre des comptes in Nérac and recorded that he spent 970 livres in doing so. All the while, Venier's servant, François LaFargue, ferried back and forth between Venier and

---

[66]These expenses, entered as *dépenses communes*, quadrupled in most accounts between 1562 and 1595.

Navarre's officers in Paris at an additional charge of 466 livres. When Venier finally tallied the total cost of his commission as special envoy, including his salary and those of the family accountants, his expenses amounted to almost 1,100 livres.[67]

Repairs comprised an even greater charge on domanial treasuries, and the frugal treasurers—out of whose pockets deficits and debts were paid—frequently chose to forgo all but the most necessary repairs until more pressing expenditures were settled.[68] Of the latter, we must certainly count the rebates handed out to farmers whose fields had been damaged by troop movements. After wages, which remained fairly stable, rebates probably comprised the greatest drain on a treasurer's disposable income.

The Albrets considered the random granting of rebates a dangerous enough threat to their income to issue stringent regulations concerning their award and vehement injunctions against any farmer or agent found guilty of fabricating evidence.[69] In the years immediately before and after the Religious Wars, estate officials granted rebates to lessees who were unable to claim the full fruits of their lease for any number of reasons. In 1604, for example, Henri IV ordered members of his Chambre des comptes at Pau to investigate damages caused by a hailstorm in his kingdom of Navarre and grant due compensation where the domain had been ruined.[70] But in the late sixteenth century in the wake of the Religious Wars, estate officials were so flooded with claims that they risked losing most of their receipts to rent reductions. As the ranks of farmers clamoring for relief burgeoned and rebates—both those granted and those pending verification—became an irrepressible charge on domanial budgets, Navarre was ultimately forced to respond by tightening the conditions under which rebates were granted. "The farmers of the said domain cannot claim any reduction in the lease for any reason or fortune except if there is war or plague in the countryside." So read the preamble to the general leasing contract of the county of Bigorre in 1597.[71] The text stipulated that farmers of properties in or near garrisoned towns were not eligible for rebates of any kind. Navarre showed no clemency to his subjects in the duchy of Albret in 1589–90. There, rebates which had been mounting over the

---

[67] AD-PA, B1710. See also, Neuschel, *Word of Honor*, 170–71, for a discussion of the administrative costs and travel expenses of noble household officers.

[68] Repairs usually amounted to between 2 and 10 percent of domanial expenses.

[69] AD-PA, B1013.

[70] AD-PA, E382.

[71] AD-PA, B1025.

years reached 3,037 livres in 1585–86 and 1,622 livres in 1587–88.[72] When leases came open in 1589, all leasing contracts included a special clause requiring farmers to renounce any right to claim rebates during the three-year contract period from 1589 to 1592.[73] Contracts apparently carried the same requirement three years later because the treasurer was obliged to explain an entry in his accounts in 1594–95 of 30 livres to one Bernard Durant, farmer of the seigneury of Laussignan. Launay, the treasurer, insisted that the rebate was due only to Catherine de Bourbon's touching "liberality . . . notwithstanding the renunciation of all rebates in the said country."[74] The treasurer of Rodez, in his accounts, indicated that edicts proscribing rebates were promulgated in his jurisdiction in the early nineties. In 1593, he recorded that Guillaume de Revessac paid his rent of 325 écus for the domains around Caussade "without any hope of a rebate."[75]

The county of Armagnac provides perhaps the clearest example of the wild surge in rebates which took place during the civil wars (see table 1.7). There awards doubled between 1583 and 1586–87; a year later they had more than doubled again. In just four years rent refunds rose from 876 livres in 1583–84 to 3,872 livres in 1587–88. Even so, farmers' claims far exceeded the agents' magnanimity. In 1583–84, Armagnac lessees demanded a total of 1,602 livres in refunds. Agents suspended payment of almost half of this sum—726 livres—pending further investigation of these claims. Undaunted, farmers continued to press their claims, which by 1587–88 had more than quintupled. A whopping 11,585 livres (more than rents received) was charged to the treasurer's account that year. Estate officials anxious to stem the rising tide and weed out fraudulent or exaggerated claims contested nearly two out of every three cases submitted for consideration. Nevertheless, for several more years the value of those claims in which fraud or collusion was suspected continued to exceed the value of claims actually granted. Only after almost a decade of peace rebate figures dropped significantly, although estate officials still found it difficult to break farmers' rebate claims. The treasurer for Armagnac recorded in 1604–5 that rebates worth 407 livres—out of 867 livres claimed—were suspended, pending investigation. The worst economic consequences of the Religious Wars had been weathered and rental receipts were once again rising on the lands of the house of Foix-Navarre-Albret.

[72]AD-PA, B1473, B1477, B1478.
[73]AD-PA, B1480.
[74]AD-PA, B1486.
[75]AD-PA, B1950.

Table 1.7 Rent Rebates in the County of Armagnac (in *livres tournois*)

Year	1574-5[c]	1578-9[c]	1583-4[c]	1586-7[d]	1587-8[e]	1589-90[c]	1595-6[c]	1604-5[c]
Rebates Granted[a]	738	1200	876	1680	3872	969	318	460
Rebates Pending[b]	22	—	726	—	7713	2658	2664	407
Total Rebates Claimed	760	1200	1602	1680	11585	3627	2982	867
Total Rents Received	23920	25604	24955	—	893	5676	19529	18863

AD-PA Source, repectively by year: B1591, B1594, B1600, B1605, B1606, B1610, B1621, B1674

[a] *Alloué*
[b] *En surcéance*: rebates claimed by farmers, but not paid pending further investigation.
[c] The fiscal year ran from one Saint John the Baptist's Day to the next.
[d] Not a full treasurer's account; a statement listing only those properties from which rebates were claimed.
[e] Rents received in this term covered only half year.

V. Rents in Kind and Sales of Produce

The Albrets clearly derived the bulk of their fortunes from monetary leases. In most of the regions under their control, payments in kind comprised only a small—sometimes negligible—part of total revenues. In Navarre, for example, fiefholders still paid their annual dues with chickens, grains, and fava beans.[76] In the local marketplace, these fixed payments in kind—seventeen chickens, six *conques* of wheat, fifty-six *conques* of rye, and two sacks of fava beans—never brought more than an additional thirty livres into the domanial coffers.[77] This represented less than 1 percent of the Albrets' total annual income for their Pyrenean kingdom. Treasurers held the accounting of these revenues to be more time-consuming than profitable and frequently only reckoned them into the overall account in the postscript. In many domains, revenues paid in kind were never converted into cash, but served instead as part of the complex system of payments and perquisites by which estates officials were remunerated. Revenues from the seigneury of Aurillac in the county of Armagnac always included twelve *pipes* of wine, which were promptly handed over to the county syndic as one of the perquisites of office.[78] In Périgord, the leaseholder of the seigneury of Montignac owed six *carteaux* of wheat and rye and twelve *pipes* of wine to the captain of the castle in addition to his money lease.[79] In Foix, treasurers recorded a much longer list of revenues paid in kind—wheat, rye, millet, hens, and iron—all of which were absorbed by the county.[80]

Only in the duchy of Albret did rents paid in kind ever amount to sizable sums. Here the great mills in the barony of Nérac were farmed out to leaseholders for a share of their produce every year. These mills produced between six hindred and nine hundred *carteaux* of grain annually for the house of Foix-Navarre-Albret. Payments were so high that they warranted a special account. In the 1570s, the Albrets contracted with Pierre Assezat, the famous Huguenot merchant of Toulouse, to market the grain for them.[81] Not surprisingly, Assezat sold the grain at ever-increasing rates, and receipts from grain sales nearly tripled in the decade between 1576 and 1586 as the figures in table 1.8 make clear.

---

[76] AD-PA, B1412.
[77] AD-PA, B1412, B1414, B1417, B1420, B1425.
[78] AD-PA, B1591, B1606, B1673, B1674.
[79] AD-PA, B1862.
[80] AD-PA, B1072.
[81] AD-PA, B1468, E587.

Table 1.8 Revenues from Wheat in the Duchy of Albret (in *livres tournois*)

Year	Income in *Livres*	Average Price/ Carteau
1576–7	2,243	3£ 6s
1582–3	6,955	3£ 16s
1585–6	4,757	3£ 15s
1586–7	6,312	4£
1594–5	2,553	5£ 5s/ 6£
AD-PA Source, respectively by year: B1468, B1473, B1476, B1477, B1486		

Rents might even have been higher had the disruption of war not compelled Navarre to grant rebates to a number of beleaguered millers, while an even greater number defaulted on payments. According to the treasurer's accounts for 1586, 316 *carteaux* of wheat, 16 *carteaux* of millet, and 2 *carteaux* of hay could not be collected. And in the years following, grain receipts so dwindled that even rising prices could not compensate for the loss. In 1594, Albret agents sold less than 400 *carteaux* of grain.[82]

The only domain which the Albrets kept consistently in hand were their forests, although when the opportunity presented itself they were more than willing to auction off several hundred *arpents* of timber to satisfy pressing debts and personal obligations. Unlike the sale of real property which was often complicated by customary law and competing familial claims, the sale of timber could normally be accomplished with little fanfare and could yield enormous profits. The combined pressures of population growth, urbanization, and industrial development created a ready market for wood—even of the poorest quality—in the sixteenth century, often driving noble proprietors and their agents to exploit their forests ruthlessly with little concern for the continuing vitality of their woodlands. Just how important forest revenues could be to noble fortunes—middling and great—has been demonstrated by Jonathan Dewald in his study of the Norman barony of Pont St. Pierre,

[82] AD-PA, B1486.

where the Roncherolles saw the value of each *arpent* cut in their forest of Longbouel climb from two livres between 1501 and 1504 to fifty-seven livres by 1574. The Roncherolles found it difficult to remain immune to the lure of such quick profits and exploited their forests so zealously, according to Jean Bodin, that they "devastated nearly two leagues of countryside" by 1570.[83]

Great court nobles, such as the Albrets, were also shrewdly aware of the value of their forests.[84] Where profits matched financial exigency, the Albrets treated their trees less as a crop to be culled annually than as a vast reserve of potential capital to be drawn upon in times of crisis. In 1584, for example, in desperate need of money, Navarre ordered his treasurer, Vincent de Pedesclaux, to sell outright the woodlands belonging to his barony of Tournay "for maintenance of our affairs which we have to undertake every day."[85] Twenty years later, he commissioned the wholesale felling of 4,334 trees in Manciet to finance the repurchase of his alienated seigneury there. In the contract of sale, Navarre ceded the right to harvest these trees to two merchants from Bayonne "for the sum of 13,000 livres."[86] The forests in Périgord, in particular, were never systematically farmed, but were sold off instead for great lump sums which financed the Albrets' royal pretensions and their Huguenot armies.[87]

An even more ready source of funds than the Albrets' Périgourdan forestland were their forests in their estates of Vendômois, Marle, and Beaumont. To satisfy family debts estimated at 1,500,000 livres at Jeanne's death in 1577, family officials sold outright the forestland of Vendômois.[88] Forests in the county of Marle and the duchy of Beaumont were protected and still comprised from 15 to 20 percent of total revenues a year later. But by 1602, Henry IV ruthlessly exploited his forest of Saint Gobain in Marle ordering his agents to raise 15,000 écus from the timber sales to cover the salaries of his officers in the royal Chambre des comptes.[89] Timber harvesting on such a massive scale sometimes drew the criticism of the surrounding community and involved the Albrets in costly litigation and judicial proceedings. Saint

---

[83]See Jonathan Dewald, *Pont-St-Pierre*, 198–205.
[84]See Michel Devèze, *La vie de la forêt française au XVIe siècle*, 2 vols. (Paris: S.E.V.P.E.N., 1961), 1:202–3, for a comparison of the Albrets' forestland vis-à-vis other nobles.
[85]AD-PA, B1602.
[86]AD-PA, B1676.
[87] See, for example, AD-PA, B1608.
[88] Devèze, *La vie de la forêt*, 1:256.
[89]AD-PA, A4.

Gobain locals complained in 1602, for example, that Navarre's orders jeopardized traditional communal grazing rights, in spite of agents' protests that the harvest represented only a fraction (*la superficie*) of the lush forests of Saint Gobain which sprawled over four thousand *arpents* (roughly twenty-five hundred acres).[90]

Where geography and commerce combined to encourage a kind of rudimentary tree farming, there is evidence in notarial records and administrative documents that the Albrets and their agents pursued a well-reasoned policy of timber cultivation. In Armagnac especially, the Albrets treated their forests as a precious and increasingly valuable resource which they handled in a manner worthy of the most enterprising merchant.[91] Here, the plenitude of small rivers, all flowing into the great Garonne, made transport to the markets of Toulouse, where timber and wood fetched high prices, a relatively easy and inexpensive affair. This transportation naturally made Armagnac wood especially attractive to traders. Well aware of the profits to be had, the Albrets employed eight guards to watch their forests and paid the captain of the château at L'Ile Jourdain to lease out or sell selected sections of forest every year to traders. In many cases, the contract of lease or sale prohibited the wholesale felling of trees. The forests were divided into small sections between four and nine *arpents* in size and auctioned off. Treasurers increasingly distinguished between ordinary cuts (*coupes ordinaires*), where the purchasers felled only marked trees, and specialized sales, where traders could harvest every tree on the lot. Thus exploited, the forests of Bacone, Saint Gerbaige, and Glandaigon produced between 2,000 and 6,000 livres annually for the Armagnac treasury until League activities made it virtually impossible to find willing lessees and the years of war finally took their toll. Receipts from wood sales began dwindling in the early eighties and by 1587 revenues had completely dried up. For the next decade the only profit Navarre realized from his formerly lush woodlands in Armagnac was 400 livres from the sale of 100 *arpents* of woodland burned and destroyed by Catholic troops. The next substantial sale of woodlands occurred in 1598; receipts still fluctuated for another decade and never reached the levels achieved earlier in the century (see table 1.9).

In part, low profits in the first decade of the seventeenth century reflect not only the slow process of recovery but also the willingness of

---

[90]AD-PA, A4.

[91]For a discussion of Henri d'Albret's early efforts to regulate the exploitation of his forests in Armagnac, particularly the forest of Bacone, see Devèze, *La vie de la forêt*, 2:103–4.

agents to forgo the immediate profit if waiting might yield a higher return. The value of each *arpent* cut plummeted between 1578 and 1600, reflecting the widespread devastation of Armagnac forests. By 1600 agents auctioned off woods for one-fifth of their value in 1578. Agents carefully monitored the market for wood and refused to sell for less than the going rates. In 1607, for example, Henri IV commissioned his officers to auction off forty *arpents* of woodland in the forest of Bacone. When the trumpet sounded on the morning of October 26, the crowd gathered in the public square was too small, so judged the commission, to elicit any kind of competitive bidding. In hopes that many of the prospective bidders were simply tardy, the commissioners postponed the auction twice (October 27 and 28) until it became apparent that there was just no market for wood in L'Ile Jourdain. After much discussion, the commissioners decided to take the auction to Toulouse. There, however, they still had difficulty getting their projected price and chose instead to defer the sale until 1608.[92]

The Albrets routinely consulted with estate officials and the local population before converting any rich forest into pasture by the widespread harvesting of trees. In so doing, they tapped a wellspring of resident wisdom and peasant common sense which proved to be eminently useful and illuminating. When Navarre made plans in 1578 to sell one hundred *arpents* of so-called forest in Loblie, he sent a group of his councilors to investigate first. The councilors questioned a bevy of resident experts, from the local seigneur to the forest guards to a young yeoman farmer whose worldly possessions amounted to only twenty-five écus. The overwhelming consensus was that this forest, unexploited for over twenty-five years, would not bring much money into the domanial coffers if farmed as woodland. One after the other, the provincial sages testified that it would be to Navarre's greater advantage to rent the land *à nouveau fief* and make his money from entry fines and the imposition of seigneurial dues rather than attempt to sell trees, which were, in their words, "only bushes and not large enough to make good timber or logs."[93] The forest guards further discouraged Navarre's commissioners from recommending the future exploitation of these bushes, arguing that the forest was subject to the constant degradations of peasants in the surrounding villages. "These ruffians," Gaillard Jullien disdainfully explained, "creep into the woods under cover of night and steal anything they can find."[94] As Jean Garrigues, guard-

---

[92]AD-PA, E122.
[93]Ibid.
[94]Ibid.

40 • The Economics of Power

Table 1.9 Revenue from Woodlands in the County of Armagnac

Year	Gross Income from Woods	Wages Forest Guards	Wages/Maître des Bois	Auction and Harvesting Costs	Net Income	Percentage of Total Revenue	Total Revenue for the County
1569-72	3,139	—[a]	—[a]	—[a]	—[a]	—	—[a]
1574-75	6,203	192	25	44	5,942	19.8	30,019
1576-77	4,474	210	25	—[b]	4,239	11.8	35,872
1577-78	5,156	216	25	—[f]	4,915	14.7	33,481
1578-79	5,984	216	25	—[f]	5,743	15.6	36,754
1582-83[c]	3,686	216	25	1010	2,435	8.1	30,045
1583-84[c]	2,286	153	25	267	1,841	5.2	35,372
1587-88[c]	0	0	0	0	0	—	4,998
1588-89[c]	0	0	0	0	0	—	7,404
1589-90[c]	0	0	0	0	0	—	9,434
1595-96	400[d]	0	25	16	359	1.3	28,110
1598-99	2,726	0[e]	25	—[f]	—	—	25,749
1600-01	1,815	0[e]	25	—[f]	—	—	27,539
1604-05	1,376			291			20,284

(continued next page)

Table 1.9 (continued)

Year	Gross Income from Woods	Wages Forest Guards	Wages/ Maître des Bois	Auction and Harvesting Costs	Net Income	Percentage of Total Revenue	Total Revenue for the County
1602-03	840	63	25	—[f]	—	—	19,367
1604-05	1,376	—[f]	—[f]	291	1,085	5.3	20,284
1605-06	860	—[f]	—[f]	—[f]	—	—	12,760
1606-07	1,821	—[f]	—[f]	1100	721	2.9	24,475

AD-PA Source, respectively by year: B1588, B1591, B1592, B1593, B1594, B1598, B1600, B1606, B1608, B1610, B1621, B1636, B1652, B1657, B1673, B1674, B1685

[a] Some pages from this account are missing, including the ones listing expenses and total revenue.
[b] An entry for travel expenses to L'Ile Jourdain to collect income from wood sales is left blank.
[c] This account was originally figured in écus, which I have converted into livres at the rate of 1:3.
[d] These monies come from the sale of woods burned by marauders and troops.
[e] These expenses are not specifically delineated in my notes.
[f] Litigation costs are included under this heading.

witness, protested, no matter how vigilant the watch, "these scavengers cannot be stopped."[95] Navarre's commission thus saved him the considerable expense of assaying and auctioning off scrub forest which was, in the end, better leased to local peasants than farmed for timber.

Decisions about how to best exploit forest land, so it appears, followed extensive investigations of all the factors at play in the economy. Albret agents took into consideration geography, market trends, local custom, and human nature—the likelihood that peasants would pilfer the Loblie reserve, for example—when they wrote their reports. In general, the Albrets preferred to sell their woods uncut to merchants and traders, who came in and absorbed the considerable costs of harvesting the timber and transporting it to market, and commissioners supported this system of exploitation with strikingly elaborate calculations of probable profits and losses. The dossier submitted by the commission investigating the newly purchased woods of Barousse in 1585 is no doubt typical of many such reports read and approved by the Albrets. In it, the commissioners calculated that it would cost close to 15,000 livres simply to cut and transport fifteen to eighteen thousand logs (*une menée*) from the forest of Barousse to the nearest waterway, the fairly shallow River Losse. Another 2,400 livres would have to be paid to the men who performed the skilled task of guiding such an unwieldy cargo down the Losse into the Garonne and then into Toulouse. At current market prices, the commissioners estimated that the timber might fetch as much as 45,000 livres, from which even the enterprising merchant could expect to deduct another 5,000 livres for losses due to theft and damage. With all expenses deducted, the lucky farmer might clear 20,000 livres. It would still seem a case of clear profit, but Navarre's agents warned that it was not so simple. The Losse, they argued, was frequently too low to make timber transport easy, except in years of extraordinary snow or rainfall. In normal years, buyers were slow to present themselves, "fearing as it is impossible due to the great cost and the unaccommodating River Losse."[96] To maximize profits and minimize the risks, agents recommended that Navarre search for possible buyers willing to "cut and put the timber outside of the forest and in the water...at their own cost and expense."[97]

---

[95] Ibid.
[96] AD-PA, E387.
[97] Ibid.

VI. Conclusion

Recent studies in general have emphasized that the sixteenth century witnessed the first sustained challenge to the nobility's control over rural society and the rural economy through seigneurialism. Tax revolts masquerading as religious rebellion, open warfare, a surge in population growth, and inflation, all challenged the traditional privileges that nobles had exercised over land and threatened the various revenues that nobles customarily drew from it. Great nobles, such as the Albrets, nevertheless were singularly well positioned to turn crisis into profit; they had access to the experts necessary to deal with the increasingly complex issues of the management of estates and their resources in the sixteenth century. Consigned by the pressing concerns of politics and religion to a less active role on many of their estates, they maintained their dominance over the rural economy by mixing modern management and marketing methods with older, more traditional patterns of exploitation. From about 1550 to 1580, Albret agents manipulated rental structures to take advantage of the general surge in population, which became a driving force behind rising land rents and offset the deleterious effects of the Religious Wars until very late in the century. When military maneuvers finally depressed the rental value of the Albrets' landed resources, they encouraged their agents to alter time-honored proscriptions, rules, and regulations in order to reinvigorate the lagging market for land. As a result, demand for land and, consequently, rents remained high enough on certain estates that peasant tenants were pushed out of their leaseholds by noble aspirants—often *capitaines de ville*—who had made their fortunes while warmongering. Furthermore, these small noblemen were drawn into the frenzied patronage economy practiced by the Albrets during the Religious Wars, as we will see in chapter 3, and thus ended up enriched by the wars rather than defeated by them. In southwestern France nobles, great and small, enhanced their proprietorship over the land and the rural economy during the sixteenth century. Indeed, the problems posed by religious wars paved the way for a new generation of noble landlords, more rapacious than their predecessors, who would struggle with the developing capitalist economy and the increasingly powerful forces of an absolutist state in their efforts to succeed.

Two

The Fruits of Office and the Bounty of Kings

Revenues from land and seigneurial fees comprised the most significant part of most noble family fortunes, but for many a second fortune was made in the glittering corridors of the royal court and in the possession of the great offices of the realm. "From earliest feudal times," writes Lawrence Stone, "the fortunes of the nobility have depended as much upon the favors and ferocities of the monarch as upon their hereditary sources."[1] Royal pensions and the legal and extralegal perquisites of office considerably enriched even the most illustrious noble houses and certainly saved many a genteel one from extinction. Gifts and salaries from the royal purse amounting to tens of thousands, occasionally even hundreds of thousands, of livres were not uncommon, and the political influence and social prestige that derived from close proximity to the king could bring a cornucopia of less easily calculable fruits to the determined and fortunate few.

Most sixteenth-century French nobles were quick to recognize the importance of royal patronage and court service and to commend it to their contemporaries. In his famous memoirs, the Gascon adventurer and *guerrier*, Blaise de Monluc, repeatedly acknowledged the integral part that royal patronage played in his rise to prominence and in the establishment of his legendary fortune. "It is then just to confess," this master of boasts humbly concludes after several hundred pages of self-glorification, "that we could do nothing without the bounty and favor of

---

[1]Stone, *Crisis of the Aristocracy*, 398.

kings."[2] Monluc's contemporary, Louis de Gonzague, duc de Nevers, was more precise about the financial benefits of royal service and office holding. By his own careful calculation, Nevers claimed to have collected 513,997 livres from the crown during twenty-nine years of faithful service.[3] Perhaps the most compelling example of the rewards of royal service, however, is Anne de Montmorency, who, as Francis I's royal favorite, enjoyed offices and pensions worth 56,450 livres annually by 1538, thus establishing himself in the minds of many as the first in a long line of royal *mignons*, whose annual demands of the royal exchequer compromised the financial stability and political credibility of the Valois monarchy. Even after his first disgrace and dismissal from court in 1541, Montmorency kept a running account of the value of his pensions, which were restored to him in full, in addition to 225,000 livres for arrears, by Henri II in 1545. For Montmorency, royal pensions provided the means with which to enlarge his landed patrimony by a factor of ten by 1561.[4]

By the mid-sixteenth century the most distinguished members of the *noblesse d'épée* willingly acknowledged the pivotal role of royal service in the accumulation of landed wealth and political prestige. Gaspard de Saulx-Tavanes, who reputedly garnered over 100,000 livres in unofficial income while serving as governor of Burgundy, pointedly reminded his successors to disdain neither the fruits of office nor those who sought nobility through office holding. In one of those ubiquitous manuals on education in which noblemen of the Ancien Régime penned paternal advice, Saulx-Tavanes warned his children of the dangers of taking office holding and officeholders too lightly. "Stupid is the opinion of brutes," he wrote, "that presidents and councilors of *parlements* are not gentlemen."[5]

---

[2]Blaise de Monluc, *Military Mémoires,* ed. Ian Roy (London: Longman, 1972), 226.
[3]Robert Harding, *Anatomy of a Power Elite,* 143–49. Nevers' final assessment of the value of royal service was less positive. With the same fastidiousness that led him to calculate his revenues from the Crown, he also kept track of his losses which, he implied, amounted to 377,000 livres in unpaid gifts and arrears in pensions in addition to an unstipulated number of heavy charges he incurred while in the entourage of the king's brother at the siege of La Rochelle in 1572 and with the future Henri III in Poland in 1574.
[4]Greengrass, "Property and Politics," 374–80.
[5]*Mémoire de Gaspard de Saulx-Tavanes*, as quoted in Robert Forster, *The House of Saulx-Tavanes: Versailles and Burgundy, 1700–1830* (Baltimore: Johns Hopkins University Press, 1971). The Protestant preacher, Theodore de Bèze, expressed his amazement at the size of Saulx-Tavanes' fortune in his *Histoire écclésiastique des églises réformées au royaume de France,* eds. G. Baum and E. Cublitz, 3 vols. (Paris, 1889) 1:524. For an excellent overview of noble attitudes toward the economic and political values of office

For Saulx-Tavanes and other noblemen, court pensions were rarely considered to be "begging money from the monarchy," but rather legitimate and lucrative sources of income to be as assiduously cultivated as the family domains.[6] As Montmorency's case makes clear, sixteenth-century nobles treated their pensions, gifts, and offices like private property, calculating and collecting arrears in payment. They assigned or alienated their pensions to creditors to cover debts with none of the legal problems associated with mortgaging family estates.[7] Indeed, royal offices and the pensions derived from them comprised an increasingly large share of noble fortunes during the first half of the sixteenth century and were crucial to the financial stability of many noble houses. The realignment of royal pensions with the pressures of wartime finance and royal bankruptcy in the 1550s and 1560s posed a real and continuing challenge to this crucial source of noble income during the second half of the century. How did the Albrets cultivate the fruits of office? How did they respond to threats to this lucrative source of income? To what extent did they build their fortunes on royal service?

I. In Pursuit of Royalty

Henri d'Albret was the last scion of the illustrious house of Foix-Navarre-Albret to spend his formative years on the family estates in southern France. His delayed entry into court in 1515 at the advanced age of twelve—when many heirs of the great noble houses of France would already be in attendance, if not in service—was occasioned by the troubles which had raged in the family's kingdom of Navarre since the 1490s.[8] For almost thirty years, the Pyrenean kingdom of Navarre had been a continuous source of tension and hostility between Jean d'Albret, Henri's father, who claimed possession of Navarre by his marriage to Catherine de Foix, and Ferdinand of Aragon, who maintained the claim of his second wife, Germaine de Foix, who came from a cadet branch of the family. Ferdinand of Aragon, who desperately wanted to annex the territory to his own kingdom to enhance his bid for power in

---

holding and toward the *anoblis* administrative elites of early modern France, see Donna Bohanan, *Old and New Nobility in Aix* (Baton Rouge: Louisiana State University Press, 1992), 21–24, 79–96, 120–32.

[6]William Weary, "Royal Policy and Patronage in Renaissance France, 71.

[7]Greengrass, "Property and Politics," 379.

[8]For a discussion of the enduring conflict between Spain and the viscounty of Béarn, see Frederic J. Baumgartner, *Henry II: King of France, 1547–1559* (Durham: Duke University Press, 1988), 11, 15; Dartigue-Peyrou, *Vicomté*, 189–221; G. Bascle de Lagrèze, *La Navarre française*, 2 vols. (Paris, 1881), 1:253–319.

Spain, exploited local tensions between the Navarrese and the house of Foix-Navarre-Albret, as well as the ambitions and fears of the last of the Capetian monarchs of France, in order to do so. Between 1494 and 1512, Ferdinand attempted to annex Navarre largely through diplomatic channels; offers and counteroffers between Ferdinand and Charles VIII, and later Louis XII of France, were regularly exchanged, including a bid in 1497 to guarantee Charles VIII the Italian kingdom of Naples in return for Navarre. Catherine of Foix, Henri's mother, plotted and conspired as well to maintain her increasingly tenuous control challenged by Ferdinand's invocation of the Salic Law, which in France prohibited female succession. Finally in 1512, Ferdinand, weary of decades of fruitless diplomacy, invaded and summarily conquered the fertile valley of southern Navarre, known henceforth as Haute-Navarre; in the process he challenged the royal pretensions of the scions of the house of Foix-Navarre-Albret, who, nonetheless, continued to call themselves "kings" and "queens" and to claim royal prerogatives at the French court. The loss of Haute-Navarre was an enormous blow to the Albrets, including young Henri who had been born in the Pyrenean kingdom. With the memories of the ignominious defeat at the hands of the Spaniards still burning in his mind, Jean d'Albret finally made preparations to present his son, Henri, at the French court in 1515. And so, in a very real way, the events of 1512 intensified the importance of the Albrets' feudal connections to the French monarchy, which they hoped to exploit to raise troops and moneys to regain Navarre.

A clever adolescent, Henri understood from the beginning that his presentation at court was a serious diplomatic expedition from which his father hoped to garner royal favor and support for future forays against Spain.[9] Once at court, Henri quickly established himself as part of the entourage surrounding the twenty-one-year-old Francis I. Even when the Béarnais Estates clamored for Henri's immediate return after the inopportune death of his father in 1517, Henri remained at court for another two years under the guidance of his grandfather, Alain d'Albret, the official regent of his vast interests in the southwest. Henri intended to stay at court at all costs to achieve his objective: to install himself in the king's graces so that all manner of favors might be bestowed, including troops and moneys to reclaim the lost kingdom of Navarre.[10]

---

[9]See Dartique-Peyrou, *Vicomté*, 148–49, for a discussion of the formative influence of the Navarre question on young Henri d'Albret, which forged, he argued, an unusually sensitive and independent character and which made Henri aware of the great political and diplomatic latitude he possessed because of his domains in Béarn and Navarre.

[10]Ibid., 493.

The various perquisites and pensions which Henri received during his career as a courtier and confidant of the kings of France, as well as his royal marriage to Marguerite d'Angoulême, Francis I's only sibling, must be placed within the context of the Navarre question which remained very problematic for the Valois monarchs who were engaged in their own struggles with the Spanish Hapsburgs. Certainly, Francis I was not eager to enhance in any substantive fashion the royal claims of the Albrets, who were already difficult vassals to control. But nothing short of the phantom kingdom could fulfill Henri's expectations, and thus it became Francis I's constant challenge to placate the passionate, self-styled king of Navarre with open-ended pledges and important military positions which seemed to promise a resolution to the Navarre problem. It took twelve years of concerted attention to the affairs of court and costly expeditions on behalf of the French Crown—including the famous incarceration at Pavia—before Henri reaped any substantial political or financial benefits from royal service.

From 1515 to 1529, Henri served Francis I by fulfilling his chivalric responsibilities as head of one of the great noble houses of France. His attendance at court and on royal campaigns was only sporadically interrupted by perfunctory visits to his domains to plead for money from his estates. As one of the peers of France, and hence one of Francis's privy councilors, he received a modest pension, but none of the great military offices of the realm and their lucrative perquisites were his.[11] The royal muster rolls bear testimony to the *campagnie d'ordonnance* which Henri commanded in 1521.[12] Undoubtedly, he received the customary captain's pension of 800 livres,[13] but he also persuaded the Estates of Béarn to vote him an additional 5,000 écus to help defray the heavy expenses incurred while in royal service. The *ex gratia* gratifications which Henri regularly received from the Estates of Béarn were an enormously important source of additional revenue, especially during his sojourns at court and during his campaigns in Italy. Unlike many of his noble contemporaries, who received periodic donations

---

[11]Alain le Grand, Henri's grandfather, received pensions from the Crown as one of the peers of France. The amount, Achille Luchaire argues, fluctuated according to his standing at court and was even suppressed for a number of years when he was out of favor. See A. Luchaire, *Alain le Grand*, 15. It is reasonable to suspect that the pension was continued with Francis I, particularly as Henri d'Albret was one of the premier members of his entourage. See, for example, the royal *état* from 1523, entitling Henri to a 10,000-livre pension in Roger Doucet, *L'état des finances de 1523* (Paris: Imprimerie Nationale, 1923).

[12]BN, Collections Clairambault, 360, fo. 261.

[13]Harding, *Anatomy of a Power Elite*, 140.

from provincial estates in their capacity as governors, Henri's estate revenues were not subject to royal control. Moreover, the gratifications offered by the Estates of Béarn were given in recognition of Henri's sovereign status, distributed almost annually, and by the 1520s were around 10,000 écus a year.[14] In 1524, for example, the Béarnais Estates again bore the burden of Henri's service on behalf of the Crown of France in Italy. In two notable sessions held within the walls of the venerable cathedral at Lescar, the estates voted to award their peripatetic viscount "par delà les monts" a donation of 10,000 écus, which was supplemented only seven months later by a subsidy of 11,000 écus for Henri, "toujours en Italie."[15]

Indeed, it was while in Italy with Francis I, on the last of the French missions across the Alps, that Henri finally succeeded in his quest for royal support, recognition, and royal office. Taken prisoner with Francis I at Pavia in 1525, he made a dramatic escape from his prison using a rope ladder, and returned to France to bask in the admiration of his fellow courtiers, including Marguerite d'Angoulême who negotiated her brother's more prosaic release over the next year. Marguerite's admiration blossomed as the hero of Pavia seriously began to court her attentions. Widowed, ten years Henri's senior, a distinguished scholar of philosophy and religion, Marguerite seemed an odd match, on a personal level at least, for the dashing Gascon adventurer, who clearly adored warmongering. On a political level, however, it was a union which suited the larger ambitions of both royal houses. More than one historian has noted that the motives behind Francis's gifts were unambiguously political.[16] While Henri plainly expected that marriage to Marguerite would grant him permanent access to the king's ear on matters concerning Navarre, Francis, for his part, hoped that the marriage and its many financial perquisites, would satisfy Albret's royal pretensions and bring an end to his infernal scheming. When Henri's demands intensified after 1527, the wily king of France proceeded to shower his brother-in-law with royal pensions and perquisites on a grand scale in order to deflect attention from the sensitive subject of southern Navarre.

As a sign of his approval of the marriage, Francis had blessed this new union with touching displays of royal largess.[17] According to the terms of the marital agreement, Marguerite brought to the marriage

---

[14]For a nearly complete record of the donations of the Estates of Béarn between 1517 and 1555, see Dartigue-Peyrou, *Vicomté*, 494–97.
[15]Ibid.
[16]Ibid.
[17]See Roelker, *Queen of Navarre*, 2–8; P. Jourda, *Marguerite d'Angoulême*, 2 vols. (Paris: Champion, 1930), 1: 146.

the rich counties of Rodez and Armagnac and the viscounty of Fézenzaguet, which increased Henri's landed revenues by nearly 10,000 livres annually. And within the first two years of his marriage Henri received offices and preferments at Francis's hands which doubled his total annual income.[18]

Henri's first major military appointment came within eighteen months of his marriage to Marguerite. With a rapidity that was rare in the sixteenth century, Francis appointed Henri lieutenant general and governor of Guyenne in August 1528, just two weeks after the death of Odet de Foix, seigneur de Lautrec, who had served as governor of the province since Francis's accession to the throne.[19] Provincial governorships were among the most coveted royal appointments in sixteenth-century France, reserved only for the great nobility and carrying responsibilities which significantly complemented the political influence of the holder. Of the eleven military provinces into which France was divided during the sixteenth century, the *gouvernement* of Guyenne was one of the most prestigious and lucrative. Covering virtually the whole of southwestern France and bordering on Spain, Guyenne was considered to be of strategic importance and the pension and salary granted to Albret in 1528 reflected its significance. Despite Dartique-Peyrou's assertions that Henri received only 10,000 livres a year as governor of Guyenne, decrees issued to the treasurer of the *Epargne* indicate that his official pension and salary for the position stood at 24,000 livres annually and were paid in regular quarterly increments.[20] With such an income, Henri was one of the most highly remunerated governors in sixteenth-century France. His contemporary Jean de Laval, seigneur de Châteaubriant, was awarded only 16,000 livres as salary and pension for his position as governor of Brittany.[21] And Francis's favorite, Philippe Chabot, seigneur de Brion, collected only 2,000 livres more than Laval for his post as governor of the frontier province of Burgundy.[22] According to Robert Harding, pensions and salaries awarded to major governors from the *Epargne* averaged between 14,000 and 18,000 livres between 1523 and 1549, which would mean that Henri's pension was 6,000 to 10,000 livres above the norm.[23]

---

[18]Dartigue-Peyrou, *Vicomté*, 245–53.
[19]*Actes de François Ier*, 1:596; and Harding, *Anatomy of a Power Elite*, 223.
[20]Dartique-Peyrou, *Vicomté*; and *Actes de François Ier*, 2:133, 460, 526, 726.
[21]Ibid., 3:21.
[22]Ibid., 2:236.
[23]Harding, *Anatomy of a Power Elite*, 121.

The records indicate that Henri was paid his pension promptly and regularly throughout most of his career. From 1532 onward the treasurer of the *Epargne* disbursed funds to Henri every three to six months. The only hint of difficulty in payment dates from Henri's first three years as governor (1528–32) when he was caught in the grip of the king's own problematic finances. Instead of receiving money directly from the *Epargne* in 1531, Henri was assigned revenues from a variety of sources: 6,293£. 4s. 6d. from the *octroi* levied on the nobility and free towns of France, 10,000 livres from the balance that royal officers estimated would be left in royal accounts at the end of the fiscal year, and 7,716£. 15s. 3d. from the *plus-values* in the general treasury the following year.[24] Only one other instance of arrears in payment to Albret appears among the King's ordinances: an outstanding payment of 1,200 livres from 1530 was finally ordered to be paid in 1533.[25] Thus it seems clear that Henri was generally untroubled by arrears in payment and uncertain revenue assignments after 1532.

Francis's liberality toward his brother-in-law extended beyond the governorship of Guyenne. On January 22,1529, he consolidated Henri's already considerable political weight in the southwest by offering him the admiralty of Guyenne, with its extensive powers and fiscal prerogatives over the conduct of maritime maneuvers and commerce along the Bordelais coast.[26] A year later, Francis extended Henri's jurisdiction to include the Charentais territories of Saintonge, Poitou, and La Rochelle.[27] While the office of admiral carried with it a modest pension of 3,000 livres, the unofficial perquisites of office considerably enhanced the political and financial appeal of the office. Certainly for Henri the greatest appeal of the admiralty was the opportunity it offered to direct naval maneuvers almost at will in Guyenne. According to an edict issued by the Crown in 1517, the Admiral of Guyenne had the right to marshall soldiers, artillery, munitions, victuals, and "all that is necessary for war," prerogatives of enormous breadth which could be used to the admiral's own political and financial advantage.[28] Under the prior admiral, Lautrec, these privileges had scarcely been

---

[24]*Actes de François Ier*, 2:345, 362; 7:610, 619.
[25]Ibid., 7:704.
[26]Ibid., 1:630.
[27]Ibid., 1:686; 7:619.
[28]Marcel Gouron, *L'Amirauté de Guienne: depuis le premier Amiral anglais en Guinne jusqu'a la Revolution* (Paris: Librairie du Recueil Sirey, 1938), 174–78; Robert Boutruche, et al., *Histoire de Bordeaux*, 8 vols. *Bordeaux de 1453–1751* (Bordeaux: Fédération historique de sud-ouest, 1966), 4:285–86.

used except to ensure free and easy traffic for merchant ships into French ports. Henri d'Albret, however, seized the opportunity offered by his charge to build up the naval fleet in Guyenne and conduct reconnaissance missions along the Spanish coast in his determined effort to harass and challenge the rulers who had stolen his kingdom.[29]

It would be a mistake, however, to argue that Henri's interest in the office was solely political and not also economic. As viscount of Béarn, Henri had proved himself capable of pursuing even the most insignificant seigneurial dues and privileges with a doggedness that proved to be extremely effective, and the Admiralty of Guyenne carried with it perquisites which must have been attractive to this sharp-eyed landlord. Notable among them were the right to share in the proceeds from the sale of goods recovered from shipwrecks or confiscated from pirate or enemy ships and the right to pocket the receipts from the sale of sailing permits, anchorage fees, and passports.[30] Indeed, admiralty revenues in Guyenne were sufficiently large to generate great jurisdictional conflicts with the royal Admiral of France, Anne de Montmorency, who frequently tried to collect the money himself, as well as with provincial admirals.[31] There are unfortunately no extant admiralty receipts from Henri's years in office which would enable us to understand the full scope of his opportunities for material gain. But his numerous missives to Francis I concerning the quick and expedient registration of his appointments and privileges in the provincial parlements suggest that he intended to make full use of his prerogatives and to apply himself assiduously to the task of recovering errant maritime revenues for the Crown and for his own pocket.[32]

The Parlement of Bordeaux was sufficiently alarmed by Henri's reputation and the political and financial implications of his dual appointment as governor and admiral of Guyenne to resist registration of the letters patent confirming his appointment.[33] What could stop Albret, they protested, with his considerable seigneurial claims in Guyenne and the governorship and admiralty at his disposal, from abusing his powers and appropriating additional perquisites for himself to the detriment of the province's longstanding traditions and liberties? Only

---

[29]Gouron, *L'Amirauté en Guienne*, 175.
[30]Ibid., 186–200.
[31]Ibid., 179–200; see also Bergin, *Cardinal Richelieu*, 96–103, for a fascinating discussion of Richelieu's attempts to undermine the authority of provincial admirals in order to collect the enormous revenues from their office.
[32]Gouron, *L'Amirauté en Guyenne*, 171.
[33]Ibid., 150–52.

after Francis I reissued his decrees in December 1529 demanding compliance in no uncertain terms did the *parlementaires* of Bordeaux reluctantly agree to register the appointment. At the same time, however, opposition to Henri's extensive administrative power in the Charentes continued unabated. Leading members of the local nobility in Saintonge resented the new admiral's intrusion into their affairs, particularly his attempts to recover certain maritime revenues which they had come to enjoy under the rather desultory guardianship of Admiral Saluces. Arguing that Henri's rights over the territories of Poitou, Saintonge, and La Rochelle, which were officially under the jurisdiction of the Parlement of Paris, had never been properly registered by that august body, the local seigneurs refused to give up their "time-honored" fiscal privileges and liberties. An additional royal decree issued in January 1530 and the acquiescence of the Parisian parlement brought the Saintongeais seigneurs to heel.[34] Roughly a year after his first official appointment by the crown, Henri d'Albret was finally vested with his full powers as admiral.

By early modern standards, a one-year lag between a royal decree and parlementary approval was remarkably short. Henri's success is telling testimony to his skill and persistence in the pursuit of income in whatever guise. A century later the eminently able Cardinal Richelieu would have to wait four years for the Parlement of Bordeaux to accept his appointment as Grand Master of the Admiralty.[35] Regrettably, Henri had only begun to realize the full potential of his office and to regularize the receipt of his extraordinary revenues when Francis I unexpectedly asked him to resign in February 1533 in favor of the king's current court favorite, Philippe Chabot, seigneur de Brion.[36] Politics as much as personal favoritism prompted the change in personnel. Henri's repeated demands on behalf of Navarre and the small naval missions along the northern Spanish coast, particularly at the moment when Francis was moving towards an increasingly peaceful stance with the Hapsburgs, made Henri's tenure as admiral a liability to the crown.[37] Custom frequently prescribed compensation, but Henri's resignation came under less than salutary circumstances. Apart from the pension which was prorated from the first of January to the day of resignation in February, there is no indication in the royal ordinances to suggest that Albret was compensated for the loss of his office. Whatever

---

[34]Ibid., 182.
[35]Bergin, *Cardinal Richelieu*, 99–100.
[36]*Actes de François Ier*, 2:236.
[37]Gouron, *L'Amirauté en Guienne*, 154–55.

the financial arrangements were, Henri clearly harbored no ill will against his successor, and as evidence of his goodwill he used his prerogatives as governor of Guyenne to nominate Chabot's son, Charles, as the governor and captain of La Rochelle.[38]

Royal favor again shone on the house of Foix-Navarre-Albret long before Henri's reappointment as Admiral of Guyenne upon Chabot's death in November 1543, but the first hint of Francis's intentions to put Henri back in charge of the naval resources of southern France came in January 1543 when he named Albret "lieutenant general for the king on the Ponant and Levant coasts, in Guyenne and Poitou, and Languedoc and Provence."[39] This office in effect made Henri d'Albret the military overlord of all southern France, and offered even greater opportunities to avenge the loss of Haute-Navarre.[40]

Henri's excitement and anticipation at the prospect of controlling the military resources of virtually one-third of France was barely contained. Even before receiving the official letters of provision, he began to take action against his enemies. As a cautionary measure against the English, who had just concluded an alliance with Charles V, he ordered the incarceration of English subjects living within or around the environs of La Rochelle and the seizure of their belongings. In June 1543, he assembled a squadron of twenty galleons in the harbor of La Rochelle to ward off English and Spanish ships which were menacing the port. Only a short while later, Henri commissioned the construction of a dozen ships to protect the Basque ports of Bayonne, Saint-Jean-de-Luz, and Cap breton from both English and Spanish attacks.[41] As lieutenant general, Henri enjoyed virtually all the prerogatives of the Admiralty of Guyenne for nearly a year before receiving the formal appointment from the Crown. When the letters patent were finally issued in November 1543, six months after the death of Philippe Chabot, they merely made official what was already true in practice—that Henri was master of the Atlantic as well as the Mediterranean—and gave him the opportunity to claim another royal pension.[42]

During his second tenure as admiral, Albret's privileges went largely uncontested by the *parlementaires* of Bordeaux, but at times they were seriously jeopardized by civil unrest and the continuing hostilities with England and Spain. During the infamous revolt against the *gabelle* in Guyenne in 1548, admiralty officials in La Rochelle, in all

---

[38]Ibid.
[39]*Actes de François Ier*, 4:396.
[40]Gouron, *L'Amirauté en Guienne*, 150.
[41]Ibid.
[42]*Actes de François Ier*, 4:519. The original ordinance is in AD-PA, E574.

the confusion and in their haste to dispatch a serviceable fleet to Guyenne, failed to issue sailing permits and passports. Almost as soon as Albret received the news of their negligence, he ordered an immediate remedial action. Determined to recover the lost revenues, Henri ordered all ships entering Bordeaux or any ports along the Atlantic coast from La Rochelle to Hendaye to be searched for proper credentials and fined accordingly if lacking them.[43]

By the 1550s, the wars and rumors of war between the Valois and Hapsburg monarchies occasionally compromised Henri's extraordinary revenues from his *droits d'ancrage*, *congés*, and passports, but they probably also encouraged a spectacular increase in the revenues he derived from the confiscation and seizure of enemy ships. Seizures and confiscations naturally increased during wartime, and it is highly probable that Henri's revenues from his traditional *dixième de prise* rose after 1551, offsetting the losses from his other extraordinary revenues. With the declaration of war on the Holy Roman Emperor in 1551, Henri received official orders from Henri II of France to commence offensive efforts against the Spanish navy and to seize and sell the belongings of Spanish subjects within Guyenne to the profit of the Admiralty. The inevitable skirmishes which occurred in the Atlantic between French and Spanish ships meant enormous profits, especially when cunning subordinates were watching carefully to ensure that the admiral's prerogatives (and perhaps their own) were properly respected. Only one tantalizing bit of correspondence from an admiralty official to Albret remains from this tumultuous period, but it suggests the profits which could be made during wartime. In 1552, Henri's lieutenant in Saintonge, one Estissac, wrote to his patron to apprise him of a Spanish ship which had been seized by French sailors, or perhaps privateers, off the Atlantic coast with a cargo of sugar, silver, and copper worth more than 400,000 écus. Albret's traditional share of the take as admiral, Estissac calculated, might run as high as 60,000 to 80,000 *"bons francs"* if the ship was moored in La Rochelle. But, unfortunately, under orders from Anne de Montmorency, then Admiral of France, the ship had been taken to the Breton port of Belmar, far beyond the reach of Albret's administration. The wily lieutenant urged Albret to press his case with Montmorency, arguing that the ship had been seized within the vicinity of La Rochelle and so should be assigned there. "I beg you," Estissac

---

[43]For a discussion of this revolt, see Stephane Claude Gison, *Contribution à l'histoire de l'impôt sous l'ancien régime: La révolte de la gabelle en Guyenne* (Paris, 1906); and more recently, Jean Bouchet and Guillaume Paradin, *La Révolte de la gabelle en Guyenne et à Bordeaux en 1548* (Bordeaux: Atelier Aldo Monvzio, 1981).

concluded this missive, "to put a swift end to this debacle with Monsieur l'Amiral because it will be of great profit to you and to La Rochelle also."[44]

If Albret's extraordinary revenues as admiral lie largely hidden from view, those from his governorship are only marginally easier to trace. As governor of Guyenne, Henri periodically received donations from the Estates of Guyenne, probably intended to buy his goodwill and a certain leniency with regard to the implementation of royal policies and taxes. Upon his nomination as governor of Guyenne in 1528, for example, both the Estates of Guyenne and officials in the county of Périgord offered him lavish gifts of money amounting to thousands of livres, but it is unclear if these donations continued to be given on a regular basis.[45] In addition to the income Henri garnered from his military appointments, a plethora of smaller offices, privileges, and exemptions which were Francis's to give were transferred to Henri and Marguerite. These liberalities, according to the sixteenth-century sense of the term, demonstrated a recognition of the value of generosity, even in small things.[46] In 1537, for example, Francis confirmed the ancient right of the family of Albret to nominate notaries and sergeants in the counties under their lordship and to collect the profits from the sale of offices, in spite of the fact that French law prohibited governors from nominating notaries and sergeants in their provinces.[47] By 1546, Henri's revenues from these sources amounted to slightly over 200 livres.[48]

The most frequent demonstrations of royal largess, probably because they least directly drained royal finances, came in the form of special exemptions and gratuities which helped to defray the burdens of "living nobly." In 1535, for example, Francis had designated that all Henri's revenues were to be vested with all of the privileges associated with royal revenues, which meant practically that Henri was to be accorded first preference by his debtors. Later he exempted Henri from all export and transport duties on Gascon wine. Years later, Charles IX accorded the same exemption to Antoine de Bourbon, Jeanne's hus-

---

[44]Gouron, *L'Amirauté en Guienne*, 150.

[45]*Actes de François Ier*, 2:237–38. These practices are well documented by J. Russell Major in his *Representative Government in Early Modern France* (New Haven: Yale University Press, 1980), 322. See also Greengrass, "Property and Politics," 380–82.

[46]For a discussion of the various distinctions made between the meanings of "liberality," "magnificence," "generosity," and "largess" see Felicity Heal, *Hospitality in Early Modern England* (Oxford: Oxford University Press, 1990), 23–26, 99–100.

[47]*Actes de François Ier*, 4:300, 592, 728; 6:175.

[48]AD-PA, B4.

band, which meant a savings of up to 2,100 livres annually.[49] At the same time that Francis exempted Henri and Marguerite from certain commercial impositions, he also permitted them to increase their revenues by creating commercial impositions of their own. At Albret's request, Francis ordered the establishment of three fairs and a weekly market at Monjoux in the county of Rodez. Two years later, the duke and duchess of Armagnac obtained the right to establish biweekly markets in the city of Auch. All these fairs attracted foreign traders who were subject to import duties and tariffs and local merchants who had to pay vendor's fees.[50] The revenues from these sources were relatively minor, but in 1544 Francis's generosity reached a new high when he issued letters patent according Henri the right to levy taxes "at his profit" on all merchandise exported from the counties of Foix, Nébouzan, and Bigorre into Spain.[51] There were almost certainly other rights which would be difficult to trace, and which were as much affirmations of his sovereign status as they were significant sources of income.[52] Together with Henri's official pensions and appointments, however, their value may have surpassed even Henri's income from landed revenues by the 1540s.

By all accounts, during the early years of his marriage Henri's official pensions from the crown comprised the most significant part of his total annual income next to his domanial revenues. By the 1540s, income from royal pensions surpassed all other sources of revenue. A surviving *état* from 1546 shows that Henri's various pensions from the Crown amounted to 36,376 livres or 48.4 percent of his total income (see table 2.1). If we also allow for the extraordinary, often concealed, revenues that Joseph Bergin and others have called the sine qua non of early modern office holding, Albret's revenues from royal offices and pensions may well have comprised the majority of his income.[53] And indeed, the addition of Marguerite's 25,000-livre pension considerably enriched the family treasury and contributed to the structural transformation of the Alberts' fortunes.

---

[49]*Actes de François Ier*, 7:633; *IAD, Gironde*, sér. C, 2:377.

[50]Ibid., 3: 513; 2:187; for Henri's aggressive pursuit of revenues from such sources in his viscounty of Béarn, see Dartigue-Peyrou, *Vicomté*, 258, 302–6.

[51]*Actes de François Ier*, 4:611.

[52]Mark Greengrass, "Property and Politics," 382, draws similar conclusions about the many liberalities extended to Montmorency.

[53]See, for example, Bergin, *Cardinal Richelieu*, 92–94, 97–102, 114–18, for the careful distinction he draws between official and unofficial revenues of office and the particular importance he gives to the latter. For the definitive work on the sale of offices in early modern France, see Roland Mousnier, *La Vénalité*.

Table 2.1 Sources of Income, Henri d'Albret, 1546 (in livres tournois)

Nature of Income	Amount[a]	Percentage
Domain	27,945	37.1
Pensions[b]	36,375	48.4
Donations (Provincial Estates)[c]	4,375	5.8
Gambling Wins	2,957	4.0
Sales of Offices	947	1.3
Seigneurial Fees	200	0.3
Sales of Produce	95	0.1
Miscellaneous	2,241	3.0
Total	75,135	100.0
AD-PA Source: B4		

[a]Rounded to the nearest *livre tournois*.
[b]Does not include Marguerite d'Angoulême's 25,000 livres pension.
[c]Does not include donations from the estates of Foix, Béarn, and Navarre, which were not recorded in the 1546 account.

Given the critical role that royal largess and service played in the development of the Albret fortune by 1546, Marguerite lost no time writing to her principal agent at court, the Sieur d'Izernay, when her brother died a year later, with instructions to plead her case with the new king, Henri II. "Above all," she enjoined, "do me the service of pressing my affairs [at court] of which the greatest is the security of my 25,000 livres [pension] without which you know it would be impossible for me to maintain my station."[54] D'Izernay's petitions on behalf of Marguerite and her husband brought the desired results. When the royal *état* appeared enumerating royal pensions for 1548, Henri II had honored his father's bequests to the King and Queen of Navarre. Marguerite was listed to receive her pension of 25,000 livres; Henri received his pension of 24,000 livres, as well as an additional 6,000 livres to defray the extraordinary costs of his governorship of Guyenne,

[54]F. Génin, ed., *Lettres de Marguerite d'Angoulême*, 2 vols. (Paris, 1841), II:383–84.

and another 4,000 livres for the admiralty. In all, 59,000 livres was to be disbursed from the public treasury in Paris to fill the coffers in Pau and Nérac.[55]

If we are to believe the numerous missives dispatched to d'Izernay during 1547 and 1548, however, the 59,000 livres that Henri and Marguerite netted from the royal *caisse* just barely gave them the resources to live according to their station and to keep Jeanne, now a mature young woman, in sufficient style at court. Moreover, the "liberalities" which had been tendered as expressions of Francis's great affection for his only sister and her devoted, almost obsessive attentions towards him were probably not continued after the accession of Henri II in 1547, with one exception. In 1548, the Parlement of Bordeaux was further obliged by royal decree from Henri II to exempt Henri d'Albret from river tolls and charges on wood sent from the family domains in Périgord and Limousin down the Garonne and Dordogne rivers to Bordeaux for sale and shipment.[56] In general, however, the dogmatic young king felt no particular fondness for his aunt who dabbled in reformed theology and philosophy, and Marguerite was thus reduced to soliciting royal favors indirectly from Anne de Montmorency, a staunch Catholic and Henri II's chief advisor-confidante.[57]

Only one instance of additional royal largess towards Henri d'Albret can be documented after 1547, and the circumstances surrounding the grant reveal the depth to which the so-called king of Navarre had fallen in court circles in spite of his strenuous efforts to manipulate court intrigues and diplomacy to his benefit. In July 1547, Albret attended and assisted at the coronation of Henri II, but his sojourn at court was soon sullied by his schemes to marry off Jeanne (recently released from her tragic adolescent marriage to the Duke of Cleves) to one of the princes of the house of Hapsburg, as the first step in a larger plan to bring the ever-elusive kingdom of Navarre back into his possession. Henri's schemes were at complete odds with the royal will. The new king had no desire to see the extensive holdings of the Albret family drawn firmly into the Hapsburg orbit and pushed hard instead for an alliance with a loyal French prince of the blood, the dashing Antoine de Bourbon. To delay decision on the matter, Albret took a fortuitous tour of his estates in southern France in the fall of 1547, lin-

---

[55] Ibid.

[56] *Actes de François Ier*, 4:258.

[57] Roelker, *Queen of Navarre*, 69; for a discussion of the evolution of Henri's relationship with Marguerite, see Baumgartner, *Henry II*, 5–7.

gering in Béarn where he could more easily continue negotiations with the Holy Roman Emperor.

Eventually, however, the royal will proved to be too strong, and in feverish desperation Albret returned his attentions to Henri II in hopes of negotiating some compensatory payment for his frustrated plans. When the two met at Moulins in October 1547, Albret asked for an additional annual pension of 15,000 francs in return for his consent to the Bourbon marriage. Henri II was delighted and considered it a minor coup of sorts to have settled the delicate matter so easily. As he commented cavalierly to his chief confidante, "The contracts are ready, the marriage will take place on Sunday. I am getting out of it cheaply; I only have to give him 15,000 francs a year toward the expense of his kingdom."[58] The royal pension lists over the next few years tellingly reveal who was the shrewdest politician. Only a single payment was ever made on this extra pension.[59]

II. Jeanne d'Albret and Antoine de Bourbon

To what extent did royal largess continue to grace the next generations of Béarnais sovereigns? As an illustrious princess of the blood, Jeanne d'Albret, even as a woman, wielded enormous power over the vast patronage network she controlled. As head of an extensive household with close to two hundred officers and servants by 1556, Jeanne controlled the distribution of some of the most prized and potentially most lucrative household offices in France, positions which will be discussed more fully in the following chapter.[60] Beyond the domestic patronage Jeanne controlled within the context of her household, she also exercised, albeit indirectly, considerable patronage power in the public arena, particularly at court, where she frequently acted as a broker of papal and royal patronage for office seekers connected to her domestic network and for members of her own family. For example, Jeanne successfully petitioned Pius IV and Cardinals Georges d'Armagnac and Jean du Bellay on behalf of her great uncle, Louis d'Albret,

---

[58]Roelker, *Queen of Navarre*, 73.
[59]H. Noel Williams, *Henri II: His Court and Times* (New York: Methuen and Co., Ltd., 1910), 251.
[60]For an extensive discussion of the patronage power of French noblemen and noblewomen in the sixteenth century, with a number of references to Jeanne d'Albret and her daughter, Catherine de Bourbon, see Sharon Kettering, "The Patronage Power of Early Modern French Noblewomen," *The Historical Journal* 32 (1989): 817–41.

who was interested in the lucrative bishopric of Lescar in Béarn.[61] But apart from royal gifts which were doubtless distributed to Jeanne and her husband, Antoine de Bourbon, on the eve of their marriage in 1548, there is no record in Jeanne's accounts of any royal pension she herself gathered from the crown.[62] By 1565, her extraordinary receipts, so her treasurer noted, were largely comprised of loans negotiated to defray household expenses and the fairly meager returns from the sale of a number of minor offices in her territories. Most of these—offices, notaries, and sergeancies in particular—only brought 5 to 10 livres at a time into the coffers, totaling only 162£. 10s.[63]

While Jeanne herself could not exercise the military appointments and royal offices which Henri d'Albret had governed for the house of Foix-Navarre-Albret between 1527 and 1555, she was instrumental in securing these appointments for her husband, Antoine, who safeguarded the Albrets' dynastic interests in them. Moreover, Antoine proved to be just as driven to possess the phantom kingdom of Navarre as his Gascon father-in-law had been. He resisted the Crown's tempting offer, tendered as soon as Henri d'Albret's death seemed imminent in 1555, to exchange Béarn for important territories in the center of France which would have rounded out his own patrimonial holdings in the Vendômois.[64] And on his father-in-law's death on May 24, 1555, Antoine offered his resignation as governor of the northern province of Picardy, where his family held extensive lands and had held the governorship for two generations, in order to pursue his claim to the government of Guyenne. Within two weeks, Antoine saw himself confirmed as the new governor of Guyenne.[65] His confirmation as Admiral of Guyenne followed soon after, provoking strong parlementary opposition.[66]

In his new post, Bourbon harbored even grander illusions than had Henri d'Albret. As admiral, he proposed an ill-fated attack on the Spanish Navarrais port of Fontarabie and dreamed of basing a strategic fleet of ships along the northern African coast in order to expand his operations against Spain after the Treaty of Cateau-Cambrésis. The defeat dashed his hopes for a French-sponsored invasion through

---

[61]Ibid., 830, 833–37.
[62]AD-PA, B6.
[63]AD-PA, B8.
[64]For a discussion of Antoine's obsession, see Roelker, *Queen of Navarre*, 79–80; for the royal intrigues surrounding the Béarn regime, 106.
[65]Harding, *Anatomy of a Power Elite*, 223.
[66]Gouron, *L'Amirauté en Guienne*, 159–60.

the Pyrenees.[67] There is little evidence to suggest that Bourbon aggressively pursued the economic opportunities of his position—he was first and foremost a warrior. Additionally, he was increasingly drawn into the whirl of religious politicking which characterized French political life in the later 1550s and early 1560s; this inclination may have precluded many active efforts to recover the extraordinary revenues of his offices. At any rate, Bourbon's tenure as governor and admiral was short. The civil wars took him to the battlefield for the Catholic cause where he died in October 1562 in the siege of Rouen. His untimely death left one large question: Would the great offices he had held transfer to his nine-year-old son?

III. Henri de Navarre

Writing in 1602, the author of *La Maladie de la France* noted somewhat nostalgically that under Francis I governorships had been recruited on the basis of a "judgment of the virtue and merit of a man chosen among many to be entrusted with power and a public charge."[68] But sometime during the sixteenth century, the writer lamented, the practice had changed and governorships had become the private property of great noble houses. The house of Foix-Navarre-Albret certainly stood to profit from royal policy, particularly after Antoine de Bourbon's death in 1562. Within five weeks of his death, Bourbon's only male heir, Henri de Navarre, then but a child of nine, was confirmed by royal decree as the new governor of Guyenne. At such a tender age, Navarre was hardly in the position to perform the numerous duties required of a governor, so a deputy lieutenant was appointed by the Crown until Henri reached majority.[69]

To Jeanne's great consternation, the man chosen to rule in Henri's name was none other than the great Gascon blackguard, Blaise de Monluc, who, as lieutenant general of Guyenne, had despoiled Jeanne's properties only nine months earlier and had conspired with Philip II of Spain to launch an invasion into the heart of her domains, the viscounty of Béarn itself. In typical style, the lusty warrior had even joked that he intended, if he ever managed to breach the boundaries of Béarn, to despoil its sovereign in order to find out "if it was as much fun to sleep with Queens as with other women."[70] Jeanne immediately pro-

---

[67]Ibid.
[68]J. Leschassier, "La Maladie de la France," [1602] in *Oeuvres*, as cited in Harding, *Anatomy of a Power Elite*, 119–20.
[69]Roelker, *Queen of Navarre*, 197.
[70]Ibid., 195–97.

tested the appointment, fearing that Monluc might try to jeopardize Henri's ultimate control of the office. In a letter to Catherine de Medici, queen regent, written in late February or early March 1563, she deftly tried to discredit Monluc's reliability and faithfulness by recalling that he had once been a client of the house of Foix-Navarre-Albret only to betray its interests in the first Religious War. She also stressed his overtly greedy designs on the office.[71] But Catherine remained firm. Monluc was put in place; ultimately it would be Jeanne herself who would jeopardize Henri's authority in his government of Guyenne.

As titular head of the province of Guyenne, Henri received all the pensions and perquisites due his estate, including a royal commission in the king's ordinance companies as a captain of one hundred *lances*. A function normally ascribed to provincial governors, the office carried an annual salary between 1,200 and 2,800 livres.[72] An extant receipt from the royal treasury shows that Henri was also rewarded 450 livres in November 1562 as the captain of a company of five hundred men-at-arms.[73] Even before the Religious Wars upset the political balance of the kingdom, child captains were not uncommon. Royal records show that French kings were not especially chary about commissioning mere babes as captains in their gendarmerie. Particularly germane to the discussion here is the case of the young Comte de Saint-Pol, who was given the governorship of Dauphiné and a captain's commission in an ordinance company in 1545 when he was only nine years old,[74] the same age Henri de Navarre would be in 1562 when he became governor of Guyenne.

While kings refused to be bound by legal principles or established decorum when handing out the great offices of the realm, provincial parlements rigorously held to the letter of the law as the signature of their authority and as a counterweight to the growth of royal power. Thus, when Catherine de Medici bestowed the last of Bourbon's titles and perquisites, the Admiralty of Guyenne, on nine-year-old Henri in 1562, the *parlementaires* of Paris and Bordeaux protested and refused to register the letters of provision. Particularly galling was not only that Henri was a minor according to French law, but also that as a future sovereign in his own right, he was exempted from doing homage for the position. When the Crown reissued the letters patent six months later and demanded compliance, the *parlementaires* consented

---

[71]Ibid., 204–5.
[72]Antoine de Ruble, *Jeanne d'Albret et la guerre civile* (Paris: E. Paul et Guillemin, 1897), 306.
[73]de Ruble, *Jeanne d'Albret*, 305.
[74]Harding, *Anatomy of a Power Elite*, 21.

but not without registering a reservation of their own: they declared that the Admiralty's alleged right to approve royal letters was, in fact, an infringement upon parlementary prerogative. Only after nine long months of parlementary maneuvering with the crown were the letters patent and all the special details and formalities of the appointment finally registered.[75]

Henri's final confirmation of the full power of his offices of governor and admiral occurred with great pomp and circumstance on July 7, 1568, when he reached the age of fifteen. Only three months later, he was deprived of them because he was "in the power of the enemies of the crown."[76] Jeanne's open espousal of the Huguenot cause in the fall of 1568—after nearly a decade of nonpartisan politics—led to this stunning divestiture which officially lasted until 1575 when Henri was reinstated in his offices shortly before the Peace of Monsieur. Between 1568 and 1575, Henri received none of his pensions from the Crown, and even his salary as a captain in the gendarmerie was suspended.[77]

In practice, however, Henri continued to exercise many of the privileges of his office, especially in the Protestant stronghold of La Rochelle, where he functioned as admiral de facto if not de jure and insisted on enjoying the full prerogatives of his office. There, admiralty revenues bounteously poured into the family coffers and even enriched the treasury of the Protestant party, in flagrant disregard of official sanctions against it. One-fifth of the proceeds from confiscated ships and merchandise coming into the Protestant port were earmarked for the Huguenot cause; another one-tenth went to Navarre's private purse as part of the admiral's traditional *dixième de prise*. In one year alone, Henri's portion of the admiralty prizes amounted to 300,000 livres.[78]

Outside of La Rochelle Navarre's powers were more severely circumscribed. Local notables tried to take advantage of Navarre's temporary fall from royal grace and the confusion of the civil wars to claim certain magisterial prerogatives for themselves, not the least of which were rights to administer the prodigious revenues coming into the Admiralty's treasury. In the ever-epic prose of Fernand Braudel, the civil wars saw a "rolling back of the processes of time, a return to independent urban life, to the city-state."[79] Even after the Crown recon-

---

[75]Gouron, *L'Amirauté en Guienne*, 160.
[76]Ibid., 161.
[77]Ibid., 163.
[78]Ibid., 164.
[79]Fernand Braudel, *La Méditerranée et le monde méditerranéen à l'époque de Philippe II* (Paris: Armand Colin, 1949), 495.

firmed Navarre's appointment as admiral in 1575, many local officials and notables refused to recognize his influence. The avidly royalist *parlementaires* of Bordeaux not only refused to register the new letters patent confirming Navarre's privileges, they went so far as to deny him entry into the city until October 1576.[80] Not surprisingly, they vehemently disputed Henri's claims to the proceeds from anchorage fees, arguing that the Crown had traditionally rewarded the city with these revenues; eventually, the magistrates were so persuasive that Henri III granted them the privilege. So matters stood until 1600 when Navarre, as Henri IV of France, revoked the concession.[81]

Even in La Rochelle, Navarre's rule was not undisputed, and his right to enjoy certain revenues of office was subject to constant review by the town elite during the Religious Wars. With the revival of hostilities in 1576, the forced loans and "voluntary" contributions that had characterized Jeanne d'Albret's domination of the city in 1569–70 resumed. But many of the town's leading citizens balked at such highhanded conduct and demanded a share of the funds that were being raised or pirated outright for the Huguenot party. After an absence from the Protestant port in 1577, for example, Navarre returned only to find that his lieutenant, the Prince de Condé, had been forced to grant the city councilors "one-half of one-fifth of the booty being within the enclosure of the said city walls." A further indignity required a city-appointed commissioner to serve alongside the Admiralty official who oversaw the proceeds from confiscations and seizures, presumably to safeguard the city's portion of the proceeds. By 1579, the actions and attitudes of the Rochellais elite had so provoked the representatives of the Reformed Church that the delegates came to Navarre's defense and in the *cahiers de doléances* they presented to the king in October they insisted on his right to enjoy "the real and full possession of the admiralty."[82]

The pension lists of 1576 and 1578 show that Henri and numerous other declared "rebels" continued to appear on the royal *états* as salaried servants of the state after the new cycle of religious violence broke out in the spring of 1576; this time little attempt was made to divest them of their titles. Navarre and his coreligionists were the happy beneficiaries of a philosophy gaining favor among the chief counselors at court who argued that royal interests would be better served if the great Protestant nobles were curried rather than cut off. Certain per-

---

[80] Gouron, *L'Amirauté en Guienne*, 190–91.
[81] Ibid.
[82] Ibid., 164.

suasive court theorists held that the kingdom would be restored only when the Protestant *grands* and the lesser nobles who made up their clientèles, so firmly entrenched in the Midi and virtually institutionalized in power by various political assemblies, were placated with gifts, pensions, and demonstrations of royal largess. Thus, it was believed that a certain portion of the royal treasury should be reserved for these fractious subjects of the king in order to draw them back into the established order.[83] Long before Lucien Romier wrote his history of the origins of the Religious Wars, contemporary observers suggested that cupidity and not a sudden religious sensitivity explained the preponderant involvement of the nobility in the Wars of Religion.[84] Owing to these royal policies, Navarre's official pensions from the crown totaled 48,000 livres by 1579, a figure almost double the pension and salary his grandfather received in 1532.

Collecting these pensions, however, proved increasingly difficult as Henri suffered from the common plight of many royal pensioners during the Wars of Religion; pensions promised, guaranteed, and backed up by nearly useless assignments were rarely disbursed on time, if at all. The infamous instability of French royal finances in the sixteenth century, beginning with the great bankruptcy of 1559, was only exacerbated by decades of religious and civil disorder and unrestrained spending by French monarchs. By 1579, the generosity of Henri III and, even more importantly, decades of war had largely depleted the royal treasury, making Navarre's pensions tediously difficult to claim.[85] His agents often showed up at the appointed *caisse* only to discover that the various treasurers and accountants had orders not to disburse funds or simply had no funds to disburse. When the councilors of the Chambre des comptes in Pau finally reconciled Navarre's 1579 accounts nearly two years later, they were constrained to cancel

---

[83]Harding, *Anatomy of a Power Elite*, 141–42.

[84]Lucien Romier's classic explanation of the political motivation behind the Religious Wars, *Les Origines politiques des guerres de religion*, 2 vols. (Paris: Perrin et cie, 1913–14), has shaped historical writing and interpretation for almost a century.

[85]For a lucid discussion of the notorious disarray in the royal finances in the 1580s, see Mark Greengrass, *France in the Age of Henri IV: The Struggle for Stability* (New York: Longman, 1984), 14–25. The ever-prudent *parlementaire* Pierre de L'Estoile waxes eloquent on the prodigality of Henri III; see *Mémoires-journaux, 1574–1661* 4 vols. (Paris: Tallandier, 1882), 1:141–43, 188–89, 253–54. 263. See also, Nancy Roelker, ed., *The Paris of Henry of Navarre* (Cambridge: Harvard University Press, 1958), 52, 59, 64, 67. For a somewhat subdued portrait of the flamboyant king, see Jacqueline Boucher's revisionary *Société et mentalités autour de Henri III*, 4 vols. (Lille: Champion, 1981).

the figures for the royal pension, which a hopeful treasurer had written in, because the funds had never been received.[86]

Navarre pursued his errant pensions with a doggedness worthy of his ancestry. In the five years of nominal peace following the Treaty of Fleix in November 1580, he proposed creative ways of recouping his unpaid pensions—totaling in the hundreds of thousands of livres—without straining the feeble reserves of the *Epargne*. In 1581, for example, he outlined a plan to find Henri III an additional 100,000 livres on the condition that his overdue pensions for his governorship would be paid in part from the proceeds. Henri III readily agreed and granted Navarre the right to pocket one-tenth of the sums he raised.[87] In the same year, Henri III also began to settle accounts with Navarre concerning his unpaid salary for his post as a captain of an ordinance company. In October 1581, the king finally issued a decree to his treasurer of the *Epargne* ordering payment of Navarre's unpaid salary from 1572–74, which amounted to 3,200 écus. Administrative oversight, however, continued to delay payment when the obviously observant treasurer balked at disbursing such a significant sum from the royal *caisse* without proper documentation in the muster rolls. Henri III was thus forced to issue two other decrees almost a year later demanding the disbursal of the funds, "notwithstanding the fact that he [Navarre] is not listed on the rolls and *états* of the said gendarmerie for the said year." This explanation apparently settled the matter and Navarre's agent collected the payment.[88]

Mounting royal debts made it nearly impossible for Henri III to fulfill his promises, and Navarre's pensions and gifts went unpaid in 1582. But the importunate Protestant chief was not left empty-handed because Henri III attempted to make up the deficit by bestowing venal offices and other revenues on Navarre. Money from the sale of offices brought in 18,353 livres, river tolls collected along the Garonne amounted to 14,650 livres, and an impressive 52,000 livres came from the sale of government bonds (*compositions*) in Périgueux. In all, these revenues totaled 85,002 livres, nearly double what Navarre would have expected from the *Epargne*.[89] In 1586, Marguerite de Valois, Henri's wife, garnered 25,500 livres for her private *caisse* from similar awards.[90] One cautionary note needs to be added. It is true, as Harding has noted, that "a large proportion of royal gifts to governors were actu-

---

[86]AD-PA, B2527.
[87]*IAD, Basses-Pyrénées*, sér. B2007.
[88]AN, K101, fo. 31.
[89]AD-PA, B157.
[90]Harding, *Anatomy of a Power Elite*, 141.

ally reimbursements for advances that they had made to buy supplies and repair fortifications," and Navarre's military expenses in 1582 were prodigious, as we will see in detail in chapter 6.[91] But this military practice does not diminish the fact that Navarre continued to be a beneficiary of the Crown, and the revenue he received from taxes, government bonds, and other royal sources restored some balance to his accounts, where expenditures were almost spiraling out of control.

As the century progressed royal pensions and salaries came to comprise a smaller and smaller share of the Albrets' total revenues on the male side. Whereas Henri d'Albret had relied on his royal pensions for almost 50 percent of his income in 1546, Navarre's returns were negligible from this source in 1582. (see tables 2.1 and 2.2).

Table 2.2 Sources of Income, Henri de Navarre, 1582 (in *livres tournois*)[a]

Nature of Income	Amount	Percentage
Land Rents	162,020	36.9
Land Sales	140,000	31.9
Estates Donation[b]	30,240	7.0
Ecclesiastical Land	6,339	1.4
Tolls, Taxes, Royal Grants	66,650	15.2
Sale of Offices	18,353	4.2
Seigneurial fees	157	0.1
Party Moneys	1,500	0.3
Adjusted Receipts[c]	438,759	100.0
Total Receipts	748,179	—
AD-PA Source: B157		

[a]Rounded to the nearest *livre tournois*.
[b]Includes only the donation from the Estates of Béarn; donations from other provincial estates are not specifically listed in the account. Includes part of the 200,000 livres donation voted to Navarre by the Assembly of Churches in 1579.
[c]Not included are sums listed as receipts which were actually expenditures where payment was suspended, and a miscellaneous receipt of 224,893 livres transferred into the treasury by Vincent de Pedesclaux "from the coffers." It cannot be determined if this large lump sum was actually "revenue."

[91]Ibid., 138.

The salary Navarre received in his post as captain of an ordinance company was four times what Albret had earned in 1521; but compared to overall revenues, it was a relatively minor receipt. Tolls, gifts from the Crown, and *parties casuelles* accounted for 15.2 percent of his income, but the weight of influence had shifted and clearly lay with the land and family domains, which were rented and sold at ever increasing prices.

The two decades Henri spent cajoling money from the hands of royal treasurers and accountants convinced him of the political value of royal donations and bribes which bound even a recalcitrant nobility to the Crown. Keenly aware of the mechanisms of patronage, both as a patron to his own circle of followers and as a client of the Crown, Henri would use bribes and donations to bring both Huguenot and Catholic nobles under his authority after he assumed the throne in 1589, and thus restored a measure of stability to France. Royal patronage thus became an even more significant and concrete way of identifying the nobility's own advancement with the well-being of the state after 1589.

IV. Catherine de Bourbon

The importance of court pensions and perquisites to members of the house of Foix-Navarre-Albret is perhaps best illustrated by the case of Catherine de Bourbon. A child of thirteen when Jeanne d'Albret died, Catherine was, of course, too young to receive her mother's legacy in her own right. The records show that the bulk of her expenses in 1572 were paid with receipts from Bourbon territories in Flanders, Picardy, and Vendômois.[92] Catherine's household expenses, however, more than doubled over the next two years, and her brother Henri, in desperate financial straits himself, assigned 10,000 livres to her account from the treasury of the duchy of Albret. Collection proved difficult, forcing Catherine to write a solicitous request to Henri's general treasurer in Albret, Imbert LeVenier, for complete satisfaction of the charge. As she explained,

> Be assured that it will serve me well since I have no other means to remedy the extreme necessity which is at present in my house. And I beg you to also work out with Monsieur Assezat [the famous Toulousan Protestant and merchant who also served as one of Henri's farmers-general] that I am paid the 5,000 livres which he owes me that I am assigned from the general farm in Albret.[93]

[92] AD-PA, B22.
[93] Raymond Ritter, ed., *Lettres et poésies de Catherine de Bourbon* (Paris: Champion, 1927), 2.

Such requests were clearly an integral feature of sixteenth-century finance; unpaid assignments were routine, and in 1576, the household treasurer noted in his accounts that 11,587£. 1s. 3d. finally passed through his hands from the farmers-general of Albret.[94] The frustration of dealing with family business in such a drawn out manner and the increasing charges of Catherine's household eventually prompted Henri to offer a number of pensions to his sister. In 1579, he granted Catherine an annual pension of 10,000 livres from confiscated church lands in Béarn "in order to underwrite in part" the maintenance of her household.[95] This pension was followed by an additional 25,000 livres from Henri's coffers and receipts from the treasurers of Armagnac and Albret. To facilitate payments over the next few years, Henri made Catherine the beneficiary of the receipts of Béarn, Foix, and Bigorre. In all three provinces Catherine served as regent, and the weight of her authority and the relative peace enjoyed in these territories, particularly Béarn, after 1579 meant rich returns in land rents. Moreover, the provincial estates in these territories traditionally voted generous donations to the house of Foix-Navarre-Albret, making these domains all the more valuable. The Estates of Béarn, in particular, favored Catherine with significant annual subsidies. In 1583, this meant an additional 12,000 livres in Catherine's coffers; by 1585 specially appointed receivers turned in 11,360 livres to Catherine's account; in 1587, this sum had risen to 15,000 livres. (see table 2.3)[96]

Even with these estates' donations, Catherine needed additional funds to cover her expenses. Here fortune and position favored her. Beginning in 1583, the household treasurer acknowledged the receipt of 12,000 livres annually from the Crown, but never formally entered the amount into his accounts, noting that these "sums" were put in her coffers "without having passed through the hands of the said accountant which the said lady always has disposed as it seemed good to her." Catherine continued to receive a pension from the Crown throughout the 1580s as well as undisclosed sums from "the subjects of the king of Navarre."[97] It is difficult to assess the importance of these royal pensions and extraordinary gifts before 1590 when these moneys were formally integrated into the household accounts. It is reasonable to suspect that these sums were used to acquit outstanding debts.

---

[94]AD-PA, B32.
[95]AD-PA, B48bis.
[96]AD-PA, B83, B111.
[97]See for example, AD-PA, B83.

And what of Navarre's largess towards his sister after his ascension to the Crown of France? To what extent did Catherine benefit from her position as the *soeur unique* of the King of France? According to Sully's *Mémoires*, Catherine charged Henri with a certain meanness in 1595 in the heat of their *embrouillement* over her love affair with the Comte de Soissons, and accused him of keeping her in financial straits by delaying the distribution of her legacy in order to force her hand.[98] The treasurer's accounts after 1594 do reveal a dramatic structural change in Catherine's revenues which lends a certain credence to her charge. Income from land rents plummeted between 1591 and 1594 from 54,035 to 23,148 livres, but the treasurer's accounts also show that the erosion of Catherine's land rents was offset by generous compensations from the Crown which suggest that Catherine may have been guilty of a little histrionics. (see table 2.3) Henri offered her 60,000 livres as compensation for the patrimonial lands over which he kept control (*non-jouissance*); one wonders if she would have garnered as much from leases when we have already seen that the first years of the 1590s brought unmitigated disaster to so many of the family domains.[99]

Henri's record with royal pensions and gifts to Catherine was equally openhanded. In the first year of his de facto reign he continued the pension of 12,000 livres and granted Catherine the right to sell a number of offices which earned another 2,076 livres for her private coffers. But these gestures appear miserly when compared with his actions between 1594 and 1598. Over these years, Catherine's income more than tripled, almost entirely as a result of court favors and pensions. (see table 2.3) In 1594, for example, 222,900 livres were delivered into Catherine's treasury by Francis Hotman, the Protestant apologist and propagandist, who had parlayed his political beliefs into a position in the new government. In 1595, the *Epargne* disbursed a similar gift of 180,000 livres to cover "the great expense that Catherine makes close to His Majesty."[100]

To defray further the lavish expenditures which Catherine was obliged to make as a fixture in the royal entourage, Henri confirmed Catherine's right to exact extraordinary revenues from the administra-

---

[98]Ritter, ed., *Lettres de Catherine de Bourbon*, 118–23. For Henri's soothing letter to Catherine on June 22, 1596, trying to solve the issue, see L. Dussienx, ed., *Lettres intimes d'Henri IV* (Paris, 1876), 251.

[99]See chap. 1.

[100]AD-PA, B138, 139. Catherine was recalled from Béarn, where she had served as Henri's regent, to court in 1592. For a description of her entry, see Roelker, ed., *The Paris of Henry of Navarre*, 262, 269–70.

Table 2.3 Catherine De Bourbon's Treasury Receipts 1579–1598[a]

Nature of Receipts	1579	1583	1587	1590	1591	1594[b]	1598[b]
Royal Pensions and *dons*	25,000	12,000[c]	12,000[c]	12,000	—	222,900	180,000[a]
%	50.0	18.6	17.9	13.5		61.3	51.4
Béarnais Estates	—	12,000	15,000	17,771[d]	27,220	—	—
%		18.6	22.4	20.0	26.9		
Confiscated Church Properties	10,000	10,000	10,000	10,000	10,000	10,000	10,000
%	20.0	15.5	14.9	11.2	9.8	2.7	2.9
Parties Casuelles	—	—	—	2,076	3,073	14,483	23,253
%				2.3	3.1	4.0	6.6
Land-Leases	15,000	30,500	30,000	47,140	54,035	23,148	54,015
%	30.0	47.3	44.8	53.0	53.3	6.4	15.4
Non-*jouissance* Land-leases	—	—	—	—	—	60,000	60,000
%						16.5	17.1

(continued next page)

Table 2.3 (continued)[a]

Nature of Receipts	1579	1583	1587	1590	1591	1594[b]	1598[b]
Land Sales	—	—	—	—	—	26,664	—
%						7.3	
Miscellaneous	—	—	—	—	7,000[e]	6,150	23,019[f]
%					6.9	1.7	6.6
Total Receipts	50,000	64,500	67,000	88,987	101,328	363,345	350,287
AD-PA Source, respectively by year: B48bis, B83, B129, B136, B138, B142							

[a]Account is figured in *livres tournois*. Receipts are rounded off to nearest livres.
[b]This account is given in écus, which were converted to livres at the rate of 1:3.
[c]Noted in the account but not officially entered and tallied into total receipts.
[d]Includes donation of the Estates of Navarre.
[e]Made up from tolls levied along the Charentes and Garonne rivers.
[f]Funds from seigneurial dues and fines on counterfeiters in Normandy; gifts from Henry IV.

tive officials on the family domains. Proceeds from these *parties casuelles* brought increasingly significant sums into her private treasury. From a mere 2,040 livres in 1590, returns leaped upwards to 14,472 livres in 1594 and peaked at 23,252 livres in 1598. In less than a decade Catherine's revenues from this source had increased tenfold! (see table 2.3) To what extent this movement was due to the duplication—even the multiplication—of administrative offices is difficult to gauge because we know so little about the pattern of office holding during this period. In his seminal study on the sale of offices under Henri IV, Roland Mousnier offers figures to indicate that royal revenues from the sale of offices increased because of the wide-scale creation of offices and multiple officeholders.[101] It would be tempting to argue that Catherine's revenues from *parties casuelles* increased through a similar increase in sale of local offices. But scattered evidence from the Chambre des comptes in Pau suggests that Henri was actually trying to reduce the number of administrative officials in the family domains in order to save the expense of their salary. In 1596, for example, he ordered eliminating the position of the alternate treasurer of accounts.[102]

Catherine's accounts do give us some basis for comment, however. First, it is obvious that the dramatic increase in revenues comes only in small part from the movements in the price of offices. Between 1556 and 1590 the price of even minor offices more than tripled; but between 1591 and 1598 the value of sergeancies and notaries remained fairly stable at 30 livres. A far more important reason for the increasing revenues from *parties casuelles* was the kind of offices in which Catherine dealt, offices which commanded a higher price than the minor sergeancies and notaries of Jeanne's day.[103] While Catherine certainly never disdained the small sums that were to be made from the sale of minor offices, she doubtless appreciated Henri's confirmation of her right to pocket the proceeds of the *parties casuelles* from the important legal and financial offices of her estates. In 1594, for example, the sale of the post of *juge-mage* in Lectoure alone brought 1,200 écus into her treasury.[104] The average price of offices sold in 1591 was 413 livres as compared to 775 livres in 1598.[105] Despite the considerable income Catherine derived from the sale of office, proceeds from *parties*

---

[101]Mousnier, *La Vénalité*, 104.

[102]*IAD, Basses-Pyrénées*, 257.

[103]See, for example, the sale of offices in Jeanne's accounts, AD-PA, B144, as compared with those of Catherine.

[104]AD-PA, B138.

[105]AD-PA, B137, B148.

casuelles comprised only a small part of her total annual income. Profits from the sale of offices never amounted to more than 7 percent of her total revenues.

By far the bulk of Catherine's moneys came from royal pensions and gifts. (see table 2.3) These large grants from the *Epargne* were frequently supplemented by other subventionary measures, perquisites, and assignations designed to assist Catherine in procuring additional revenues. One grant in particular deserves mention. Early in his reign, Henri ordered the establishment of a new *chambre de grenier à sel* (salt storehouse) with instructions that Catherine was to receive "some small sum" from the proceeds of salt sales to "help her meet the expenses of her household."[106] But as the tenor and repetition of letters to the royal Chambre des comptes at Rouen suggest, it was one thing for Henri to order these payments, but it was quite another for Catherine to collect. In October 1595, Catherine rather testily reminded the royal officials in Rouen of their responsibilities:

> Once again the King my Lord and brother gives you to understand by the letters that he writes you, that his intention is that you proceed at once to the edict that his Majesty sent for the establishment of a salt storehouse, which, although I doubt that you will ever satisfy the goodwill that you carry for his service; Nevertheless, so much does he desire to bestow upon me some small sum of the monies that should come from the said edict, in order to help defray the expense of my house, that I have decided to send you this word of advice and beg you to bring to this all possible diligence.[107]

The administrative inertia in Rouen provoked a flurry of letters from Catherine's hand to royal councilors and treasurers all over the kingdom. In desperation she wrote to Bauldry, one of Henri's treasurers in Tours, asking him to help her extricate "some fruit" from salt sales elsewhere to satisfy her due.[108] Not content with money alone, Catherine asked him to intervene personally in the situation in Rouen. All of this indicates the formidable obstacles which sometimes attended the realization of royal gifts, particularly when they entailed changes in the administrative system. These difficulties notwithstanding, incoming revenues to Catherine's private treasury reached 350,087 livres in 1598, thanks to generous royal donations and

[106]Ritter, ed., *Lettres de Catherine de Bourbon,* 122.
[107]Ibid., 123.
[108]Ibid., 125.

patronage. Over the next six years, until her untimely death in 1604, she dramatically increased her complement of servants and occasioned expenditures which could only have been acquitted with the help of lavish royal pensions.[109]

V. Conclusion

The increasing political, financial, and cultural value of royal offices and pensions to the great nobility is one of the indisputable features of early modern France, a telling testimony to the growth of monarchical power and influence. By the mid-seventeenth century, access to court pensions and royal offices determined the political health and financial wealth of great noble dynasties in France. Those without access to the corridors of power found themselves gradually consigned to the life of a petty rural seigneur, with little but a noble toponym to distinguish themselves from the prosperous peasant *coq du village*. Even by the sixteenth century, however, royal pensions, offices, and periodic demonstrations of royal largess contributed substantially to the fortunes of many great court nobles and often provided them with the liquidity necessary to maintain and preserve their varied interests and activities. Royal pensions and offices permitted nobles, such as Blaise de Monluc, Anne de Montmorency, Gaspard de Saulx-Tavanes, Henri d'Albret, and Henri de Navarre, to preserve and expand their landed patrimony, to fulfill their military obligations to wage war, even for the Huguenot cause, and to engage in conspicuous consumption in court circles. Indeed, by the sixteenth century, royal service and the benefits accrued from it were viewed as crucial to any effort to live "nobly," according to the dictates of fashion. For the Albrets, the sixteenth century witnessed the beginnings of the family's dynastic claims to the most important royal offices and military appointments doled out by the French monarchy. Francis I's royal grants survived even Antoine de Bourbon's untimely death, Henri de Navarre's succession to the family titles at the unlikely age of nine, and Henri's conversion to Calvinism. While Navarre was briefly divested of his title and pensions during the early days of the Religious Wars, he and many of his coreligionists were reintegrated into the royal *état* in 1576 as salaried servants of the state, beneficiaries of royal efforts to bring potentially rebellious or contentious nobles to heel through bribery. Thanks to these policies, Navarre's pensions and gifts from the

---

[109]For a record of Catherine de Bourbon's household and household expenditures, see AD, Meurthe-et-Moselle, B1266, B1282.

Crown lagged only slightly behind wheat prices and probably kept pace with prices in general which did not climb as much as grain prices.

The Albrets' success in pursuing their pensions and preserving their offices even in the face of chronic royal bankruptcies, religious war, and regency governments emphasizes their dogged pursuit of revenues in whatever form. Indeed, even as the amazing growth of landed revenues dwarfed the value of Navarre's pensions within the context of his overall fortunes, he continued to devise creative ways to collect them. Moreover, as grateful recipients of royal largess, the Albrets were careful to engage in similar demonstrations of liberality and generosity to their own household officers, followers, companions, and *fidèles*. Indeed, by cultivating the loyalties of their clientèles through gifts of household appointments, pensions, and preferment, they established a sound structural basis for their bid for power during the Religious Wars.

Three

The Economy of Patronage

After the deeds and the exploits of war, which are claims to glory, the household is the first thing that strikes the eyes, and which it is therefore most necessary to arrange well."[1] So wrote the chronicler Georges Chastellain in 1453 when the court of Charles the Bold of Burgundy ranked as one of the most magnificent and ordered households in Europe. A century later, Chastellain's prescription for the art of living nobly still exerted a compelling call to order and magnificence to the *haute noblesse* of France. For most great aristocrats in Renaissance France, the key to power—and to giving the illusion of power—lay in the maintenance of the extensive patronage networks which had been developed and nourished over the centuries. At the heart of these networks was the household, where protégés of proven loyalties were rewarded with honorific titles and pensions, and the younger sons and daughters of the lower nobility were trained in the arts of war and society.[2]

---

[1] As quoted in Johan Huizinga, *The Waning of the Middle Ages* (New York: Anchor Books, 1954), 41.

[2] See, for example, Neuschel's discussion of the role of aristocratic service in the socialization of young nobles in *Word of Honor*, 78–90; see also Harding's discussion of the main patronage networks of major governors in Renaissance France, and the role of the household in those networks, in *Anatomy of a Power Elite*, 21–31, 182–89; see also Mack Holt, *The Duke of Anjou and the Politique Struggle during the Wars of Religion* (Cambridge: Cambridge University Press, 1986), 16–17; idem, "Patterns of Clientèle and Economic Opportunity at Court during the Wars of Religion: The Household of François, Duke of Anjou," *French Historical Studies* 13 (1984):305–22; Sharon Kettering, *Patrons, Brokers, and Clients in Seventeenth-Century France* (Oxford: Oxford University Press,

Contemporary moralists repeatedly emphasized that servants and masters, clients and patrons were bound inextricably to one another by ties of *affection* and *fidélité*.[3] Noble and nonnoble alike subscribed to the belief that the affective ties created by aristocratic service were crucial to the preservation of public order. Delegates to the Estates General in 1576, for example, argued vehemently that household service was the only effective antidote to the spread of random confessional violence, carried out by bands of young provincial nobles inspired as much by boredom as by religious enthusiasm. Members of the Third Estate appealed to the wives of *les grands* to maintain well-ordered households, where the children of the lesser nobility could be "nourished in virtue," so that "peace and tranquility" could be returned to the realm.[4] For these concerned delegates, aristocratic households were a force for permanence and stability in a world of flux and change.

Relying heavily on political treatises and public discourse, such as statements made by the Third Estate at the Estates General of 1576, Roland Mousnier argued frequently in the 1970s that the ties of *affection* and *fidélité* created between patron and client through household service militated against any expression of materialistic self-interest, which was alien, in the first place, to the noble values of honor and quality.[5] Much of the best recent scholarship has emphasized, however, the fluidity that characterized most noble households and the complexities that shaped noble relationships.[6] By the late 1560s and 1570s, the constant threat and practice of civil and religious war had militarized the households of many noble governors, who tendered the

---

1986), 34–36; Mark Greengrass, "Noble Affinities in Early Modern France: The Case of Henri I de Montmorency, Constable of France," *European History Quarterly* 16 (1986):275–311; Pierre Lefebvre, "Aspects de la 'fidélité' en France au XVIIe siècle: Le Cas des agents des Princes de Condé," *Revue historique* 250 (1973):59–106.

[3]Roland Mousnier, *Les Institutions de la France sous la monarchie absolue, 1598–1789*, I (Paris: Presses Universitaires de France, 1974), 85–93; idem, "Les concepts d'ordres, d'états, et de fidélité et de monarchie absolue en France de la fin du XVe siècle à la fin du XVIIIe siècle," *Revue historique* 147 (1972): 289–312; for a response to Mousnier's view of early modern French society as a "society of orders," see the festschrift in his honor, Yves Durand, ed., *Hommage à Roland Mousnier: Clientèles et fidélités en Europe à l'époque moderne* (Paris: Presses Universitaires de France, 1981).

[4]As quoted in Harding, *Anatomy of a Power Elite*, 27.

[5]See Roland Mousnier, *Les Hiérachies sociales de 1450 à nos jours* (Paris: Presses Universitaires de France, 1969); and idem, *Les Institutions de la France*.

[6]See J. H. M. Salmon, "Storm over the Noblesse," *Journal of Modern History* 53 (1981):242–57; William Beik, *Absolutism and Society*, 6–9; and the extensive critique of Mousnier and the current state of the discussion on the problem of clientage in Neuschel, *Word of Honor*, 9–12, 15, 18.

enormous resources at their disposal, including offices in their own household, to compensate members of their military clientele for services rendered and to draw potential clients into their network of influence. Robert Harding, for example, has stressed that the expectation of material gain was an important motivation behind aristocratic service, prompting many so-called "faithful" clients of Catholic governors to desert their patrons and the service of the crown in favor of Calvinist governors, who offered them lavish bribes and pensions.[7] In his study of the household of the Duke of Anjou during the Wars of Religion, Mack Holt has demonstrated that many of Anjou's leading officers found nothing improper or indecorous about seeking service and preferment from nobles of rival confessions when it brought justifiable economic gain.[8] Most recently, Sharon Kettering has dismissed Mousnier's interpretation as being too simplistic and monochromatic. "Fidelity relationships as described by Mousnier," she writes, "certainly existed in seventeenth-century France, but they were not the most prevalent type of patron-client relationship. The ordinary garden variety was less durable and more materialistic."[9]

The sixteenth century witnessed significant alterations in the size and structure of aristocratic households and in the conditions that bound master to servant and client to patron. The courtly conventions of the Renaissance, the development of religiously based parties, and the emergence of religious wars all placed enormous demands on the patronage networks of the great nobility. Even before the Religious Wars, according to Robert Harding, "the cost of maintaining the throng of household officers and pages was the largest type of private expenditure" most great nobles made.[10] The implications of these changes in personal and household relationships are significant for any discussion of noble fortunes.

[7]Harding, *Anatomy of a Power Elite*, 48.
[8]Mack Holt, "Patterns of Clientèle," 305–22.
[9]Kettering, *Patrons, Brokers and Clients*, 22; see also 35–36 where she discusses the mechanism of patronage within the households of great nobles.
[10]Harding, *Anatomy of a Power Elite*, 28.

I. Household Structure

By the sixteenth century, the households of great court aristocrats were carefully modeled after households of the royal family, down to the smallest detail.[11] Roland Mousnier has stressed that the personnel in the royal household represented "a cross-section of the social stratification of the kingdom as a whole."[12] In like manner, men and women from all walks of life, from prominent nobles to illustrious clerics to day laborers, could be found on the Albrets' household rolls; their presence in the household reinforced, in highly visible terms, the extensive influence that the Albrets exercised over all three social orders in French provincial society.[13]

Like the royal household, the Albrets' households were divided into three departments: the bedchamber, the stable, and the kitchens. The bedchamber was widely considered to be the most prestigious department of the household, in part, because it permitted the greatest physical intimacy with the master or mistress of the household. Indeed, many officers of the bedchamber were already close advisors, companions, and favorites (*les intimes*) of the lord or lady, who had garnered their privileged positions as a result of a long tradition of family service or a long and trustworthy friendship. Often they slept and ate in close proximity to the master or mistress of the household and were often trusted to perform delicate diplomatic and personal tasks which

---

[11]For a description of the functioning of royal households in France, see Roger Doucet, *Les Institutions de la France au XVIe siècle*, I (Paris: A. et J. Picard, 1948), 102–30; and Mousnier, *Les Institutions de la France*, II: 115–31; Ruth Kleinman, "Social Dynamics at the French Court: The Household of Anne of Austria," *French Historical Studies* 16 (1990): 517–35. A lucid description of the Duke of Alençon's household which appears in Mack Holt, "A Prince of the Blood in the French Wars of Religion: François de Valois, Duke of Alençon and of Anjou, 1555–1584," unpublished Ph.D. diss., Emory University, 1982, 68–81.

[12]Mousnier, *Les Institutions de la France*, II: 124.

[13] The literature on the organization of noble households in early modern Europe is also extensive and much of it is fairly recent and responsive to the new cultural history. For works in this vein, see Neuschel, "Noble Households"; idem, *Word of Honor*; F. William Kent, *Household and Lineage in Renaissance Florence* (Princeton: Princeton University Press, 1977); Kate Mertes, *The English Noble Household, 1250–1600: Good Governance and Politic Rule* (London: Basil Blackwell, 1988); Heal, *Hospitality in Early Modern England*, esp. chaps. 2 and 4. The ratio of men to women in the households was always in favor of men. Indeed, in Henri d'Albret's household no women were listed on the domestic rolls, although some figured on the pension lists. In households headed by women, there were naturally women serving in honorific positions and in domestic roles—such as the laundry and bath. But men still performed the administrative functions and domestic jobs, even in the kitchens. For a more detailed discussion of the male-dominated households of the Renaissance, see Boucher, *Société et mentalités*, 1:156–57.

required the utmost secrecy.[14] By virtue of their service in the bedchamber, these nobles publicly declared themselves clients and subordinates, even if in private they demonstrated an easy familiarity. Accordingly, the Albrets tried to attract members of the most distinguished provincial nobility into these positions. In the earliest extant account of Henri d'Albret's household dating from 1518, members of some of the most important Béarnais and Gascon noble families—Miossens, Andouins, La Motte, Lavedan—all held offices in the bedchamber. As *chamberllans, maîtres de la garderobe*, and maîtres d'hôtel, they held some of the most lucrative positions in the household and exercised duties which required handling and dispensing significant sums of money and jewelry as well as state secrets. While officers of the bedchamber often engaged in diplomatic missions of the highest order, the menial task of looking after the personal needs of the Albrets fell to the valets, or *filles de chambre* in female-headed households, who were often also nobles, but frequently from less illustrious lineages than the other officers of the bedchamber. For many, a position in the bedchamber served as a springboard to other posts and perquisites beyond the household and later to important positions within the Huguenot party structure.[15]

Male members of the Albret family also kept fully manned stables, the officers of which ranked second in importance behind those of the bedchamber. At the head of the stables (*écurie*) were men of noble extraction, whose primary responsibility was to oversee the military and courtly education of the host of young noblemen attached to the households as pages. The first squire (*écuyer*) of the stables took charge of a staff, which included a tutor, dancemaster, and fencing instructor as well as the numerous grooms and their aides. These latter servants were generally of peasant stock with little hope of social advancement within the household, who performed the more inglorious and laborious tasks in the stables, while the noble pages were trained in the chevalric arts. Noble officers in the stables were also responsible for all household transportation, which meant servicing the numerous carriages, coaches, and wagons needed for a peripatetic household. They also worked in tandem with the leading squires in the kennels to orga-

---

[14]Mertes, *English Noble Households*, 42–46; Neuschel, *Word of Honor*, 173–78.

[15]Until 1515, the title *valet de chambre* had been used to designate the most intimate companions of the king. But upon his accession, Francis I decided that the title had become debased and ordered thenceforce that his aristocratic companions would be styled as "gentlemen," a title far better suited to their social eminence. See R. J. Knecht, *Francis I* (Cambridge: Cambridge University Press, 1982), 89. By 1518 Henri d'Albret had already incorporated this refinement into his own household, AD-PA E561.

nize the Albrets' hunting activities and sport. While often not as highly paid as the gentlemen of the bedchamber, squires in the stables were looked upon as guardians of the traditional virtues and values of the nobility. Frequently they were rewarded with annual pensions which, in combination with their salaries, placed them on an equal economic footing with leading officers in the household. On the other hand, the grooms and aides in the stables were probably among the most poorly paid servants in the household, who often were given only room and board.

Perhaps the most diversely figured part of the household, and the least prestigious, was the kitchen staff. Its numbers were composed mainly of nonnobles—the numerous cooks, pastrymakers, saucemakers, porters, aides, and spit turners necessary to provision and feed the Albrets' massive household and throng of hangers-on. But lesser nobles often filled the top positions in the kitchens and added a ceremonial, indeed almost sacramental, character to the banquets prepared and served by the cooks and their assistants. Sometimes styled *gentilshommes servans*, these younger sons of the nobility performed rituals which were holdovers from the feudal past. With great pomp and circumstance, these breadmasters and cupbearers carried the bread and wine to the table and tasted the food, if required, to guard against poisoning.[16] In spite of the occupational hazards of their position, they were paid poorly in comparison to their noble colleagues in the stables and chambers. Salaries for noble positions in the kitchens were sometimes half those of the bedchamber, and often they were no more than the wages paid to the cooks and other nonnoble professionals in the household.

To oversee and assure the smooth functioning of a household and its general accounts was an enormous task, one which fell to the superintendent of finances. He was assisted in his massive endeavor by a number of general comptrollers, serving by quarter, who were usually nonnobles with proven financial acumen. They verified and approved expenditures made in all parts of the household and coordinated the multifarious activities of the officers of the households. Numerous *maréchaux de logis* and *fourriers* managed the complicated logistics of

---

[16]See the discussion on the dignities surrounding the kitchens and banquet tables of Charles the Bold in Huizinga, *The Waning of the Middle Ages*, 42–43. Olivier de La Marche, Huizinga notes, treated the kitchen "in a respectful and quasi-scholastic tone." La Marche maintained that the breadmasters and cupbearers should be noble "because they are in charge of the bread and wine, to which the sacrament gives a holy character."

moving a household of two hundred through the barely civilized countryside of early modern France. These admirable teams (many of whose members served in similar capacities in the Albrets' ordinance companies) both forged ahead of the cumbersome household to arrange for lodgings and extra provisions and stayed behind to settle accounts with local merchants and innkeepers when the household moved on to a new location.

A number of trained bureaucrats transcended the traditional divisions of bedchamber, stables, and kitchens and were attached to the household to manage the weighty correspondence and to perform the diplomatic duties that characterized the interests and obligations of the great nobility. The chancellor was one of the most highly paid members of the household, second only to the superintendent of finance. Beneath him were a score of secretaries, many of whom were trained as lawyers or humanists, and some were recognized as among the most famous legal and literary minds of the French Renaissance. Victor Brodeau, the protégé of the famous poet and linguist, Clément Marot, for example, spent his formative years as a secretary to Jeanne d'Albret, and after her death offered his services to Henri de Navarre. In his post as secretary to Navarre, he often carried out important diplomatic duties, serving as an ambassador and agent at courts, both foreign and French.

The Albrets also employed qualified doctors, surgeons, pharmacists, preachers, and chaplains; these professionals saw to the daily physical and spiritual needs of their patrons and were amply rewarded for their expertise. In addition, there was always a group of artists and artisans in train—painters, poets, jewelers, tapestry makers—who frequently received only meager remunerations for their talents, but who also received room and board. Moreover, their numbers dramatically increased over the century as a consequence of the increasing political stature of the house of Foix-Navarre-Albret. As their fortunes permitted, the Albrets also subscribed to the idiosyncrasies of fashion. For instance, Jeanne kept a female dwarf, Thomette, as one of her attendants and amused herself by dressing the midget in lavish costumes. She quite literally showered gifts of clothing upon Thomette, and eventually bestowed upon her a private valet and a lifetime pension. Henri de Navarre, too, added a little exotic cachet to his entourage by including a dwarf and a fool among his attendants.[17] Such extrava-

---

[17]For an illuminating discussion of sixteenth-century sensibilities vis-à-vis the young and the miniature, see David Hunt, *Parents and Children in History* (New York: Basic Books, 1970), 161–75.

gances were countered by the comptrollers' constant attempts to eliminate superfluous domestics, who were a burden to the household and to the food budget.[18] But their efforts at economy were to little effect against the inflationary price cycle and the demands of social convention.

II. The Politics of Numbers

"The sixteenth century was an age," according to Lawrence Stone, "when a man's status was judged by the number of attendants he had and the scale of his hospitality."[19] More than any other factor, Stone maintains, even more than the rise in prices, it was this obsession with display, publicity, and numerical quantity which plagued noble fortunes and drained private treasuries.[20] In France the royal court itself set the increasingly competitive pace and provided the model for noble households. Over the course of the century, the households of the French royal family grew larger and grander, nearly quadrupling in size when compared to their fifteenth-century counterparts. Several factors encouraged this dramatic evolution, most prominently the drive toward centralization and the desire of Valois kings to establish themselves as more than primus inter pares. Perhaps as important was the need to compete on the world stage among charismatic figures like Henry VIII, Charles V, and Phillip II. Accordingly, French Renaissance monarchs engaged in games of cultural one-upsmanship with these other potentates, a contest which included increasing the entourage of their households.[21] Where Louis XII had been content to have slightly over 200 courtiers and servants close to his person, Francis I counted 622 on his household rolls by 1535.[22] By 1584, the profligate Henri III

---

[18]See a grant to Jean Fousteau, an aide in the wine cellars, on October 21, 1585; he was given twelve livres and sent home "because of the great numbers of aides who are in the kitchens," AD-PA, B2545.

[19]Stone, *Crisis of the Aristocracy*, 266.

[20]Ibid., 547–586.

[21]For a discussion of the changing nature and political ambitions of the French monarchy during the sixteenth century, see R. J. Knecht, *Francis I and Absolute Monarchy* (London: Historical Association, 1969); J. Russell Major, *Representative Institutions in Renaissance France, 1421–1559* (Madison: University of Wisconsin Press, 1960); and idem, *Representative Government in Early Modern France* (New Haven: Yale University Press, 1980). For the lively rivalry between Francis and Charles V, see F. Mignet, *La Rivalité de François Ier et de Charles-Quint*, 2 vols. (Paris: Didier, 1875).

[22]Knecht, *Francis I*, 89; see also Doucet, *L'état des finances de 1523*, 87–88, for expenditures on the royal households; total expenditures for the households reached 543,800 livres, and not 60,000 livres as Mack Holt noted in his article "Patterns of Clientèle," 311–12.

drew the opprobrium of contemporary chroniclers with a household of 1,096.[23] While households headed by women, even queens and princesses of the blood, were always smaller than their male counterparts, the same moves toward grandeur can be documented. Most telling is the expansion which took place in Catherine de Medici's domestic rolls between 1569 and 1585, when her household went from 316 to 666 members.[24]

As heir of one of the great feudal dynasties of the Middle Ages, a hereditary duke in France, sovereign of Béarn, and erstwhile ruler of the kingdom of Navarre, Henri d'Albret maintained a large household that reflected his place in the social hierarchy at court and in France at large. While Albret could not afford to match the grandeur of the house of Valois, he strove, nonetheless, to match the evolution of the royal household in degree, if not in kind. He surrounded himself with an entourage of officials and servants, paid and unpaid, which rivaled and surpassed those of the greatest aristocratic clans in France. During his first sojourn at court in 1518 Henri d'Albret counted seventy-one attendants and servants on his household rolls,[25] including many Gascon nobles who had been summoned especially by Catherine de Foix to accompany the young viscount on his first trip to court. For a young nobleman who had just reached his majority, Henri's household at court was a large and auspicious one, and it permitted him to hold his own against some formidable court fixtures, such as Louis de la Trémoille, one of the great pensioners of the crown, who could boast a household of only slightly over fifty.[26] Over the next three decades, Henri d'Albret and his daughter, Jeanne, increased their complement of servants as their fortunes improved; thus, by midcentury they could lay claim to one of the most illustrious noble households in all of France. They strove to maintain at least numerical parity with the indomitable Guise clan, whose undeniable presence and influence at court had given them a virtual stranglehold on royal patronage by 1560. Household records show that the duc de Guise employed 113 servants and officials in his household in 1542; his son François de Lorraine, as governor of Dauphiné, had 159 on his domestic rolls by 1556

---

[23]Boucher, *Société et mentalités*, I:147–51; idem, "L'évolution de la maison du roi des derniers Valois aux premiers Bourbons," *XVIIe siècle*, 34 (1982):359–79. Note that her figures are too large for Louis XIII's households because of a hasty use of E. Griselle, ed., *État de la maison du roi Louis XIII* (Paris: Paul Catin, 1912).

[24]Boucher, *Société et mentalités*, I: 148.

[25]AD-PA, E561.

[26]Weary, "Royal Policy and Patronage," 84.

and 164 by 1562.[27] During roughly the same period, Henri d'Albret counted 117 on his household rolls in 1547, while his daughter, Jeanne, increased her household from 141 to 242 in 1565.[28]

The cost of maintaining such a large entourage of followers entailed more than doling out salaries and small gifts at Christmas. All family retainers, including the little *tournebroches* who were never listed on the household rolls, received room and board commensurate with their status while in the Albrets' employ. Just keeping the stable hands and kennel grooms within reach of inflation taxed the ingenuity of the superintendent of finance. Food costs, clothing for liveried servants, and small liberalities and gifts consumed a substantial part of incoming revenues each year.[29]

While there were periodic attempts to economize by reducing the numbers on the household rolls, the Albrets were ruefully mindful of how crucial their show of numbers was in assessing political status and social stature, especially at court and on the road. Separated from more permanent signs of their power and influence, such as the family châteaux and estates, the Albrets were obliged to recreate their power in specifically human terms. Even their superintendents of finance, whose principal duty it was to control expenses, recognized the absolute necessity of maintaining, even inflating, the Albrets' household numbers while at court. The Albrets' visibility and viability in court politics depended to a large extent on the show of strength they demonstrated by their household numbers and thus, their typically conservative superintendent of finance often searched for ways to cut expenditures without reducing household numbers. In 1547, for example, Marguerite d'Angoulême wrote repeatedly to the Sieur d'Izernay, Jeanne's superintendent of finance, to urge him to limit Jeanne's expenditures at court. When Marguerite pressed him to reduce the numbers in Jeanne's household, which was "marvelously grand" according to all eyewitness accounts, the exasperated d'Izernay produced a detailed memorandum from Fontainebleau, a sort of compte rendu, in which he accounted for every expenditure made on Jeanne's behalf, and strenuously argued against the reduction of Jeanne's

---

[27]Robert Harding, "Provincial Governorships of Early Modern France: Anatomy of a Power Elite," unpublished Ph.D. diss., Yale University, 1974, 41. These figures do not appear in the published version of this work, *Anatomy of a Power Elite*.
[28]AD-PA, B5, B6, B15.
[29]For estimates of the house of Foix-Navarre-Albret, see chaps. 4 and 5. For other noble households, see Harding, *Anatomy of a Power Elite*, 28; Neuschel, *Word of Honor*, 162–66; Mertes, *English Noble Household*, 43–44, 216–18; Heal, *Hospitality in Early Modern England*, 46–48.

household, whose numbers were only befitting a young princess of the blood. In a letter penned in January 1548, Marguerite was forced to relent:

> I have received your letter from Fountainebleau in which I see what needs to be done for the maintenance of the household of my daughter, which makes me understand its not being smaller and that my daughter being at court it is not possible to have fewer household officers than she has.[30]

Great nobles played the politics of numbers with more than their household servants. Whenever they toured their territories or sojourned at court, they "padded" their entourage with retinues of mounted noblemen (*fidèles* and *compagnons*), regimental guards, and Swiss mercenaries, whose presence in the entourage underscored the extent of their masters' political and social influence.[31] To many court theorists, it was an unwelcome visual reminder of the tentative nature of political order and monarchical power in early modern France. The great humanist, Etienne Pasquier, for example, was terrified by the image of the mounted noble with his entourage of mounted clients and argued that such retinues revived the ancient power of the aristocracy to the detriment of both subject and king. "What used to be the crime of *lèse majesté*," he declared pointedly, "is today called *fidélité*."[32] Henri II was intimidated enough by these mounted cavalcades to prohibit aristocrats from travelling with such retinues. As Pasquier notes, this proscription was even extended to include the king of Navarre, Henri d'Albret.[33] But attempts to enforce these decrees were eventually abandoned because great nobles refused to give up their troops of mounted and armed men. By 1556, Jeanne d'Albret still regularly employed a regiment of Swiss guards on her household rolls and routinely traveled around the countryside with an armed retinue.[34] Indeed, when she made the journey to court in 1558 to present young Henri de Navarre to the king, the retinue of servants, vassals, and armed retainers that followed in train was so large that both the

---

[30]Génin, ed., *Lettres*, 1:390–92.

[31]For examples, see J. Russell Major's seminal article, "The Crown and the Aristocracy in Renaissance France," *American Historical Review*, 69 (1964):631–45; Harding, *Anatomy of a Power Elite*, 21, 38, 174–75.

[32]As quoted in Harding, *Anatomy of a Power Elite*, 38.

[33]Ibid.

[34]See for example, AD-PA, B16. Payment to Jeanne's Swiss guard, consisting of one captain and twelve soldiers, was 1,786 livres.

English ambassador and the Duke of Albuquerque reported that it seemed like an army on the march.[35]

In many respects, this assessment of Jeanne's entourage was a chilling intimation of things to come and reflects an important social reality; the same clients who could be summoned to swell Jeanne's courtly entourage during peacetime could also be summoned to follow the Albrets into war. By the 1570s and 1580s, the conflation of the Albrets' domestic and military clienteles would indeed transform their households into "an army on the march."[36]

III. The Wars of Religion

There is every reason to suspect that the advent of Religious Wars and the development of religious parties, as well as court politics, contributed to the increase in the Albret household after 1560. According to Robert Harding, the effect of the royal bankruptcy and the Guises' rise to power in 1559 and 1560 within the patronage networks of provincial governors was disastrous. Within a year, the royal pensions that sustained many nobles and their clienteles were cut by one-third. Without royal means to show their gratitude toward their clients, governors, in turn, reported to the crown that disenchanted followers were abandoning them in droves to join up with the Huguenots who offered them bribes. One such turncoat, the Gascon memoirist, Blaise de Monluc revelled in describing the 120,000 livres he had allegedly been promised by the Calvinists.[37] Mack Holt has verified the general trend behind Monluc's boasting by showing how the household of the Duke of Anjou tripled in size between 1576 and 1578 after he offered his services to the Huguenot cause and formally allied himself with William of Orange.[38] And is it any coincidence that Catherine de Medici's household doubled between 1569 and 1588 during the most intense and vicious phase of the Religious Wars? What impact, then, did the religious wars in France have on the Albrets' households?

Even before her conversion to Calvinism in 1560, Jeanne d'Albret began increasing the numbers in her entourage as a consequence of her enhanced political role as Henri d'Albret's sole heir. Within a few months of her father's death in 1555, Jeanne added nearly twenty

---

[35]Roelker, *Queen of Navarre*, 111.
[36]For a trenchant analysis of the three main clienteles—military, domestic, and political—directed by Renaissance governors, see Harding, *Anatomy of a Power Elite*, 21–31.
[37]Harding, *Anatomy of a Power Elite*.
[38]Holt, "Patterns of Clientèle," 305–22.

names to her household rolls.[39] By 1559, she supported a household, which in size and perhaps even in luster surpassed the household of the late Marguerite d'Angoulême; 190 officials and servants were listed on Jeanne's domestic rolls, including two archbishops of France.[40] The most dramatic change in the household, however, was the number of high-ranking administrative officials—secretaries, finance counselors, chamberlains, and the like—who were added to the roster to manage Jeanne's extensive financial and political interests.

Jeanne's open espousal of Protestantism in 1560 led slowly to structural changes in her household. Her sojourn at court in 1561 only confirmed her Calvinist convictions. And there, with the support of similarly minded nobles, notably the Condés and Châtillons, she began making tentative gestures on behalf of the faith. In addition to holding Protestant services in her apartments and welcoming itinerant evangelists within her doors, Jeanne began to offer positions in her household to young men and women with Protestant inclinations.[41] Perhaps the most interesting case of this kind involved Catherine du Bellay, the daughter of a minor noble family with a record of service in the Bourbon household. Sometime in 1561, it came to Jeanne's attention that young Catherine, on the strength of her religious convictions, had refused to attend Mass with her mother, Madame de Langey. When rumors spread that Madame de Langey was severely punishing her daughter for her heretical leanings, Jeanne immediately intervened with offers to raise the recalcitrant girl as a member of her own household, ostensibly to honor the long ties of affection and fidelity that existed between the Bourbon and Bellay families. With great subtlety, Jeanne employed the concepts of honor, fidelity, and affection to convince Madame de Langey to release Catherine to her custody. But the uses of these terms, as the letter reveals, involved a redefinition of their meaning.

> I cannot think [Jeanne wrote] that as the mother of so virtuous a girl that it is possible for you to treat her with such inhumanity and cruelty . . . greatly damaging your reputation. . . . You must realize that God's word separates fathers from chil-

---

[39] AD-PA, B6. For the evolution of Jeanne's household from early childhood onward, see Jacques Boulenger and Abel Le Franc, eds., *Comptes de Louise de Savoie et de Marguerite d'Angoulême* (Paris: Champion, 1905), 94; and Roelker's treatment of her early childhood and adolescence, *Queen of Navarre*, 25–26, 31–34.

[40] AD-PA, B144.

[41] For Jeanne's religious politicking at court in 1561, see Roelker, *Queen of Navarre*, 163–73.

dren and husbands from wives [an irony Jeanne could well appreciate by 1561]. It recognizes nothing else in the world but serving purely the glory of Him, who told us that any who showed more affection to his father and mother than Him was not worthy of Him.[42]

In the face of such clever casuistry Madame de Langey could do nothing more than prepare her daughter "out-fitted in a manner worthy of her family with dresses and jewels" to enter Jeanne's service.[43]

How many other young noblewomen and noblemen in similar circumstances were "trained in virtue" in Jeanne's household? Between 1559 and 1565, the ranks of the household swelled from 190 to 245; in Jeanne's bedchamber alone, at least eight maids-in-waiting and five new valets made their appearance on the rolls.[44] Were many of these new household members young Protestants whom Jeanne protected by enlisting them in her service? In 1562–63, we know that Jeanne welcomed the daughter of young Henri's Huguenot tutor, La Gaucherie, into her household, after the convinced Protestant had been abruptly dismissed from his post by Antoine de Bourbon.[45] She also encouraged young Protestant devotees in the household, like Georgette de Montenay, to hold to the faith. After a brief term of service in the household, Georgette continued to spread the Reformed faith to her own network of servants and protégés.[46]

Between 1559 and 1565 court politics fused inextricably with religious patronage and encouraged the rapid growth in Jeanne's household numbers. Henri II's sudden death in 1559 while jousting at the marriage celebrations of his daughter Elizabeth left the real exercise of royal power tenuously in the hands of Catherine de Medici, who helped her sickly sixteen-year-old son, Francis II, administer the kingdom along with his ambitious uncles, the Duc de Guise and the Cardinal de Lorraine. The obvious weakness of royal power encouraged many nobles, on both sides of the religious divide, to strengthen their

---

[42]Ibid., 171–72.
[43]Ibid.
[44]AD-PA, B144, B13.
[45]AD-PA, B13; La Gaucherie's Calvinist views earned him the disapproval of the Church as early as 1560 when he was excommunicated by a papal bull; see Nicholas de Bordenave, *Histoire de Béarn et Navarre, 1517 à 1572*, ed. P. Raymond (Paris, 1873), 86, 115.
[46]Roelker, *Queen of Navarre*, 182–83; for Montenay's career after she left Jeanne's household, see Régine Reynolds-Cornell, "Reflets d'une époque: Les devises ou emblèmes chrestiennes de Georgette de Montenay," *Bibliothèque d'Humanisme et Renaissance* 48 (1986):373–86.

patronage networks, including their domestic households, in a bid for increased power. Francis II's death in 1560, after a tumultuous one-year reign, and the succession of ten-year-old Charles IX plunged France into a regency government and contributed to widespread unrest, which flared into civil and religious war in 1562–63. In the aftermath of war, Catherine, as queen regent, fashioned many strategies to bolster the sagging fortunes of the Valois monarchy, including an unprecedented tour of France in 1564 to assess the war-torn kingdom. Catherine's preemptive summons to Jeanne in the spring of 1564 to join the royal court on its tour of France prompted the viscountess of Béarn to rally loyal family clients and *fidèles* around her.[47]

Although Jeanne had not actively cooperated with the Huguenot party when religious war first broke out in 1562, she was still considered a potential threat by the established powers and a possible ally by the Huguenots. Excommunicated by the pope in late 1563, Jeanne had chosen this moment to incorporate the daughters of the many prominent Gascon noble families, such as the damoiselle de Bénac, into her household, in recognition of the the dangerous game she was playing in which a show of numerical strength was a necessity.[48] And while Catherine de Medici had proven to be a staunch ally during the papal struggle, Jeanne had no desire to be upstaged by a queen of France at what appeared to be a critical juncture in the fortunes of the house of Foix-Navarre-Albret and of the French aristocracy generally. Meanwhile, Catherine had issued royal decrees in 1564 prohibiting nobles who joined the royal tour from traveling with more than their "ordinary household servants and their serving officers." In his dispatches home, the Venetian ambassador waxed eloquent about the royal train (which he described as an "entire city") and about Catherine de Medici's entourage of eighty ladies-in-waiting (which he described as a "flying squadron").[49] Nevertheless, when Jeanne joined the court mid-tour she managed to make an impression. In defiance of royal decree, Jeanne arrived in Macon on June 3, 1564, dressed in heavy mourning and

---

[47]The principal secondary sources concerning this remarkable voyage are Pierre Champion, *Catherine de Médicis présente à Charles IX son royaume* (Paris: Grasset, 1937); Victor E. Graham and W. M. Johnson, *The Royal Tour of France by Charles IX and Catherine de Medici: Festivals and Entries, 1564–1566* (Toronto: University of Toronto Press, 1979); and most recently, Jean Boutier et al., *Un tour de France royal: le voyage de Charles IX, 1564–1566* (Paris: Aubier-Montaigne, 1984). See the latter for a particularly astute analysis of the political importance of this voyage, 165–85.

[48]Philip de Montaut, baron de Bénac, was among the entourage of Béarnais gentlemen who accompanied Henri de Navarre to Basse-Navarre in 1567 to quell rebellion there. See Bordenave, *Histoire de Béarn*, 145.

[49]Boutier, et al., *Un tour de France*, 112.

accompanied by well over two hundred household members and three hundred cavalrymen, whose presence she justified by claiming that her life was threatened by Monluc's machinations and various Catholic conspiracies. Prominent among her attendants were eight Calvinist ministers in somber dress intoning passages of scripture and prayers.[50]

The stark contrast between the festive revelry which prevailed in Catherine's court and the Huguenot sobriety of Jeanne's household established the viscountess' presence in the royal entourage even more effectively than did the inflated size of her household. Nevertheless, Jeanne was neither so partisan nor so foolish as to surround herself solely with Protestant attendants. Although she had requested that the Calvinist hierarchy in Geneva relieve the charismatic minister, Jacques de Spifâme, sieur de Passy, from his ministerial duties, so that he could serve as her chancellor of affairs and general policymaker, Jeanne also continued to employ leading Catholic figures in sensitive positions in her household.[51] Most notably, she kept Claude Régin, the bishop of Oloron, in his prestigious post as her first chaplain and master of requests, even though his Tridentine sympathies were well publicized.[52]

The growth of Jeanne's household over the years was reflected in her treasurer's general accounts. Where salaries and pensions had amounted to 17,294 livres in 1556, they reached 22,617 livres in 1560, and peaked at 27,982 livres by 1565. The continuing prosperity of Jeanne's estates throughout the first twelve years of her reign made it possible for her not only to sustain these increasing charges, but also to raise the salaries and pensions of some of her closest attendants and trusted advisors. These halcyon years came to an inglorious end in 1569, however, when Jeanne's own domains were invaded by Antoine de Lomagne, the Baron Terride, on the express order of Charles IX as punishment for her overt support of the Huguenot cause. The impact of Terride's brief overlordship in Béarn, where Jeanne enjoyed the prerogatives of sovereignty, was devastating both psychologically and financially. In the Protestant stronghold of La Rochelle, where Jeanne had taken refuge, she recoiled in horror upon reading diplomatic missives that "three out of four" of her Béarnais subjects had turned on her, among them some of her most trusted retainers. Claude Régin,

---

[50]Roelker, *Queen of Navarre*, 229; Boutier et al., *Un tour royal*, 100–52.

[51]For Jeanne's tumultuous relationship with Spifâme and its tragic denouement, see Roelker, *Queen of Navarre*, 225–29, 249–50, 366–67.

[52]Bordenave, *Histoire de Béarn*, 130–34.

Jeanne's first chaplain and master of requests, for example, had offered his services to Terride and almost gleefully helped the Baron so thoroughly despoil the viscounty that receipts only slowly trickled into the treasury in 1570, a year after Béarn had been liberated.[53] Revolts in Navarre and troop movements in Armagnac and Bigorre further diminished Jeanne's income from these traditionally prosperous domains.[54]

What impact did this disastrous set of affairs have on the shape of Jeanne's patronage network, particularly on her household? In the public sphere, Jeanne, who had been remarkably charitable to conspirators through much of the 1560s, was quick to wreak her own revenge. In 1569–70 she ordered the confiscation of the estates and belongings of rebel leaders, stripped them of their offices in a humiliating ceremony staged by the Estates of Béarn, and imposed an order that permitted only her coreligionists to hold administrative office in her realm.[55] Huguenot officials in Béarn welcomed Jeanne's decrees as a useful tool with which to consolidate their growing political presence in Béarn and vehemently protested any perceived infractions of the decree. Following through with the decree, however, proved nearly impossible in an era when trained legal minds and accomplished administrators were still in short supply; thus, within weeks of her return to Pau, Jeanne appointed Catholics of proven abilities to important offices.[56] In the private sphere, Jeanne was forced by principle as well as by economics to dismiss attendants of long standing from her employ and to pare down her household until it resembled the small entourage of her adolescence. Not only was Claude Régin's salary slashed from the 1569 accounts, but a number of the salaries of other officers were also stricken from the accounts, most for the sake of financial expediency. Of the 190 people who remained in Jeanne's employ in 1569, only 120 actually received their stipends.[57] By 1570, Jeanne's contingent of servants fell to a mere 102. As a result of these staff cuts, her wage bill came to only 18,263 livres, while daily expenditures on food and necessities fell from one-half to one-third of her total budget.[58] Such econo-

---

[53]Roelker, *Queen of Navarre*, 279–80.

[54]See chap. 1 for a discussion of the impact of the 1568 revolts. See also Major, "Noble Income," 29–34.

[55]Roelker, *Queen of Navarre*, 283.

[56]When Jeanne appointed Arnaud Rospide, a staunch Catholic, as one of her personal household councilors in 1571, officials in the Chambre des Comptes bitterly remonstrated their sovereign for ceding a lucrative office to a renowned papist. Jeanne replied that her personal servitors were not affected by the decree. For this exchange, see "Extraits du registre de la Chambre des comptes de Pau," *Revue de L'histoire de Gascoigne et Aquitaine* (1898):271; see also Roelker, *Queen of Navarre*, 283–88.

[57]AD-PA, B16.

[58]Ibid.

mies helped to restore some balance to Jeanne's private accounts, which were sorely strained by lost revenues and high expenses. Even so, a minister of the king estimated that Jeanne's debts and fixed obligations still amounted to more than twice her incoming receipts in 1571. Financial hardships, however, did not keep Jeanne from rewarding those who had remained loyal during the revolt. Concierges, valets, *capitaines de guerre* received letters lavish with praises, gifts, and even, in some cases, salaries in arrears.[59] Continued efforts at economy and Jeanne's premature death in 1572 kept the salary bill at only 14,648 livres.[60]

The household records for 1569 to 1572 demonstrate that Jeanne practiced a policy of selective economy which permitted her to redirect her limited resources as necessary. Between 1571 and 1572, for example, Jeanne shifted the burden of household expenditures toward the forms of conspicuous consumption necessary in the marriage negotiations for her son, Henri de Navarre. Thus salaries accounted for only 7 percent of Jeanne's total expenditures in 1572, while expenditures on clothes, horses, and jewels (wedding presents for Henri) rose dramatically. To make ends meet, Jeanne suppressed many of the ceremonial conceits of her household, such as the seeming indispensable contingent of Swiss guards, to allow for these "necessary luxuries."[61]

The growth of Henri's and Catherine's own households and clienteles meant that Jeanne's retrenchments in patronage between 1569 and 1572 did not significantly alter the Albrets' patronage network nor seriously divert their solid core of family servitors and *fidèles* from a sense of devotion to the house of Foix-Navarre-Albret. Many of those dismissed from Jeanne's service in 1570 and 1571 found jobs in Navarre's household, which by 1572 was at least as large as Jeanne's had been at its peak, and which cost Navarre 27,000 livres in salaries and pensions.[62] Moreover, many of Baron Terride's chief conspirators, including De Luxe and L'Audaux, who Jeanne staunchly refused to pardon, were pardoned by her son and restored to important posts in Catherine de Bourbon's household. Many of them owed their restoration to members of Navarre's household who had used proximity to the young viscount to broker pardons for their clients.[63]

In the years following Jeanne's death in 1572, Navarre assumed a position of leadership within the Huguenot party quite unlike any posi-

---

[59]Roelker, *Queen of Navarre*, 288–89.
[60]Ibid.
[61]AD-PA, B35, B148.
[62]See BN FF 3948 for the record of wages in Henri's household.
[63]Roelker, *Queen of Navarre*, 290; AD-PA, B32.

tion Jeanne had ever held as a woman. As one of the great noble *chefs du parti*, it was nearly impossible for Navarre to practice his mother's economizing efforts with equal facility. During his four-year captivity at court after the St. Bartholomew's Day Massacre, Navarre had a household which was fairly modest in size by royal standards. His flight from court in February 1576, however, changed him from a mere courtier to the leader of a massive resistance movement against the Crown.[64] As a result, his household expenditures on salaries and pensions spiraled upward. As titular head of the Protestant party after 1576, Henri de Navarre naturally attracted a number of ambitious, but poor gentlemen, war captains, and soldiers, seeking wealth, office, title, and fame in his service. Many simply joined the throngs of hangers-on, unsolicited and unpaid, styling themselves as zealous partisans of the cause, or even more flatteringly, as *fidèles* and *compagnons* of Navarre himself. From the back ranks of the train, these aspiring (or perhaps conspiring) heroes hoped eventually to win an honorable charge in the household or in Navarre's ordinance company. At the very least, they expected to garner some small reward for feats of military bravery.

For Navarre, it certainly was tempting to reward the dreams of these soldiers, particularly when he so desperately needed to build a loyal clientele among Huguenot elites in southwestern France. The years at court, particularly his playful intimacies with the Guise clan, had tarnished his image among Protestants in the Midi, while many avidly Catholic areas within his government of Guyenne refused to acknowledge his authority.[65] Eager to create a strong party around his leadership, Henri increased his circle of patronage and added many new men to his household rolls. Military men were given various positions in the household. Moreover, honorary titles were handed out to nobles who had long been loyal to the house of Foix-Navarre-Albret and had answered the summons to join Henri in the fight against religious tyranny. By 1578, he counted 263 paid officers and servants on his domestic rolls, while numerous unsalaried others ate at his tables.[66] A year later, Navarre had 281 officers and servants on his household rolls, including a full complement of officers and aides in the stables and kennels. Military expenses, however, left the general account short of funds and forced him to suspend payment or reduce the wages of over half of his officers. Most of these deferred wages were promptly paid off

[64] See Harding, *Anatomy of a Power Elite*, 21–31.
[65] For Henri's relationship with the Guise clan while at court, see Jean-Pierre Babelon, Henri IV (Paris: Fayard, 1982), 193–214; David Buisseret, *Henry IV* (London: G. Allen and Unwin, 1984), 8; Holt, *Duke of Anjou*, 37–56.
[66] AD-PA, B2324.

the following year with incoming receipts, and only an unfortunate few had to wait long to receive their wages.[67]

The Treaty of Fleix, signed in November 1580, initiated five years of nominal peace in the provinces, but Navarre was left with a cavalcade of military officers and fighting men whom he could not easily and deftly dismiss. Indeed, it is doubtful that he wanted to dismiss the impressive entourage which guaranteed him a measure of strength and power against the newly formed Catholic leagues in the southwest. Over the next two years, Henri summoned more loyal family friends and their armed retainers, granting pensions (or at the very least, small stipends) to these seasoned warriors whose experience and skill he so desperately needed. Henri de Navarre still saved the most lucrative positions of the bedchamber for the young scions of the southern nobility. His first gentleman was his cousin and childhood companion, Henri d'Albret, seigneur de Miossens.[68] Serving as one of his masters of requests was Pierre de Mesmes, seigneur de Ravignan, whose grandfather had been among the entourage of Gascon gentlemen who had accompanied Henri d'Albret to Paris in 1515.[69] But sharing the privilege of serving Navarre with these Gascon youngbloods (such as seigneurs de Bénac, Frontenac, and Belsunce) were men whose roots came from northern and central France, such as the seigneurs de Vallon and Beauvoir.[70] Henri's domestic rolls thus listed 290 officers and servants in attendance. In addition, some 20 leading nobles were appended to the pension list under the illustrious title, "gentlemen in the suite of the king." Henri also took advantage of the momentary lull in hostilities to begin the process of redeeming the promissory notes for back salaries and pensions of old family retainers at a cost of 44,215 livres.[71] On the local level, domanial treasurers disbursed enormous sums to maintain lines of fidelity that had been established through generations of feudal rule. In 1581, the accounts of Béarn weighed heavy with the charge of pensions to retired servants and war captains. Important nobles in Navarre received pensions of 100 to 600 livres to insure their continued faithfulness.[72]

By 1585, the demands for place and position in the household had increased so dramatically that Henri began to duplicate offices on a grand scale, offering certain men in his entourage the option of serving

---

[67]AD-PA, B154.
[68]AD-PA, B157.
[69]AD-PA, E558.
[70]AD-PA, B157.
[71]Ibid.
[72]AD-PA, B156.

in their posts in alternate years. This time-honored practice was employed with telling effect with the largely honorific offices in the household, so coveted by regional noble elites. Between 1585 and 1586, Navarre employed fifty-six different noblemen on his rolls as gentlemen of the chamber. Yet another change in the household was the increasing number of so-called captains of war, serving in important logistical positions in the household, a telling indication of the degree to which Navarre's private domestic household had become linked to the more public purposes of the Huguenot party. Certain secretaries and financial officials in the household pulled double duty as loan agents and accountants for the party. And many domestic servants and retainers accustomed to serving quarterly continued in service beyond their terms in order to meet the needs of the burgeoning household.[73]

No retrenchment in patronage was possible after 1585 when the Wars of Religion climaxed in an apotheosis of violence. To counter the reinvigorated Catholicism and the rising passions of the League, Navarre continued to enlarge his circle of influence with offers of preferment and place. He handed out commissions and *lettres de retenus* for the honorific positions within his household at such a dizzying pace that it became impossible for the household to keep a current list of all the chamberlains, privy councilors and *gentilshommes entretenus* in his service. Appropriately, the task of organizing and arranging for the payment of these officials now fell to the viscount de Turenne, Henri's chief privy councilor, First Gentleman of the Bedchamber, and lieutenant general of Guyenne. In this latter position, Turenne commanded military forces and maneuvers of Guyenne, where he was second only to Navarre in power. So it was merely an extension of his military duties to keep a list of all the noblemen entering and exiting the household to serve in the battlefield. Most were issued receipts by Turenne, so that they could claim payment from the treasurer at the end of the year. Quite literally, tens of thousands of livres were lavished on these gentlemen-cum-soldiers in Henri's service, as we will see more fully in chapter 6. The confusion between the private and public function of Navarre's household was now complete. Even without these gentlemen-cum-soldiers on the regular domestic rolls—they had accounted for 15 to 20 percent of the household—Navarre still counted 282 servants and officers in his household in 1587.[74] Among them now for the first time were an armament officer and three superintendents of finance, who served alternately as extraordinary treasurers of war for the Huguenot party.

[73] AD-PA, B159.
[74] AD-PA, B160.

IV. The Cost of War Patronage

The cumulative effect of this steadily escalating enlistment of military men onto the household rolls was nearly disastrous for Navarre's private finances and the stability of his family's fortunes. Between 1572 and 1587, Navarre's expenditures on wages nearly tripled as a result of his participation in the Religious Wars. From a low of 27,000 livres in 1572, wage expenditures increased to 60,115 livres in 1578, to 65,337 livres in 1582, to 82,023 livres in 1585, and to 82,209 livres in 1587.[75] Moreover, as Navarre's own accountant noted in 1587, these figures were artificially low and did not represent the full charge of Navarre's clientele network on the treasury.[76] While Navarre, like his mother and grandfather before him, made every effort to pay his household regularly and fully, he began to fall seriously behind in wage payments in the 1580s. Payments disbursed to family retainers for wages and pensions in arrears routinely added another 30,000 to 40,000 livres to the household charges after 1582. The cost of provisioning Navarre's household likewise increased from 80,768 livres in 1579 to 115,582 livres in 1587.[77] Explicitly military funding provided to equip Navarre's burgeoning circle of *fidèles* (gentlemen and war captains) added crushing charges to Navarre's personal treasury, detailed more fully in chapter 6.

Landed revenues and royal pensions helped sustain Navarre's prodigious program of patronage in the early 1580s, but even these sums proved increasingly insufficient to meet the financial needs of the family's clientele network. By 1585 a number of household officers who had served their terms were not being paid; in 1590 Henri issued a decree ordering their salaries be paid.[78] Two years later, one-fourth of the servants listed on the household rolls again had wages in arrears. Many of these were high-ranking noble officials, such as the viscount de Turenne, who also advanced their own moneys to save Henri and the Huguenot party. In short, pressed for funds to sustain his armies in the field, Henri began to trade on the affection and loyalty of his household officers, and the nucleus of *fidèles* at the center of his clientele network, whose tradition of service to the house of Foix-Navarre-Albret endured even cataclysmic reversals of fortune.[79]

---

[75]BN, FF 2948; AD-PA, B2324, B154, B157, B159, B160 respectively.
[76]AD-PA, B160.
[77]AD-PA, B154, B160.
[78]AD-PA, B159.
[79]For a discussion of Navarre's military entourage during these years and a brief sketch of some of the men in his service, see Ronald S. Love, "'All the King's Horsemen': The Equestrian Army of Henry IV, 1585–1598," *The Sixteenth Century Journal* 22 (1991):

To what extent was Catherine de Bourbon drawn into this frenzied economy of patronage provoked by the Religious Wars? The records show that she, like her mother, was able to escape the worst excesses of "war patronage." In the first years after Jeanne d'Albret's death, Catherine supported a fairly modest household which numbered between sixty and seventy servants and attendants.[80] The legions of servants who were promised two years' salary and various pensions and gratuities in Jeanne's testament were paid and sent out to seek fresh employment.[81] A fortunate few appear from time to time on the Béarnais domanial accounts, but only the closest and oldest family retainers (twenty-three in all) were kept on in Catherine's service.[82] Key administrative officers were absorbed into Navarre's household, whence they handled Catherine's financial fortunes as part of their many and varied duties. According to a marginal note in Catherine's accounts, these officers "contented themselves with the status and salaries that they had on the king's rolls."[83] Catherine's household, thus, was comprised of a number of noble companions and necessary domestics. As the scope of household operations decreased, the number of valets and aides needed to keep a household diminished as well. Indeed, until Catherine's recall to court in 1592 as the *soeur unique* of the king, her household rolls and wage expenditures remained fairly static. Salary expenditures rarely reached 10,000 livres.

Household politics and numbers became important again between 1592 and 1599 when Catherine answered her brother's summons to come to Paris. At court, Catherine could not live the conspicuously simple life of a provincial noblewoman, particularly as she became the center of a vigorous faction of Protestant resistance in overwhelmingly Catholic Paris.[84] Catherine took her role as patron of the Reformed faith very seriously. Like many Huguenot nobles three decades earlier, she used her household and her private apartments as a *place de sûreté*

511–33; see also Sharon Kettering, "Clientage during the French Wars of Religion," *The Sixteenth Century Journal* 22 (1989): 221–39, who emphasizes the solid core, but shifting fringe, of many noble households and patronage networks during the Religious Wars.

[80]AD-PA, B22, B32, B48bis, B83, and B91.

[81]For an evocative discussion of the servants' plight upon the death of a patron, see Stone, *Crisis of the Aristocracy*, 262.

[82]These calculations are based on an analysis of Catherine's household records. See especially AD-PA, B22, B32 for the first three years after Jeanne's death. For Béarnais pension lists, see AD-PA, B148–B156 for the years between 1572 and 1581.

[83]AD-PA, B48bis.

[84]L'Estoile records that almost immediately upon her arrival in Paris, people began complaining about the Protestant ministers in her entourage; Roelker, ed., *The Paris of Henry of Navarre*, 262.

for beleaguered Calvinists. As a result, the Reformed Church in Paris became an extension of Catherine's household.[85] Two additional Protestant pastors were added to the household rolls,[86] and charismatic street preachers regularly were invited to her Parisian apartment to conduct services "à la mode de Genève" for the party faithful. In Pierre L'Estoile's account of court life during the reign of Henri IV, Catherine's court appears as a model of decorum, setting a sober Calvinist tone in comparison with the revelry and irreverent activities that are reported from Henri's apartments.[87] On Easter Sunday 1595, for example, Pierre L'Estoile recorded that so many people crowded into the apartments of Catherine to hear the Protestant preaching "that no one could sit down."[88] To carry out the household responsibilities that increased with all of this activity, more valets and aides were also added to the domestic rolls. Catherine employed a number of musicians, artists, and tailors in her household to help pass the hours and to provide all of the props for the masques of which she was passionately fond. By 1598, 136 servants and attendants were on the rolls at a charge of 25,240 livres.[89] Only two years later, after her marriage to the Comte de Bar, her household had doubled to 263.[90]

V. The Lure of Office

What attracted this myriad of men and women to serve in the Albrets' households? Undoubtedly, the reasons are as diverse and complex as the people who served. For the peasant boy who sought a place somewhere on the periphery of the household and had only his hands, feet, and back to offer, room and board in a noble household was compensation enough. Indeed, the spit turners in the kitchens were rarely paid, while the scullery lads and aides in the stables were paid wages which could not even have kept pace with those paid to an unskilled stonemason or farm laborer.[91] Moreover, there were other perquisites of aristocratic service: clothing was distributed on a regular basis, one

---

[85]For a discussion of the way in which religious patronage transformed the households of recusant Catholics in England, see Heal, *Hospitality in Early Modern England*, 168–78.
[86]AD-PA, B138, B139.
[87]Roelker, ed., *The Paris of Henri of Navarre*, 282–85.
[88]Ibid., 274.
[89]AD-PA, B142.
[90]Robert le Blant, "Marché de viande et poisson pour Catherine de Bourbon," *Bulletin philologie et historiques (jusqu'à 1610) du comité des travaux historiques et scientifiques (année 1968, Actes du 93 Congrès national des Sociétés savantes)* (1971):130.
[91]Le Roy Ladurie, *Les paysans de Languedoc*, 67–80. The average unskilled laborer earned four to seven sols a day, while the wages of the aides amounted to slightly under four sols per day.

had the opportunity to travel and see the dazzling sights of civilized and courtly life, and the fortunate few had the security of a pension after a long and successful term of service. A few enterprising aides even managed to establish extracurricular careers for themselves as a result of their attachment to the household.[92]

For many of the noblemen and noblewomen serving in the Albrets' households, the opportunities offered by aristocratic service differed in degree at least, and often in kind, from the service of nonnoble officers and servants. Many of the noblemen and noblewomen were kinsmen or kinswomen related by blood, marriage, or a common childhood education or nurse. Others were friends and familiars, boon companions on the battlefield, on the hunt, or at court, whose affective connection to the house of Foix-Navarre-Albret predated their household appointment. Many of them held land, either as a vassal of the house of Foix-Navarre-Albret, or as the beneficiaries of the Albrets' liberality. Some simply lived on neighboring estates and shared common territorial concerns and a common geographic culture with the Albrets. In short, an intricately complex network of beliefs, expectations, and practices connected the noblemen and noblewomen to the lord or lady of the household.[93] While it is impossible to deny the many nonmaterial concerns behind aristocratic service among the nobility, the economic benefits of service are also undeniable.

The majority of noblemen who served in Henri d'Albret's household in 1518 were from his native Béarn and surrounding estates. Most were Béarnais and Gascon noblemen interested in the perquisites and favors obtainable through aristocratic service. First, faithful service opened up employment opportunities for other family members, notably younger brothers or sons with fewer career options and smaller inheritances.[94] Most nobles in aristocratic households were aspiring

---

[92]On the benefits and evolution of domestic service in Ancien Régime France, the following studies are indispensable: Jean-Pierre Gutton, *Domestiques et serviteurs dans la France de l'Ancien Régime* (Paris: Aubier-Montaigne, 1981); Cissie Fairchild, *Domestic Enemies: Servants and their Masters in Old Regime France* (Baltimore: Johns Hopkins University Press, 1984); Sarah C. Maza, *Servants and Masters in Eighteenth-Century France: The Uses of Loyalty* (Princeton: Princeton University Press, 1981).

[93]For a nuanced explanation of aristocratic service and noble relationships, see Weary, "Royal Policy and Patronage," 88–116; Greengrass, "Noble Affinities," 275–311; Kettering, "Patronage and Kinship," 408–35; and Neuschel, *Word of Honor*, 78–92, 152–82. Neuschel, in particular, offers a fine discussion of the social composition of Antoine de Bourbon's household.

[94]In southern France, however, where primogeniture was not always practiced, the plight of the younger son was not necessarily as desperate as in other parts of France. See J. Poumarède, *Les Successions dans le Sud-Ouest de la France au Moyen Age* (Paris: Presses Universitaires de France, 1972); P. Ourliac, "La Famille pyrénéenne au Moyen Age," in *Recueil d'études sociales publiées à la mémoire de F. Le Play* (Paris, 1956), 257–63.

power brokers in their own right, avidly seeking positions for family members and their own clients. Letters of retainer to young noblemen regularly mention the loyal services of an obviously designing older sibling or relative.[95] The seigneur de la Motte, for instance, used his envious position as chamberlain in young Henri d'Albret's household to secure a position for his younger brother as *maréchal de logis* at a salary of 200 livres annually.[96] Eight years later, the younger La Motte appeared on the muster rolls of Navarre's ordinance company, along with four other members of the La Motte clan.[97] Etienne-Arnaud d'Albret, from a cadet branch of the Albret family, used his position as chamberlain to Henri d'Albret to secure a place for his son, Jean, as a gentleman attendant. Women could be just as successful in the quest for household offices. Suzanne de Bourbon-Susset, Jean d'Albret's wife and a member of the bastard branch of the Bourbon family, used her dual family connections to secure a place as governess of Henri d'Albret's grandson, Henri de Navarre. She later introduced her son, named Henri after her patron, into young Navarre's household.[98]

Second, aristocratic service was also a stepping-stone to more lucrative careers at court. Lesser nobles expected their aristocratic patrons to use their influence at court to garner favors with the king.[99] Jean-Jacques de Mesmes, for example, exploited Albret power and influence to further his own ambitions for a career at court. While Henri d'Albret was at court from 1515 to 1518, he set the stage for his climb in court circles. Mesmes used Henri's popularity with Francis I to curry the king's favor; by 1518, he had launched a career at the Parisian court which brought him prestigious sinecures. And by midcen-

[95]See Joan Davies' article, "Family Service and Family Strategies: The Household of Henri, duc de Montmorency, ca. 1590–1610," *Bulletin of the Society for Renaissance Studies* 3 (1985):27–43. She writes, "the values most enthusiastically endorsed in the household were those of acquisitiveness and advancement for the individual and his family, both cognate and affine, since career and patronage opportunities were considerable, despite the social ambiguity of posts, such as secretary. The families of some of the entourage advanced claims to old nobility, others were rather more humble (or honest), but all seem to have been more or less equally avid in their pursuit of favors," 33; see also Holt, "Patterns of Clientèle," 315–16.
[96]AD-PA, E561.
[97]BN, Collections Clairambault 360, fol. 261.
[98]*Dictionnaire de biographie française* (Paris: Letouazey et Ane, 1933) I, col. 2294, 1323–32. In 1510, Etienne Arnaud d'Albret married Françoise de Béarn, dame de Miossens, and assumed the title, sieur de Miossens. To avoid confusion with their more illustrious cousins, with whom they often shared first and last names, these Albrets are almost always referred to as the Albret de Miossens.
[99]See Harding's discussion of clients' expectations, *Anatomy of a Power Elite*, 25–37.

tury, the Mesmes family had established itself as one of the great bureaucratic dynasties of Paris.[100]

A third inducement to join Albret's household must have been even more purely economic. In 1518, salaries alone accounted for 44.7 percent of total expenditures for the year, and as such were the largest expenditures in the annual household budget. (see table 3.1) Salaries in the Albret household compared more than favorably with those offered by other members of the *haute noblesse*. Indeed, in keeping with his much-vaunted royal status, the young king of Navarre offered his closest advisor and intimate, the seigneur d'Andouins, a salary of 1,000 livres annually, which nearly approached the 1,200 livres Francis I paid to his gentlemen.[101] Henri's two favorites—Miossens and Duras—enjoyed salaries which topped 700 livres, while his ten highest councilors received an average salary of 556 livres annually. By contrast, Poitevin gentlemen in the service of Louis de la Trémoille received salaries between 120 and 200 livres annually; only one councilor received compensation above 300 livres.[102]

Table 3.1 Annual Household Expenses, Henri d'Albret, 1518

Category	Cost in *livres*	Percentage
Food (35 livres per diem or 1,050 livres monthly)	12,600	41.4
Extraordinary Expenses (clothing, purchase of horses, etc.)	3,000	9.9
Wages	13,604	44.7
Gifts, Alms, Miscellaneous Pleasures (1,000 livres monthly)	1,200	3.9
TOTAL	30,404	100.0
Source: AD-PA, E561		

---

[100]H. de Mesmes, *Mémoires, inédits de Henri de Mesmes, Seigneur de Roissy et de Maldssise*, ed. E. Frémy (Paris: E. LeRoux, 1886), 14, 128–31.
[101]AD-PA, E561.
[102]Weary, "Royal Policy and Patronage," 98–99.

A noble officer could not make his fortunes on the salary he received while in service. Indeed, beneath the privy councilors and household gentlemen were a group of noblemen serving as squires in the kitchens and stables, earning an average salary of 250 livres annually. And three noblemen in the household—the valets de chambre—were paid under 100 livres, putting them on par economically with other nonnoble professionals in the household. But the real value of offices in the household was more than this monetary income would suggest. Valets were granted stable privileges for their horses, and officers ate at Henri's tables at a cost of roughly ten sols each daily.[103]

Most of the nobles, and many of the nonnobles, however, who served in the household were not in constant attendance.[104] With the exception of the two or three key figures in the household, the greatest number of officers served only quarterly—a felicitous arrangement which permitted them ample time each year to return to their estates or to develop a more extensive network of patrons. Indeed, as the Albrets increased their fortunes, they decreased the term of service for some of the officers and professionals serving in the household. Two ministers, for instance, served in Jeanne d'Albret's household for six months in turn in 1565; by 1587, Henri de Navarre employed four Protestant preachers on his rolls for a term of service of three months each.[105] For professional officials and nobles with provincial estates, who shared their services with many clients, the advantages of quarterly service outweighed its disadvantages. But for women with their fixed portions from the family fortune, for second or third sons who served in middling positions in the household, and for the peasant boys who served in the kitchens, the benefits of rotating terms of services were dubious—particularly because they counted so heavily on their board privileges in the household. Fortunately, many of these attendants found themselves in positions which required longer terms of service or nearly year-round attendance. Jeanne d'Albret's correspondence, for example, reveals that her ladies-in-waiting left her entourage for only brief periods of time. Because many were married to

---

[103] AD-PA, E561.
[104] Those key officers, superintendent of finance, the First Gentleman of the Chamber, and First Valet, were frequently absent from the household on missions for their patron, and decrees show that they were often reimbursed for their traveling expenses. Moreover, as Turenne's career in service indicates, those who held important political or military positions, apart from their household offices, were allowed to absent themselves to fulfill the duties of these appointments. Often, as in Turenne's case, these appointments only enhanced and strengthened the Albrets' network of clients.
[105] AD-PA, B160.

officers in the household and found positions for their children there as well, long absences to attend to familial responsibilities were not necessary.[106] Kitchen servants and stable boys frequently served six to twelve months. Moreover, when they returned or were sent home, they were frequently granted small stipends to help defray the cost of their journey and their expenses apart from the household.[107]

These small liberalities of room and board were especially significant conditions of aristocratic service because they helped to counter the impact of the inflation of food prices. In general terms, wages, and salaries in the sixteenth century rose more slowly than did food prices. A cursory glance at the salary tables for the households reveals that the nominal value of individual salaries and wages of those in the Albrets' service increased very little over time. (see tables 3.2 and 3.3) In fact, in terms of real value, many salaries and wages declined quite precipitously. Overall, a servant or attendant in Navarre's employ, for example, earned a mere 16.2 percent more than his counterpart in 1518, while grain prices tripled during the same period. In households headed by female members of the Albret family, the numbers are hardly better. A comparison of salaries paid to Marguerite d'Angoulême's household in 1529 and those in Catherine de Bourbon's service in 1598 shows that only the *dames d'honneur* and the *aides à pied* managed to double their nominal salaries. In all, the salaries in Catherine's household averaged out to be only slightly higher than those paid by her grandmother seventy years earlier. The 136 employees in Catherine's household in 1598 received an average annual salary only 20.4 percent higher than that received by the 136 people in Marguerite's retinue in 1529.[108] This relatively static salary structure cut across all social boundaries in the household, except the very highest and the very lowest levels. In general, salaries in the highest echelon in the households increased dramatically. By 1578, the most important financial and administrative officers in Navarre's household were earning salaries between 2,000 and 3,000 livres, sums three to five times higher than their counterparts had received in 1518. Some professionals in the households, such as clergymen, also received considerable salary increases over the century. In the households

---

[106]See for example, letters between Madame de Thignonville and Jeanne d'Albret, some of which can be found in BN, Carrés d'Hozier, 438.

[107]Examples of these grants are scattered throughout the Albrets' personal accounts.

[108]Boulenger and Le Franc eds., *Comptes de Louise de Savoie et Marguerite d'Angoulême*, 67–77, 80–87; AD-PA, B139; as calculated by Major, "Noble Income," 38–39.

headed by Jeanne d'Albret and Catherine de Bourbon, the principal ladies-in-waiting received almost regular increases in their salaries between 1569 and 1598.

The Albrets capitalized on the fact that salaries and wages in general rose slowly in the sixteenth century to emphasize their liberality and generosity, the twin virtues of the nobility. They compensated for low wages with ostentatious demonstrations of their largess. Indeed, the static wage structure to which the Alberts and their servitors were tied only enhanced the mechanisms of the traditional gift economy, which still exerted a powerful influence over human behavior in early modern Europe. A gift, whether it came in the guise of an annual, and therefore expected, pension or an ex gratia gratification, still implied a reciprocal counter gift, which royal decrees often couched in terms of "loyalty," "fidelity", and "continued service."[109] While most of their household servitors did not receive salaries that kept pace with inflations, they were recipients of regular pensions, periodic donations, gifts, and a host of privileges which considerably increased the economic benefits of aristocratic service. As the beneficiaries of gifts, household officers and servants were thus bound more closely to the Albrets' service and continually reminded of the affective ties of their relationship. Catherine de Bourbon, for example, celebrated Jean Marcilly's twentieth anniversary in service in her household with a gift of 180 livres "for the good and agreeable services that he has done and continues to do each day for her Majesty."[110] But as Marcilly's grant makes clear, the Albrets also intended by such lavish displays of gratitude to tighten further the ties that bound master to servant. Any gift—even one for services already rendered—made the recipient further beholden and indebted to his generous patrons. Extraordinary donations were thus given not only as recognition for services rendered but also with a lively sense of services which were still to come. Such thinking permeated Navarre's gift in 1585 to his aides, Bolleau and Josset. The letters patent confirming the 300-livre donation noted that it was not just a "reward for good and loyal services" but also an advance to give them "an even better means to continue in service in the future."[111] Gifts were designed, then, to urge the servant to greater and better works. Money was inextricably bound to *affection* and

---

[109]On the role of gift-giving and the gift economy in sixteenth-century France, see Sharon Kettering, "Gift-giving and Patronage in Early Modern France," *French History* 2 (1988): 131–51.
[110]AD-PA, B137.
[111]AD-PA, B159.

Table 3.2 Salaries* in the Households of Henri d'Albret and Henri de Navarre 1518–1587 (given in *livres tournois*)

Office[a]	1518 No. / Avg. Sal.		1578 No. / Avg. Sal.		1582 No. / Avg. Sal.		1585 No. / Avg. Sal.		1587 No. / Avg. Sal.	
Chamberllan	10	556	3	600	7	600	14	600	3	600
Secrétaire[b]	—	—	19	223/600	16	600/200	17	600/200	23	600/200
Maîtres d'hôtel	2	350	5	400	5	360	4	400	4	500
Gentilshommes servans[c]	12	—	11	300	25	300	26	300	not listed	
Medicin	1	350	4	500	3	500	3	500	3	500
Chirurgien	—	—	3	400	3	400	3	400	3	400
Maréchal logis	2	250	4	300	5	300	4	300	3	300
Controlleurs	1	80	4	200	4[d]	200	5	200	4	200
Apothicaire	1	80	2	200	2	200	2	200	2	200
Trésorier	1	400	2	1500	2	1500	3	666	3	666
Gentilshommes de la chambre	1	400	7	500	11	500	29	500	not listed	
Valet de chambre	3	93	20	120	17	120	14	120	25	120

(*continued next page*)

Table 3.2 (continued)*

Huissier de chambre	2	50	5	120	4	120	4	120	4	120
Tailleur	1	50	2	30	2	30	—	—	2	30
Fourrier	—	—	8	150	9	150	9	150	8	150
Sommelier	3	80	7	160	7	160	8	160	8	160
Aide en la cuisine	1	15	2	50	2	50	2	50	2	50
Pâtissier	1	50	2	0	2	90	2	90	2	90
Fauconnier	2	90	3	200	3	200	2	500	2	500
Aumônier	4	80	1	—	1	80	1	80	1	80
Ministre	—	—	2	500	2	500	4	500	4	500

AD-PA Source, respectively by year: E561, B2324, B157, B159, B160

*Salaries given are those theoretically assigned to the office; where wages were only partially paid and reimbursement was made later, I have calculated for the full salary.
aNot all household offices are included; this table is a representative sample of wages and numbers.
bIncludes the administrative officers of the realm—*secrétaires de la finance* and *secrétaires des mandemants*—as well as the more plebeian *secrétaires ordinaires*. Under Henri d'Albret the men who performed these functions may have been listed as *chamberllans*.
cIncludes officers in the stables as well as in the *paneterie*, *cuisine*, and *éschansonerie*.
dDoes not include those at 5 livres each.

Table 3.3 Jeanne d'Albret's and Catherine de Bourbon's Households 1559–1598 (average salaries are given in *livre tournois*)

Office	1559 No.	1559 Avg. Sal.	1570 No.	1570 Avg. Sal.	1575 No.	1575 Avg. Sal.	1591 No.	1591 Avg. Sal.	1598 No.	1598 Avg. Sal.
Ministres	—	—	1	200	—	—	1	400	3	300
Dames d'honneur	1	500	2	500	1	600	2	600	2	1,200
Dames de la chambre	—	—	1	200	—	—	—	—	1	300
Dlle de la chambre	13	50	3	50	4	100	7	135	9	100
Gouvernantes	1	120	1	120	1	200	1	200	1	200
Femmes de chambre	12	73	9	62	7	64	7	77	8	78
Maîtres d'hôtel	6	300	1	300	2	600	3	400	2	400
Écuyers d'écurie	3	200	2	200	2	300	2	300	3	300
Gentilshommes servans	14	200	—	—	—	—	—	—	3	300
Médicins	4	400	2	350	1	400	—	—	3	333
Secrétaires[a]	11	154	6	150	2	200	10	200	4	200
Contrôleurs	5	120	3	150	1	500	see above		4	175
Maréchaulx logis	3	200	3	200	1	300	3	300	—	—
Fourriers	6	90	5	90	2	50	3	120	3	120

(*continued next page*)

The Economy of Patronage • 111

Table 3.3 (continued)

Huissiers de la chambre	—	—	3	100	2	100	2	120	2	120
Chappelans	2	45	—	—	2	70	—	—	—	—
Valet de chambre	14	100	12	100	3	108	7	120	13	120
Tailleurs	2	250	1	200	1	200	1	350	1	350
Tappisiers	1	40	—	—	1	50	3	70	3	120
Ophevres	1	80	—	—	—	—	1	5	1	60
Peintres	1	100	—	—	—	—	1	60	1	60
Sommeliers de la Panneterie	3	100	1	100	3	90	3	120	3	120
Aydes à Cheval	6	80	5	80	—	—	3	80	3	80
Aydes à pied	3	40	2	25	2	50	2	50	3	50
Sommeliers à l'éschansonnerie	5	100	2	75	3	90	2	120	3	120
Aydes à cheval	6	80	5	80	—	—	3	80	1	80
Aydes à pied	2	22.5	1	40	1	50	2	50	3	50

AD-PA Source, respectively by year: B144, B16, B25, B136, B142

[a]Includes administrative and financial officials of the realm, styled *secrétaires de la finance, des mandemants*.
[b]This table does not include a full roster of the households, but rather a representative example.

fidélité in the minds of these sixteenth-century masters and servants.[112]

The charges on the household accounts during the last three decades of the century clearly show that the Albrets were drawn into an increasingly magnanimous program of patronage. In 1518, for example, Henri d'Albret only allotted 100 livres a month or 1,200 livres a year for gifts, alms, and his private pleasures (*menus plaisirs*). (see table 3.1) By midcentury, Jeanne's expenditures on pensions and gifts exceeded 5,000 livres annually.[113] Catherine was more generous: she bestowed 8,920 livres of gifts on her attendants in 1588, 10,502 livres in 1591, and 23,714 livres in 1595. Thus, by 1595 Catherine spent twice as much on gifts and pensions to members of her household as on salaries. (see table 3.4) These sums appear modest, though, when compared with the prodigious amounts Navarre lavished on his attendants.[114] Awards and pensions were spread around liberally to reward attendants and servants at every level in the household. Officers in the upper echelons of the household were most likely to receive regular pensions or lavish donations, and this was especially true for the gentlemen attendants in Navarre's household. With his extraordinary pension of 3,000 livres, granted in 1576, Sire de Rocquelaure found himself drawing nearly as much money from the household coffers as the two most highly paid members of Navarre's household.[115] By 1587, Navarre doubled the value of many major offices in the household by settling annual pensions on their holders. The seigneur de Castelnau received a 1,500-livre pension instead of his 600-livre salary as chamberlain; the seigneurs de Buzemal, d'Alain, Constans, and Bremieu were awarded 700 livres pensions to supplement their 500 livres salaries; and the First Squire of the Stables, Lons, added a 500 livres pension to his salary of 600 livres. Twenty-five officers in all benefitted from Navarre's largess in 1585 and enjoyed extraordinary pensions which totaled 22,346 livres.[116] Two years later, Navarre doled out double that sum—46,525 livres—to his officers. In three cases, the value of the award had dramatically increased: seigneur de Castelnau

---

[112]See, for example, the very pointed remarks made in the decree granting one of Catherine's *fourriers*, Jean de Mayroux, an extraordinary gift of 75 livres. The grant was "to give him the courage and affection to watch over the rest of the furniture which her Majesty has left in Navarrenx," AD-PA, B137.
[113]AD-PA, B144.
[114]AD-PA, B154, B159, B160.
[115]AD-PA, B2230.
[116]AD-PA, B157.

Table 3.4 Wages, Gifts, and Pensions, Catherine de Bourbon's Household (in *livres tournois*)

Category	1575	1579	1583	1588	1591	1595	1598
Wages paid according to civil lists	7,469	8,920	10,264	10,452	13,442	12,025	18,000
Wages paid by decree	640	—	317	646	180	5,850	5,140
Back Wages	—	267	230	427	80	—	110
Gifts	—	—	—	8,920	10,502	23,714	101,473[a]
Pensions	—	—	—	—	—	1,720	1,990
Alms, Miscellaneous gifts and pleasure	831	—	—	—	2,268	—	—
TOTAL	8,940	9,187	10,811	20,445	26,472	43,309	126,713[a]

AD-PA Source, respectively by year: B25, B48bis, B83, B129, B136, B139, B142

[a] Sum somewhat inflated as a result of several entries listed as "ses affaires particulières dont son altesse n'a voullus estre faict aulcune mention ny declaration." These may not be gifts at all.

now enjoyed a pension of 3,000 livres; the seigneurs d'Alain and Constans each received 1,500 livres.[117]

Perhaps the most telling example of the way in which the gift economy pervaded aristocratic service is the career of Henri d'Albret, sieur de Miossens. As we have seen earlier, Miossens owed his position in Navarre's adult household to a tradition of family service and kinship connections dating at least as far back as 1518. His grandfather had served as chamberlain to Henri d'Albret in that year for a salary of 700 livres. Sixty years later, the salary Miossens received for services rendered was a meager 800 livres.[118] However, Miossens' wages as a gentleman attendant to the King of Navarre were supplemented by moneys he received from a number of other honorific positions and perquisites at Navarre's disposal. Among other things, he was governor of Navarre and Béarn, captain of the château-fort at Lourdes, and ensign in a royal company of ordinance. These offices, along with the pension he was granted by Navarre, brought in well over 5,000 livres annually.[119] Miossens' career as a lesser noble in service of *les grands* is a perfect illustration of the way in which many an aspiring youngblood pieced together a fortune with a number of civil and military positions and perquisites in the gift of a noble patron. Indeed, one of the principal ways in which the Albrets satisfied the hungry young men serving as attendants in the bedchamber, stables, and kitchens was to offer them governorships and captaincies in lieu of salary increases. Military preferment usually meant little strain on the family budget—these offices had to be paid regardless of who filled them—but pensions meant an additional burden on the private accounts.

It is not surprising that many of the Albrets' closest attendants received gifts and pensions which substantially raised the value of their offices. But what about those retained in the middling and lower ranks of the household—chamberwomen, valets, cooks, fourriers, and aides? Most received wages which remained fairly stable over the century; only a few had the pedigree or training to avail themselves of the perquisites of military office. How then did the Albrets induce these servants to remain in their service? First, wages for middle-ranking servants in the Albret household were comparable to wages paid in most noble households, and sometimes their wages compared favorably with those granted in royal households.[120] Shifting from one noble

[117] AD-PA, B159.
[118] *DBF*, I, col. 2294, 1323–1332.
[119] AD-PA, B154.
[120] For example, see the salaries paid in the households of Catherine de Medici, particularly those to her ladies-in-waiting and chamber attendants, in 1574, Bibliothèque Sainte-Geneviève, MSS 848; for Marguerite de Valois in 1583, BN FF, 21451; Marie de Medici in 1601, BSG MSS 848.

patron to another in search of financial gain, then, promised little to the average attendant or domestic, especially when there were so many material advantages to be gained from long terms of service.[121]

Second, the Albrets often used internal promotions rather than wage increases to satisfy the ambitions of middling members of the household. Few, usually the most menial servants, had careers like that of Michel de la Serre, who entered Jeanne d'Albret's service as a muleteer in 1565, and thirty years later was still employed in the same lowly position at the same salary of 30 livres.[122] A far more common path among the career servants in the Albret household was that taken by Jacques Daire, who began as muleteer under Jeanne d'Albret with a wage of 35 livres a year and advanced to become one of the chief kitchen stewards in 1583 with a salary of 120 livres.[123] We might also consider Jean Marcilly who began his career in Catherine's household as a *fourrier* at 50 livres a year in 1572, to become one of her chief comptrollers in 1590 earning 300 livres.[124] Through internal promotions both these men increased their salaries by 400 percent or more, outstripping the inflationary price cycle of even that most volatile of sixteenth-century commodities—wheat.

Middling officials in the household pursued financial opportunities for their children and relatives just as avidly as did their noble counterparts, and many found minor positions for their children in the kitchens and bedchambers.[125] But even in households as large as those supported by the Albrets, only a few children could be gainfully employed as clerks, valets, chambermaids, and aides. In order to appease the many anxious parents in their employ, the Albrets frequently offered annual pensions instead. These awards often stipulated that the money be used to educate the young charge to continue in the tradition of aristocratic service established by the parent. In 1592, for example, Catherine bestowed upon her godchild, Samuel La Fons, son of one of her treasurers and chamberwomen, a generous pension of 300 livres. As the letters patent confirming the pension made clear,

---

[121]The household rolls indicate that many of the servants who entered the Albrets' service stayed until retirement or death. Of the sixty-four servants who appeared on Catherine de Bourbon's household rolls in 1572, twenty-seven were still on the civil list in 1590, AD-PA, B6, B83, B137; see also Maza, *Servants and Masters in Eighteenth-Century France*, 169–71, for a discussion of the benefits of long terms of service.

[122]AD-PA, B6, B83.

[123]AD-PA, B148bis, B138.

[124]AD-PA, B138.

[125]See Davies' discussion of the relatively young age of many clerks and secretaries in Montmorency's household, which she attributes in the main to family strategies of advancement, "Family Service and Family Strategies," 30–32.

Catherine settled the award on fifteen-year-old Samuel in the hope that he would study and make himself "capable to do service for her Highness."[126] Three years later, Pierre La Fons, Samuel's younger brother, received a pension of 100 livres to the same end.[127] To the aspiring bourgeois gentlemen in the Albret households, such gifts must have offered welcome assurance that the pathway to prestige and honor was secure for another generation. Granting scholarships to children of attendants was a common convention throughout the sixteenth century for the house of Foix-Navarre-Albret. But the numbers granted increased dramatically over the century, as the Albrets attempted to reinforce the ties between master and servant with greater displays of their largess, and as they attempted to demonstrate the kind of easygoing magnanimity which was considered the mark of wealth and influence.[128] In 1529, Marguerite allotted only 474 livres to support educational efforts of the children of her attendants; by 1595 Catherine had nineteen children of household members on her pension rolls at a total charge of 1,744 livres.[129]

Calculating the real value of an office in the household of Foix-Navarre-Albret is a difficult task. Extraordinary gifts and pensions increased the value of many offices. In addition to monetary wages and salaries, servants and officers also enjoyed less calculable but no less important prerogatives and liberties which enhanced the appeal of aristocratic service. According to an extant letter of retainer, household attendants received "all honors, authorities, prerogatives, franchises, liberties, rights, profits and emoluments that pertain thereto".[130] Among the many emoluments due an attendant in the princely households of France were exemptions from the various taxes, direct and indirect, that were levied with increasing frequency by the early modern state. Household members were exempted from the *taille*, contributions to the *ban* and *arrière ban*, forced loans, and the responsibility of billeting troops. During the Religious Wars, these latter exemptions must have been especially prized. Moreover, for middling-rank nonnobles in the household, exemptions from the taille, a privilege generally granted only to members of the nobility and certain corporate groups, meant that they could style themselves as gentlemen

---

[126] AD-PA, B137.

[127] AD-PA, B139.

[128] See Davies on the self-made men in Montmorency's entourage, "Family Service and Family Strategies," 33–35.

[129] Boulenger and Le Franc, eds., *Comptes de Louise de Savoie et Marguerite d'Angoulême*, 96; AD-PA, B138.

[130] AD-PA, B2277.

and begin the process of prescription which might eventually secure noble status.[131]

Many retainers in the middle ranks of the household received additional compensations in kind. Liveried servants were outfitted free of cost. The younger ladies-in-waiting, governesses, and chambermaids were given a summer and a winter gown yearly; pages and valets received clothing as they needed it and shoes with astonishing frequency.[132] Upon betrothal, domestics generally received a money gift to be put towards the purchase of wedding clothes.[133] The extraordinary accounts show as well that kitchen servants received payments in kind which considerably increased the value of their positions. Wine stewards were paid ten sols for every wine barrel purchased, a sum which was later commuted to quarterly donations of 120 livres, roughly doubling the value of their office.[134] Maîtres d'hôtel and comptrollers received an award referred to as a *"getton d'argent,"* which amounted to 54 livres.[135] Some servants also milked extra money out of their everyday duties by contracting with officers in the household to provide necessaries for the kitchens and stables. Kitchen squires furnished greenery; valets often provided wood; grooms supplied fodder for the horses. In Catherine's stables (and presumably those of Jeanne d'Albret), Michel La Serre played the role of provisioner and was often listed as a merchant in various household accounts.[136] In the same way that other purveyors in the household received a commission for their services from the Albrets (and perhaps from the tradespeople), La Serre buoyed up his small salary by this traffic in hay and millet. Undoubtedly, the Albrets, in turn, used their servants' auxiliary incomes as justification for keeping their stable hands' wages at a minimal level.

---

[131]On the widespread practice of ennoblement by prescription, see J.-R. Bloch, *L'Anoblissement en France au temps de François Ier* (Paris: Librairie Félix Alcan, 1934), 25–31; Edouard Perroy, "Social Mobility among the French Noblesse in the Later Middle Ages," *Past and Present* 20 (1962): 345; Wood, *The Nobility of the Election of Bayeux*, 59–65.

[132]See, for example, AD-PA, B138, and the 200-livre entry in Catherine's 1594 account for the "robbes este et d'yver" for Catherine de Chivré, eldest daughter of Madame de la Barre; also 120 livres to Montguyon, *fille d'honneur*, for the "rest of her two summer and winter gowns"; and 60 livres to Madame de la Roze, governess, for her gown. Clothing usually was counted on the extraordinary rolls; see AD-PA, B20, B21.

[133]See the grant to Jacques Houdayer for 66 écus 40 sols for a wedding costume in 1594, AD-PA, B134; 20 écus to Picard, an aide in the fourrier's office, AD-PA, B138; and 33 écus 20 sols to Simone Boullenoye in 1595, AD-PA, B139.

[134]AD-PA, B26, B27, B108, B109.

[135]AD-PA, B108, B109.

[136]AD-PA, B136. B138.

The family that perhaps most clearly exploited all the benefits of service in the household of Foix-Navarre-Albret was the Selve.[137] Originally of merchant stock from the town of Marcillac in Limousin, the Selves advanced their family fortunes during the fifteenth century through fortuitous alliances with local notables and nobles. By the sixteenth century, some members of the family had shaken off the taint of their mercantile origins and entered the ranks of the minor gentry. However, a cadet branch of the family, headed by Jean de Selve, renounced provincial landholding for a life in Paris and politics. By 1520, he had established his position in the royal court by serving as First President of the Parlement of Paris and as Vice-Chancellor of the duchy of Milan during its occupation by the French. From these lofty positions, he procured places for his sons in the king's household and posts in the diplomatic service and Church. As a result of his negotiations of the Treaty of Madrid, for example, Selve secured the bishopric of Lavaur for his third son, Georges, who was only eighteen years old at the time.[138] He was less immediately fortunate in his attempts to find a position at court for his only daughter, finally settling for an appointment in the household of the king's sister, Marguerite d'Angoulême; in 1535, Marguerite de Selve entered noble service as an attendant to the young princess of Navarre, Jeanne d'Albret.[139]

Marguerite's subsequent rise in the Albret household owed much to the fact that she entered Jeanne's service when the princess was only seven years old,[140] and thus secured an early position in Jeanne's affections. She remained a fixture in the Albret household until her death in 1591, serving successively as a lady-in-waiting, governess, and finally first lady-in-waiting. As she advanced through the ranks, her salary increased from a mere 100 livres to 600 livres per annum. Moreover, she parlayed her position into places for other members of her family. Jeanne d'Albret and Antoine de Bourbon favored her marriage to Lancelot du Monceau, chevalier and seigneur de Thignonville, with a set-

---

[137]BN, Dossiers bleus, 610, Selve.

[138]Robert J. Kalas, "The Selve Family of Limousin: Members of a New Elite in Early Modern France,"*Sixteenth Century Journal* 18 (1987):147–72.

[139]For the record of her service see Boulenger and Le Franc, eds., *Comptes de Savoie et Marguerite d'Angoulême*, 94.

[140]Servants who entered the service of a young family member were usually richly rewarded. See J.-F. Massie, "Pierre de Sarrabaig: Le fils de la nourrice du prince Henri III de Navarre, ascension sociale d'une famille béarnaise," *Bulletin de la société des amis du château de Pau*, n.s., 72 (1977), 70–71; A. Communay, "Madeleine de la Fargue, nourrice du roi Henry IV," *Études historiques et religieuses du diocèse de Bayonne* (Pau, 1903): 99–110; and J.-B. LaBorde, *La maison Lareu, d'Asson: Une nourrice d'Henri IV* (Tarbes, 1923), 3–9.

tlement of 1,000 écus *d'or* and the promise of employment for the noble groom.[141] In 1553, Thignonville obtained the letters patent of his appointment to Jeanne's household as maître d'hôtel with a salary of 300 livres, as well as those declaring him exempt from the ban and arrière ban as one of the officers of the household.[142] Three years later, he became councilor and maître d'hôtel to Antoine de Bourbon.[143]

In 1569, Marguerite de Selve was promoted to governess for the young Catherine de Bourbon. Over the next few years she used her position and influence with Jeanne and Catherine to establish four first-degree relatives in Jeanne d'Albret's household. Her two daughters, Jeanne and Cécile Monceau, became ladies-in-waiting; her brother Claude de Selve was employed as a maître d'hôtel at her request in 1572; two years later, her youngest child, Jean, entered Catherine's service as a squire with a yearly recompense of 300 livres.[144] In 1578, Jean became a gentleman attendant in Henri de Navarre's household. His *lettre de retenue* as a gentleman attendant cited "the great and commendable services that his mother has done and continues to do for the sister of the Prince in her position as governess and lady-in-waiting" as Navarre's reason for retaining the young Thignonville.[145] After accompanying Navarre on his military campaigns for several years, Jean was awarded a captain's commission. In 1586, he became chamberlain of Navarre's household and was awarded a 3,000-livre pension.

As confidante of Jeanne and Catherine, Marguerite was also a considerable power broker in her own right. In addition to using her position to place her children in positions of power, aspiring nobles also sought to curry Marguerite's favor in hopes of getting their names and requests brought before the princess and the Queen of Navarre. In September 1570, for example, Marie of Clèves wrote to Marguerite to assure her of the "goodwill I bear toward you as the most affectionate friend you will ever have," and then asked her to keep the name of Clèves "always in the good graces of Madame and the Queen, her mother."[146] Such action, noted Clèves in a later letter, "will oblige me more and more to continue the goodwill that I have for you." Charles de Bourbon was more blunt in a letter he penned to Marguerite in September 1577. With promises to render service to Marguerite

---

[141]BN, Pièces originales, 1988 (Monceau).
[142]Ibid.
[143]Ibid.
[144]AD-PA, B16, B22, and B25.
[145]BN, Pièces originales, 1988 (Monceau).
[146]BN, Carrés d'Hozier, 438 (Monceau).

throughout his life, he petitioned her to employ "la bonne part" that she had for Catherine, so that the princess of Navarre would show herself more "favorable" towards his advancement.[147] As first lady-in-waiting, then, Marguerite assembled a following of her own which could be tapped for tangible favors when needed.

After Jeanne's death in 1572, Marguerite de Thignonville became First Lady-in-Waiting to Catherine de Bourbon, and as such the most highly paid member of the household. Between 1572 and her death in 1591, her salary never again increased, but her fortunes were hardly stationary. Gifts and awards had always supplemented her salary while in Jeanne's employ, and Catherine and Henri continued their mother's policy. In her testament, Jeanne d'Albret bequeathed her loyal lady-in-waiting and guardian of the family jewels, gems worth more than 8,000 écus.[148] In 1574, Henri rewarded Marguerite for her long tenure of service in the household with a large land grant: the property and goods of two of his subjects in the barony of Châteauneuf-en-Thivernais, who had been convicted of murder.[149] At the same time, Navarre granted Marguerite awards from his estates d'Assey in the duchy of Beaumont which amounted to 4,000 livres.[150] Two years later, Marguerite and Jean de Secondat, treasurer of Henri's household, were granted "all the deniers that have been judged to the King...against the inhabitants of Osses in Basse-Navarre" who had encroached upon forest rights and unlawfully cut and sold trees and wood.[151] Thus, in six years the Albrets had bestowed awards in excess of 30,000 livres upon their loyal servant, Marguerite de Thignonville.

Marguerite's fortunes in the household of Foix-Navarre-Albret were exceeded by those of her daughters. Both Jeanne and Cécile became the favorites of the princess and prince of Navarre and were in felicitous positions to benefit from the great boon to Navarre's fortunes after 1589. Even before Navarre's accession to the throne, the two sisters received munificent sums from Jeanne's two children. Upon her marriage in 1581 to Jean-Charles de Pardaillhan de Panjas, one of the most zealous partisans of the Protestant party, Jeanne was given a

---

[147]Ibid.

[148]Raymond Ritter, *La petite Tignonville* (Paris: Delmas, 1945). In 1570, Jeanne had granted Marguerite 3,500 livres as a gift to be dispensed "by the first clear monies which will come from the sale and profits of fiefs and other casual parties," but the grant had still not come through by 1572, BN, Carrés d'Hozier, 438 (Monceau).

[149]BN, Pièces originales, 1988 (Monceau).

[150]Ibid.

[151]Ibid.

marriage present totaling 4,000 écus from Navarre.[152] Catherine settled 20,000 livres on Cécile, when she married Jacques de Chivré, seigneur de la Barre, in 1584.[153] And Navarre likewise bestowed a marriage settlement upon Catherine of 4,000 écus and offered the seigneur de la Barre a position as one of his chamberlains.[154] Catherine also dramatically increased the salaries of their two favorites between 1584 and her death in 1605. In 1586, she raised their salaries to 500 livres; five years later the two received 600 livres each when they jointly accepted the role of first lady-in-waiting upon the death of their mother; and in 1594, Catherine increased their salaries to 1,200 livres. The two sisters were also rewarded with pensions which trebled their salaries (see table 3.5). Indeed, Catherine's lavish donations continued unabated, and by 1601 Barre and Panjas each received annual pensions of 3,600 livres in addition to their ordinary salaries of 1,200 livres.[155] Catherine's largess extended as well to the daughters of her confidantes, who acquired positions in the household as *damoiselles de la chambre*. At the birth of the future Louis XIII in 1601, Catherine accorded 100 écus sols to the two children of Panjas, and later a coffer of jewels containing 267 agates and gold buttons worth 497 livres.[156]

The Selve-Thignonville family bears ample testimony to the lucrative opportunities and advantages of aristocratic service. Indeed, by the seventeenth century, Jeanne du Monceau was notorious for the wealth that she had accumulated at Catherine de Bourbon's hands. Jealous contemporaries accused her of misusing her influence to deplete the princess of her fortune. After Catherine's death, Jeanne was cited before the king's council on charges of theft, corruption, and collusion by one Robert Le Bis.[157] According to the memoirs of a Parisian lawyer, Jeanne had received her "immense riches…by the unregulated exercise of her greed and desire."[158] But ultimately, the careers of Marguerite de Selve and her daughters illustrate that it was possible for household officers to serve their noble patrons loyally and enthusiastically, motivated both by affective bonds of fidelity and friendship and by desires for social and material advancement.

---

[152]BN FF 20464.

[153]BN, Pièces originales, 1988 (Monceau).

[154]Ritter, ed., *Lettres de Catherine de Bourbon*, 73. For the marriage contract, see AD-PA, E2009.

[155]Ritter, *La petite Tignonville*, 24. After Catherine's death in 1605, Henri IV continued to pay the pensions of his sister's confidante; see AD-PA, B3077, 3461.

[156]AD-PA, B139; Ritter, *La petite Tignonville*, 140.

[157]BN, MSS. Lorraine 347, fo. 54–68.

[158]As cited by Ritter, *La petite Tignonville*, 188.

Table 3.5 Wages Adjusted to Include Gifts and Pensions

Year	Attendants	Wages as Listed in Civil Rolls[a]	Increases Not in Civil Rolls[a]	Gifts/Pensions[a]	Total[a] "Wage"
1569	Dlle de Thigonville	100	—	—	100
	Cécile de Monceau	100	—	—	100
1575	Dlle de Thigonville	100	—	—	100
	Cécile de Monceau	100	—	—	100
1583	Mme de Panjas[b]	300	—	—	300
	Cécile de Monceau	100	—	—	100
1586	Mme de Panjas[c]	300	200	—	500
	Mme de La Barre	300	200	—	500
1588	Mme de Panjas	300	200	300	800
	Mme de La Barre	300	200	—	500
1591	Mme de Panjas	600	—	—	600
	Mme de La Barre	600	—	—	600
1594	Mme de Panjas	600	600	2400	3600
	Mme de La Barre	600	600	600	1800
1598	Mme de Panjas	1200	—	8250	9450
	Mme de La Barre	1200	—	6750	7950

AD-PA Source, respectively by year: B16, B25, B83, B111, B129, B136[d], B138[d], B142[d].

[a] All figures given in *livres tournois*.
[b] Jeanne de Thigonville married Sr. de Panjas in 1581 and was promoted to the position of lady-in-waiting with a yearly salary of 300 livres.
[c] Céile de Moneau married Jacques de Chivré, sr. de La Barre 18 February 1584, and accordingly was promoted from *damoiselle* to *dame*.
[d] The figures are given in écus in the MSS., and I have converted them to *livres tournois* at the rate of 3 livres or 60 sous = 1 écu.

VI. Conclusion

In 1596, Catherine de Bourbon penned this note to her brother: "I have given Madame Du Verger a vacation to look after her affairs. If you will do me the honor of keeping the promise that you have made, concerning her husband, she will want to return all the sooner to me."[159] Such blatant prodding indicates just how aware the Albrets were of the complex motives which bound their servants and attendants to their service. They had no difficulty in reconciling the desire for economic and social advancement which induced men and women into their service, on one hand, with the virtues of fidelity and affection, on the other. Both sets of motives could and did work to create a link between servant and master. The pressure to create an extensive network of clients forced the Albrets to increase their expenditures on salaries, pensions, and gifts over the course of the century. In so doing, they were not simply responding to the imperative of courtly conventions, but the Albrets were consciously constructing an image of wealth and influence to suit their political designs and aspirations. Willing to reduce their complement of servants when necessary, they also well recognized the exigencies of power and rank.

---

[159]Ritter, ed., *Lettres de Catherine de Bourbon*, 127.

---------- *Four* ----------

Dietary Conceits
and Purveyorship Contracts

The exercise of liberality and generosity, so fundamental to the self-definition of sixteenth-century nobles as well as to the definition of their sphere of influence, was expressed, first and foremost, by the gift of food and drink. A great noble's first duty was toward members of the household, servants and officers alike, many of whom routinely dined in the presence of Monsieur or Madam, though not necessarily at the same table.[1] Contemporary moralists considered the provision of food and drink so essential to social and cultural conditioning that they commonly referred to the aristocratic households where young nobles received their military and courtly training as households of "nourishment" (*nourriture*). And nobles often expressed the hope that children "nourished" (*nourri*) together in the same household, much like infants suckled by the same wet nurse, would share a common bond that would endure the highly divisive political realities of adulthood.[2] Food and drink in noble households thus served the same symbolic purposes as did the celebration of the Eucharist in the Church, which solidified the common bond of Christians. Beyond providing "nourishment" for their immediate circle of intimate friends and household retainers, great

---

[1] Jean-Louis Flandrin, "Distinctions through Taste," *A History of Private Life: Passions of the Renaissance*, ed. Roger Chartier (Cambridge: The Bellknap Press of Harvard University Press, 1989) 3:170; Neuschel, *Word of Honor*, 165–67; Heal, *Hospitality in Early Modern England*, 50–58, 154–55.

[2] For a discussion of the use of the language of "nourishment" in the sixteenth century, see Neuschel, *Word of Honor*, 85–87.

nobles were also expected to show their hospitality to a much wider circle of dependents ranging from vassals, tenants, and distant kinfolk to the occasional pilgrim, beggar, or vagrant, for whom such hospitality truly may have been life sustaining. The exercise of lavish hospitality helped create the web of social obligations and displayed the Christian responsibility (*noblesse oblige*), which in the sixteenth century distinguished the truly noble elite from the common masses.[3]

In spite of the rigorous social, cultural, and religious conventions that encouraged noble hospitality, great nobles were not the source of an inexhaustible fountain of charity showered indiscriminately on any importunate vagrant or impoverished relative. As Kristen Neuschel has argued, the gift of food and drink in noble households was "deliberate and discretionary," and certain kinds of privileges, such as reimbursement for fodder, were signs of special favor.[4] The sixteenth- and seventeenth-century proliferation of household ordinances and prescriptive literature that detailed who should and could be offered hospitality and gave dire warnings about the dangers of excess, suggests the tensions created within noble households by the exercise of hospitality. The political benefits of the practices of *noblesse oblige* were indisputable: hospitality, especially at great moments such as state banquets, publicly affirmed ties of friendship, clientage, and servitude. These practices reminded friends and rivals alike of the privileges and powers of lordship.

At the same time, the economic consequences of even a restrained policy of hospitality could be, and often were, ruinous to many family fortunes. The combined pressures of rising prices on foodstuffs, the increase of household sizes generally, the development of extensive religious and military clienteles which often fused with a great noble's personal household, and the growing emphasis on culinary refinement among noble elites produced new challenges to the practice of noble hospitality especially in the last three decades of the sixteenth century.

Until recently, historians have typically argued that great nobles met these challenges to their economic viability, especially those posed by the marketplace, with only a limited degree of success. J. H. Elliot, for example, has correlated quadrupling grain prices in sixteenth-century Europe with a loss of power by the Spanish nobility. And J. H. M. Salmon agrees that rising prices, especially on foodstuffs, destroyed

---

[3]For a discussion of the debates which raged around precisely such issues in sixteenth- and seventeenth-century England, see Heal, *Hospitality in Early Modern England*, chaps. 3 and 4.

[4]Neuschel, *Word of Honor*, 164–66.

the economic equilibrium of the French nobility after 1550.[5] In contrast to this sober scenario, much recent research has challenged that argument by showing the extent to which provincial nobles produced nearly all the food they consumed, condemned the new courtly culture and its culinary excesses, and were thus protected from the vagaries of the marketplace.[6] As consumers, rural seigneurs eschewed excess and innovation, particularly if it entailed any kind of entanglement in the market economy. Fearful of the financial risks involved in court politicking and deeply suspicious of the dubious morality of the market economy, provincial nobles chose to spend the lion's share of every year on their rural estates, where they strove, above all, to maintain an almost medieval degree of self-sufficiency. A fatherly admonition penned in 1600 by René Fleuriot, a Breton squire, captures the particular disfavor that the average provincial noble saved for profligates who purchased provisions in the marketplace.

> It would take a large book to list the number who have followed the path of those poor miserable prodigals, who consume in three months what ought to last a year for them, so much so that it is necessary to mortgage their land...and thus from expedient to expedient, the property is reduced to nothing. To avoid this, you must acquire provisions for your household...each in its own season, or else buy them at double the price, coming from day to day, as do several lords of our region as elsewhere, who by this means consume their great properties and are always in arrears.

Fleuriot's advice not only exemplifies the essence of provincial conservatism, it also points to one of the many differences which distinguished the small squires for the great court lord.[7]

---

[5]J. H. Elliot, *Imperial Spain, 1469–1617* (New York: Penguin, 1963), 300; and J. H. M. Salmon, *Society in Crisis: France in the Sixteenth Century* (London: St. Martin's Press, 1975), 40–42.

[6]The literature on the dietary patterns and practices of the nobility is quite extensive and much of it is extremely well known. The habits of Sire de Gouberville, for example, have been analyzed exhaustively in many different sources. See, for example, A. Tollemar, ed., *Un Sire de Gouberville, gentilhomme compagnard au Contentin de 1553 à 1564* (Paris: Mouton, 1972). For other works in this vein, see Pierre Charbonnier, *Guillaume de Murol: Un petit seigneur auvergnat au début du XVe siècle* (Clermont-Ferrand: Institut d'études du Massif central, 1973); idem, "La Consommation des seigneurs auvergnats du XVe au XVIIIe siècle," *Annales: Economies, Sociétés, Civilisations* 30 (1975): 465–77; Bartolomé Bennassar and Joseph Goy, "Contributions à l'histoire de la consommation alimentaire du XIVe au XIXe siècle," *Annales: Economies, Sociétés, Civilisations* 30 (1975):402–30; and Dewald, *Pont-St-Pierre*, 193–99.

[7]Dewald, *Pont-St-Pierre*, 198.

The fact remains that great nobles, like the Albrets, purchased most of the food, drink, fuel, and fodder they and their household consumed. The size and mobility of the Albret households made it impossible for them to rely on food stores and seigneurial dues from their own estates to supply their basic needs. By the early sixteenth century, most great nobles relied heavily on specialized purveyors to provide them with most of their daily necessities. This extensive use of purveyors and purveyorship contracts, as we will see later, muted the worst effects of sixteenth-century price inflation on aristocratic fortunes and provided nobles with greater resources with which to address larger and almost inescapable problems posed by expanding households, extravagant courtly conceits, and war.

I. The Albrets at Table

The emergence of large and increasingly fluid noble households in the fifteenth and sixteenth centuries in France, and all over Europe, encouraged more detailed accounting of the movement of food within those households. Maîtres d'hôtel and comptrollers often kept a daily record or journal of the food, wine, and fuel consumed by the household. These same officers sometimes included a list of the guests who dined with the household, as well as those servants, officers, and craftsmen attached to the household who were authorized to enjoy their master's or mistress's hospitality.[8] Regrettably, the Albrets' maîtres d'hôtel did not record the number of household members, invited guests, and local artisans who dined daily at the Albrets' behest, but the journals they kept, aptly referred to as "ordinary accounts," provide an invaluable guide to general dietary habits and conceits, to patterns of guesting and feasting, and to the growing expenses of the hospitality practiced by the Albrets in the last three decades of the sixteenth century.[9] They also point unquestionably to the impact of war and inflation on the household economy of great magnates.

---

[8]See, for example, Heal, *Hospitality in Early Modern England*, 49–59, 70–75; Neuschel, *Word of Honor*, 162–65. For particularly pertinent comments on the lifestyle of the provincial nobility, see Luchaire, *Alain le Grand*, 52–53; Pierre Charbonnier, *Guillaume de Murol*, 196–97, 205–6, 217–18, 233–34; idem, "La Consommation des seigneurs," 465–77; Emmanuel Le Roy Ladurie, "Introduction," in *Un Sire de Gouberville*, ed. A. Tollemer (Paris, 1972), xliii. To his credit, Lawrence Stone has argued that price rises must have affected the poor far more than the rich in his *Crisis of the Aristocracy*, 249–50.

[9]Purchases were noted in daily journals audited by the maîtres d'hôtel and comptrollers of the household. Many of these "ordinary expense" accounts survive and are classed in series B in the Archives Départementales in Pau. For a description of the way

The most striking feature of the Albrets' ordinary accounts is the enormously varied consumption of food and drink they record. Local markets, except perhaps in the most prosperous urban areas, were rarely expansive enough to accommodate the gargantuan appetites of a large noble household and the swarm of unsolicited hangers-on, who trailed behind. The Albrets and their company of cavaliers could lay waste to several dozen calves, pigs, sheep, and chickens in a single day, relishing every last tidbit of animal flesh from the cock's comb to the pig's snout. By 1572, Jeanne d'Albret's household officers and servants consumed over 300 pounds of mutton and beef daily.[10] Seven years later, Henri de Navarre's comptrollers recorded that the kitchen officers prepared 450 pounds of mutton and beef for consumption by members of the household and invited guests every day of the week.[11] These figures steadily increased during the 1580s when Navarre's growing involvement in the Religious Wars swelled the official and unofficial members of the household; Navarre's maîtres d'hôtel recorded the consumption of mutton and beef in excess of 500 pounds in a single day.[12]

Beyond mere domestic livestock, the Albrets and their entourage also feasted from platters heaped high with every imaginable wild beast of the field, bird of the air, and on holy days, fish of the sea. At a normal winter meal, when those who could afford to ate in almost gluttonous fashion, at least a dozen types of meat, game, and fowl, along with elaborately prepared patés, graced the tables. On January 9, 1572, for example, Jeanne d'Albret and her household dined on 258 pounds of mutton, 50 pounds of beef, 76 pounds of veal, 23 pounds of pork, twenty-two capons, twelve nightingales, four partridges, three rabbits, two wood pigeons, and a kid goat.[13] During one supposedly spartan Lenten repast prepared for Henri de Navarre and his entourage, even whale was featured on the menu.[14]

---

in which these accounts were kept, see AD-PA, B2350: "All [the provisions furnished] are received in the presence of the maîtres d'hôtel and the comptroller and written by the said comptroller in a paper journal from each office, which paper is carried every single evening by the household officers to the comptroller who notes what each merchant furnished and writes it in a book called the journal, which is looked at and audited each day in the office by the serving maîtres d'hôtel and at the end of each month the sums in each journal are calculated and...the said journal put in the hands of the treasurer to acquit and pay the sums contained."

[10] AD-PA, B2561
[11] AD-PA, B23, B2038.
[12] AD-PA, B100, B101, B113.
[13] AD-PA, B23.
[14] AD-PA, B60.

Such dining patterns could drain a village of supplies, and the dazzling array of delicacies that graced the Albrets' tables at even the most pedestrian of meals suggests yet another reason why local markets and domanial farmers often could not satisfy the provisioning demands of *les grands*. Beyond the staggering quantity of food and drink consumed by a large noble household was the astounding variety and quality of food and drink which great nobles expected to be served and expected to serve their guests. As Norbert Elias, Lawrence Stone, and numerous other students of aristocratic society have observed, conspicuous display and cultural competition permeated every aspect of aristocratic life, including dietary predilections and patterns.[15] The ability to command daily the bounty of creation was a powerful reminder of the earthly lordship of the nobility. Indeed, great court aristocrats increasingly distinguished themselves from the provincial nobility by consuming specialized foodstuffs from exotic New World meats to rare spices that could only be procured through a professional purveyor.[16]

Over the course of the sixteenth century, the variety of meat, fish, fowl, and game which merchant-purveyors promised to provide for the Albrets' tables steadily increased and testifies to the gradual refinement of their tastes. An extant purveyorship contract from 1538 reveals that merchant-purveyors specified 187 different kinds and cuts of meat, games, fish, and fowl that they were willing to provide for Henri d'Albret's tables; sixty years later in 1595, Catherine de Bourbon's purveyors promised an astonishing 212 different varieties of meat, game, fish, and fowl for her tables.[17] (see table 4.1) Culinary conceits, such as swan, heron, curlew, and whale figured prominently in these contracts. The rarity and semimythical quality of these birds and mammals meant that they continued to be served at banquets long

---

[15]Norbert Elias, *Court Society*, trans. Edmund Jephcott (New York: Pantheon Books, Basil Blackwell, 1983); Lawrence Stone, *Crisis of the Aristocracy*; Stephen Mennell, *All Manners of Food: Eating and Taste in England and France from the Middle Ages to the Present* (Oxford and New York, 1986).

[16]For a general discussion of the evolution of aristocratic tastes between the fifteenth and eighteenth centuries in Europe, and France particularly, see Flandrin, "Distinction through Taste," 265–308; Leonard N. Beck, *Two Loaf-Givers* (Washington, D.C.: Library of Congress, 1984); Barbara Wheaton, *Savouring the Past: The French Kitchen and Table from 1300 to 1789* (Philadelphia: University of Pennsylvania Press, 1983), 27–94; there are many treatments of diet in the *Annales: E.S.C.*; see esp. the 1975 issue which is devoted to consumption patterns in medieval and early modern Europe.

[17]AD-PA, B2038, E1998, and MC XXXVI, 23–10.

Table 4.1 *Marchés De Pourvoirie* in Meat and Fish 1538-1595

	1538[a]	1564[b]	1571[c]	1572[d]	1576[e]	1584[f]	1595[g]
BEEF							
Pound of flesh	11s	12d	12d	12d	12d	12d	3s 11d
Sirloin	2s	3s	12d	12d	12d	12d	11s 3d
Fresh tongue	8s	2s	2s	2s	2s	2s	7s 6d
Salted tongue	8s	4s	4s	4s	—	—	15s
Smoked tongue	—	—	—	—	—	—	—
Pound of marrow	7s	6s	—	6s	—	—	22s 7d
Pound of grease	2s	2s	2s	2s	—	—	7s 6d
Cow's udder	—	2s	—	2s	—	2s	7s 6d
Tripe	—	3s	3s	3s	3s	3s	11s 3d
Feet (dozen)	8s	3s	3s	12d	3s	—	3s 9d
VEAL							
Pound of flesh	30s	15d	15d	15d	15d	15d	4s 8d
Liver	2s	18d	18d	18d	18d	—	5s 7d
Head	—	2s	2s	2s	—	—	7s 6d
Feet (dozen)	6d	6d	6d	6d	6d	6d	11s 6d
MUTTON							
Pound of flesh	20s	18d	18d	18d	18d	18d	5s 7d
Feet (dozen)	—	3s	3s	3s	3s	3s	11s 3d

(continued next page)

Table 4.1 (continued)

KID		18d	18d	18d	18d	18d	
Offal	—	18d	18d	18d	18d	18d	5s 7d
Suckling pig	—	8s	8s	8s	—	—	30s
Pork chops	2s	2s	2s	2s	2s	—	7s 6d
Ribs (dozen)	8s	4s	—	4s	5s	—	15s
Feet (dozen)	12s	12d	—	12s	12s	—	3s 9d
Tongue	—	—	—	12s	12s	—	3s 9d
Ears	12s	12d	—	12s	—	—	3s 8d
Stomach	12s	15s	—	15s	12s	—	56s 3d
POULTRY, GAME							
Crane	25s	30s	—	—	—	25s	112s 6d
Heron	—	12s	12s	12s	—	12s	45s
Rabbit	—	5s	5s	5s	5s	3s	18s
Hare	11s	—	—	—	—	—	26s 3d
Small birds	2s	—	3s	2s	—	—	7s 6d
Wild goose	15s	8s	8s	8s	—	—	30s
Pheasant	25s	—	—	25s	—	25s	93s 9d
Partridge	4s	5s	5s	5s	5s	5s	18s 9d
Pigeon	16s	18d	18d	18d	18d	—	5s 7d
Chicken	25s	25s	40s/25s	25s	40s/25s	25s	56s 3d
Teal	3s	3s	3s	3s	2s	—	11s 3d
Turtle dove	3s	3s	3s	3s	—	—	11s 3d

(continued next page)

Table 4.1 (continued)

FRESH WATER FISH						
Eel	10s	8s	—	8s	—	30s
Pike (2p+)	70s	70s	—	75s	75s	281s 3d
Pike (1p+1/2+4d)	50s	50s	—	50s	50s	187s 6d
Pike (1p+1/4)	27s 1d	25s	25s	25s	25s	93s 9d
Pike (1p+4d)	—	15s	15s	15s	15s	56s 3d
Pike (1p+2d)	—	8s	8s	8s	—	30s
Pike (pied)	6s	—	—	3s	—	11s 3d
Carp (2p+)	70s	60s	—	60s	—	225s
Carp (1p+1/2+4d)	60s	40s	—	40s	40s	150s
Carp (1p+1/2)	20s	20s	—	20s	20s	75s
Carp (1p+4d)	30s/15s	10s	—	10s	10s	37s 6d
Carp (1p+2d)	25s/6s	7s	—	8s	7s	30s
Carp (pied)	4s	4s	4s	4s	4s	15s
Shrimp (100)	12s 6d	—	—	10s	—	37s 6d
Sturgeon	20s	10s	—	10s	—	37s 6d
Gudgeon (100)	3s	6s	—	5s	5s	18s 9d
Frogs (100)	10s	—	8s	8s	8s	30s
Large mullet	4s	—	3s	3s	—	11s 3d
Large perch	5s	5s	5s	4s	—	18s 9d
Medium perch	3s	4s	4s	—	4s	15s
Small perch	2s	2s	2s	2s	2s	7s

(continued next page)

Table 4.1 (continued)

Large salmon		50s	110s	—	110s	110s	130s	412s 6d
Medium salmon		40s	80s	—	80s	—	95s	300s
Small salmon		5s	40s	—	40s	—	—	150s
OCEAN FISH								
Fresh cod		10s	12s	12s	12s	—	12s	45s
Salted cod		10s	12s	—	6s	6s	12s	45s
Mussels		5s	40s	40s	40s	—	—	150s
Large skate		10s	7s 6d	—	7s 6d	—	7s 6d	28s 1d
Medium skate		10s	7s 6d	—	7s 6d	—	7s 6d	28s 1d
Fresh sardines		25s	20s	20s	20s	20s	—	75s
Tuna (pound)		—	5s	—	5s	—	—	112s 6d
Large turbot		60s	30s	—	30s	—	—	67s 4d
Medium turbot		30s	18s	—	18s	—	—	37s 6d
Small turbot		17s 6d	10s	—	10s	—	—	—
Clams		7s 6d	6s	6s	6s	6s	6s	15s
Whale (pound)		3s	4s	4s	4s	4s	—	15s

[a]Contract with Henri II d'Albret, AD-PA,B2083
[b]Contract with Jeanne d'Albret, AD-PA,E1998
[c]Contract with Jeanne d'Albret, AD-PA,B18
[d]Contract with Catherine of Navarre, AN, MCXXXVI,23-10
[e]Contract with Henri de Navarre, AD-PA,B26
[f]Contract with Henri de Navarre, AD-PA
[g]Contract with Catherine de Bourbon, AN,MCXC,159

after a plumper and tastier bird from the New World, such as turkey, was available to tempt noble palates.[18]

Throughout the century, merchant-purveyors also assured the Albrets a steady supply of pork, lamb, poultry, and fowl, and during Lent, fish and seafood. No meal was complete without several platters of pork, poultry, and assorted game. Indeed the great emphasis given to game, especially small birds, such as the Béarnais woodcock or bénaris, evoked the noble fondness for the hunt and its prominent role in noble culture, as well as provided variation in meat dishes. Proscriptions against poaching game in seigneurial and royal forests were widespread and constituted part of the popular mythology surrounding seigneurial dominance over forest and field alike. Thus, the presence of game on noble tables, even game purchased from purveyors rather than killed during the hunt, served as yet another reminder of the privileges and powers which set the seigneur apart from his dependents and the rest of society. Often, the public consumption of such "seigneurial meat" was reserved for the lord and his noble officers and guests.

Even the consumption of dietary staples, such as bread and wine, could become a sign of aristocratic preeminence. Both bread and wine were consumed in enormous quantities in the Albrets' households. Daily tallies show that by the 1570s, the Albrets, their household officers, servants, and invited guests were consuming five hundred loaves of bread a day, a figure that tripled by the end of the sixteenth century (see table 4.2). Not all of these loaves, however, were of the same quality. Bakers customarily provided two kinds of bread to the household: white bread (*pain blanc*) made of refined wheat flour, and common bread (*pain de commun*) made from various unrefined and vulgar grains, such as barley and rye.[19] The common bread of the noble household still represented a marked improvement over the daily bread consumed by the average sixteenth-century peasant, who often ate bread composed in significant part of ash, especially in regions such as Béarn where wheat was not a native crop. [20] The Albrets' maîtres d'hôtel customarily purchased several kinds of wine for daily consumption by the household, including a *vin de bouche* or common table wine intended for lesser members of the household. Finer wines, such as

---

[18]See Flandrin, "Distinction through Taste," 283–84, on the relative merits of swan, heron, and other medieval birds which often were served as much for show as for actual consumption.

[19]AD-PA, B2485, B2530.

[20]See Jean-Louis Flandrin, *Families in Former Times*, trans. Richard Southern (Cambridge: Cambridge University Press, 1979), 105; Roelker, *Queen of Navarre*, 252.

Table 4.2 Patterns of Bread Consumption

Month/Year	Dozens of Loaves Consumed	Dozens Consumed per day[a]	Cost per dozen[b]
July 1571	1214	39	6s.
January 1572	1585	51	6s.
January 1576	1542	49	8s.
July 1576	1525	49	8s.
April 1579	1927	64	8s.
September 1587	3379	112	7s. 6d.
July 1589	3598	116	9s.
AD-PA Source, respectively by year: B18, B23, B26, B26, B42, B113, B130			

[a]Figures are rounded off to the nearest whole number
[b]All prices are given in *sols tournois* and *deniers*

delicate Jurançons from Béarn, as well as wines procured from more legendary wine-growing regions, such as Bordeaux, were reserved for the Albrets, their chief officers, and invited guests.[21]

Fresh fruits, vegetables, and sweetmeats were on the table at every main meal, and further illustrated the growing refinement of taste which separated great nobles from their inferiors. The Albrets' interest in supplying their tables with fruit is evident in their efforts to cultivate both orange trees and berry bushes in their gardens in Pau and Nérac.[22] In spite of such efforts, fruits, vegetables, and sweetmeats remained delicacies reserved primarily for their own tables and the tables of visiting dignitaries and favorites. From May 8 to June 12, 1581, for example, Marquet Metraut, one of Navarre's kitchen servants, furnished eighteen livres worth of artichokes, beans, herbs, vinegar, salt, and mustard to the kitchens of the visiting ambassador from

---

[21]AD-PA, B23, B26, B65; MC, XC 167.
[22]AD-PA, B268, B514, B516; see also Dewald, *Pont-St-Pierre*, 194, for references to the comte de Pont St Pierre's efforts to cultivate melons for the same reasons in the eighteenth century.

Germany.[23] Indeed, so precious were commodities such as fresh and preserved fruits and vegetables that they were eaten in small quantities even by the Albrets themselves except on feast days. (see table 4.3)

The emphasis on variety and refinement of cuisine which was clearly a part of the development of aristocratic tastes in the sixteenth century does not imply that the Albrets engaged either in deliberate wastefulness or a disdain for certain "gross meats," such as pork, which would be eliminated from aristocratic diets a century later. The Albrets' purveyorship contracts and household records routinely mention pigs' ears, feet, snout, belly, and other by-products of butchery which vanished from aristocratic tables by 1670.[24] Indeed, no daily catalogue of meats for household consumption was complete without mention of several platters of ingeniously disguised viscera and offal. The Albrets' practice of consuming the entire animal suggests not only that aristocratic tastes, however refined, still inclined toward the gourmand rather than the gourmet, but also that they practiced a kind of household culinary economy that shunned gratuitous wastefulness. Leftover meats appeared the next day in meat pies and pastries; fruit, vegetables, and sweetmeats were consumed frugally; old bread was used as a thickening agent in sauces or fed to the hunting dogs.[25]

For reasons that had little to do with economy or religion, however, the Albrets continued to observe many of the dietary restrictions imposed by the Catholic Church long after they and most members of their households had embraced the Reformed faith.[26] The cycle of feast and fast days and liturgical seasons, which the medieval church had created to illustrate the link between the control of fleshly desires, such as gluttony, and greater spirituality very early on provided nobles with an excuse to enjoy precious and perishable delicacies, such as fish, at least three times a week. By the fifteenth century, for example, the count of Burgundy, following canon law, observed fast days (*jours d'abstinence*) on Friday and Saturday; he observed a modified fast day on Wednesday when red meat was eaten in only small quantities along with the customary fish and eggs.[27] By the 1570s and 1580s, the

---

[23]P. Raymond, "Notes extraites de comptes de Jeanne d'Albret et de ses enfants, 1556–1608," *Revue d'Aquitaine et du Languedoc*, 12 (1867):161.

[24]Flandrin, "Distinction through Taste," 273–74.

[25]AD-PA, B23; see also Neuschel, *Word of Honor*, 166; Flandrin, "Distinction through Taste," 278–80.

[26]See Heal, *Hospitality in Early Modern England*, 79, for a description of similar dietary patterns among English Protestant nobles.

[27]Monique Somme, "L'alimentation quotidienne à la cour de Bourgogne au milieu de XVe siècle," *Bulletin philologie et historique (jusqu'à 1610) du comité des travaux historiques et scientifiques* (1972):104–17.

Table 4.3 Consumption Patterns in the Household of Foix-Navarre-Albret: Feasting and Normal Meals

Dates/Repast	Bread (%)	Wine (%)	Meats (%)	Salad (%)	Pâtés (%)	Spices & Sweetmeats[a] (%)	Fruits Oils[b] (%)
14 January 1572/ Banquet at Lectoure[c]	11.2	8.7	49.9	0.6	6.9	11.5	11.2
3 February 1579/ Banquet at Nérac[d]	10.2	14.8	43.6	1.3	6.2	17.3	6.6
22 February 1579/ Banquet at Nérac[d]	13.7	11.8	51.9	0.1	8.7	10.9	2.9
7 December 1586/ Banquet at Nérac[e]	9.1	21.6	61.1	0.5	4.2	2.4	1.1
February 1579/ Normal Meals	17.1	17.6	57.6	1.2	1.8	2.3	2.4

[a]Includes sugar, spices, nuts, dates, *raisins de damas* and sweetmeats
[b]Includes figs, capers, *raisins de casse*, lemons, oranges and rich oils, such as olive and fresh butter. Occasionally spices were listed under this account and were added as part of the total fruit percentage in keeping with the *maître contrôleur's* categorization.
[c]From AD-PA, B23
[d]From AD-PA, B42
[e]From AD-PA, B102

Albrets were still practicing partial abstinence from red meat. During Lent and on traditional fast days, 60 percent of all proteins consumed by the household were fish and eggs, as opposed to 5 percent on normal days.[28]

In the Albrets' households, however, fish days were hardly fast days. Seafood was a highly prized delicacy that was difficult to transport and keep fresh and was generally reserved for banquets. Fridays thus became an excuse to eat delicacies such as oysters, salmon, and sole.[29] On fast days, the number of eggs used in the meal preparation quintupled, and butter, which was more delicate and expensive than the animal fat and lard generally used in food production, was purchased to sweeten heavily salted fish and the preserved condiments which accompanied it. Butter and eggs alone increased expenditures on food and drink by 2 to 3 percent every Friday[30].

While every meal, even on fast days, displayed in both material and symbolic terms the meaning and significance of rank in early modern French society, banquets (*festins*) revealed the full extent of the Albrets' ability to command the bounty of creation for their own pleasure, and perhaps more importantly, for the pleasure of those within their circle of influence for whom they were the source of sustenance and nourishment. Jean-Louis Flandrin has questioned whether aristocratic tables really groaned beneath the weight of huge mounds of food in the sixteenth century when artistic representations of nobles' banqueting suggest greater moderation than that practiced by their seventeenth- and eighteenth-century counterparts.[31] But judging from the Albrets' ordinary accounts and household records banquet tables truly were crowded with silver platters heaped high with meats, fruits, and vegetables. Indeed, silverplate was sometimes even rented to supplement the impressive collection of family silver which could not accommodate the number and variety of dishes served at banquets.[32] While quantitative excess was an important, indeed key, message to be conveyed to

---

[28]In January 1572, the figure was 50 percent; during Lent in April 1576, 64.3 percent.

[29]Dried and preserved fish, such as cod and herring, comprised the ordinary fare served to servants. See, for example, a 1502 inventory from the castle of Nérac in which household officers found 508 salted codfish, three barrels of herring and forty-two pounds of cheese, AD-PA, E196.

[30]During November 1579, for example, Friday expenditures were 2.5 percent higher than on normal days.

[31]Flandrin, "Distinction through Taste," 278–80.

[32]For an inventory of the Albrets' silverplate, which had not yet been pawned or melted down in return for needed cash by 1583, see AD-PA, A4; for renting practices, see AD-PA, B25.

invited guests and regular retainers alike, the growing emphasis on a variety of foods and refinement of preparation demonstrating the new courtly civility of aristocratic society was inescapable. Rare and delicate foods, as well as more common food that had been refined in the process of preparation, such as "grosser meats" into pâtés, were featured on the banquet tables. Small game birds napped in fruit sauces, fish delicately braised in butter, and oysters and other shellfish figured more prominently in total meat costs at banquets than the more commonly consumed mutton and beef. Special wines such as the *vin de Grave*, which the household apothecary, François Geoffrion "purchased in Bordeaux, had put in bottle, and carried to Nérac," were served.[33]

The most striking way in which the Albrets demonstrated their gastronomic refinement was through the consumption of rare fruits, spices, sweets, and their fondness for pâtés and pastries which required the skill of special pastry chefs. On banquet days, expenditures on luxury items which normally amounted to less than 8 percent of total food costs soared to 25 percent. (see table 4.3) The special favor given to pâtés and pastries owed much to the Renaissance "abhorrence of the simple and to the desire for refinement,"[34] driving cooks and chefs to indulge in extravagant conceits and their time-honored penchant for "stamp[ing] and strey[ning] and grynde[ing] and turn[ing] substance into accident."[35] The fascination with pies which, when cut, released flocks of live birds into the air had passed out of fashion by the sixteenth century, but pâtés decorated with the feathered heads and tails of exotic birds frequently appeared on the Albrets' tables.

The cost, both in terms of financial resources and the human-labor required to produce banquet masterpieces, was enormous. Expenditures on food and drink easily doubled on feast days.[36] Beyond the obvious expenses were the often hidden costs of "staging" such affairs: the transfer of furniture, silverplate, and tapestries from the Albrets' fortified stronghold in Navarrenx; the wages of carpenters who constructed stools, benches, and platforms for invited guests; and lodging and fodder for invited guests and their animals. These costs could double expenditures yet again. Given the enormous expense entailed in staging a proper banquet, the Albrets only rarely entertained in such a

---

[33]Beck, *Two Loaf-Givers*, 27.
[34]Ibid.
[35]AD-PA, B42.
[36]See, for example, the maître d'hôtel's tally for two banquets Henri de Navarre staged for Catherine de Medici and his *reine Margot* to celebrate the resolution of hostilities and the Peace of Nérac in February 1579. On both occasions food costs reached nearly 500 livres, or double normal daily expenditures on food and drink.

fashion. Certain traditional feast days, such as Christmas, the visit of distinguished diplomats or royalty, or the resolution of hostilities between two warring parties, required the ritual exchange of food and drink, and remained a powerful symbol of social cohesion at most levels in French society. It would be tempting to argue that the almost endless cycle of war and resolution which characterized French political life in the 1570s and 1580s drew Jeanne d'Albret, Henri de Navarre, and Catherine de Bourbon into a ruinous cycle of banqueting. The ordinary accounts suggest, however, that banquets were not an especial drain on the family fortunes. When Navarre's comptroller, for example, summed up ordinary expenditures for February 1579 during which his master had lavishly entertained the Queen Mother and his *reine Margot* with two banquets, they amounted to 1,000 livres less than January's expenses, when Henri had restrained his entertaining to economize after the festivities of Christmas.[37]

The growing distinction between the dietary patterns of the great court nobles and their household servants can be demonstrated clearly by the fluctuations that occurred in the ordinary expenses when the head of the household was absent. At those times, the amount of meat, fruit, and spices purchased for the household dropped drastically. (see table 4.4) These figures trace the variation in household expenditures during Henri de Navarre's frequent absences, when expenditures on meat and other delicacies could drop precipitously. Henri's flight from court in February 1586 provoked an 18 percent drop in expenditures on meat. His absence from the household train in July 1586, under somewhat less tense circumstances, also created changes in expenditures on food and drink. While meat costs declined only slightly, expenditures on bread, the common dietary staple of both servants and dogs in the household, increased by 7 percent.

Dietary patterns did not necessarily change nor expenditures for food and drink increase when the Albrets were in Paris or frequenting court since they customarily ate in a manner befitting their royal status and closely imitated the refinements in culinary tastes they witnessed at court. Moreover, as we will see later, purveyorship contracts protected them from fluctuations in the price of foodstuffs, even in Paris, where demographic pressures and the presence of the royal court meant prices were much higher than in the provinces. Chroniclers reported that during the years of virtual captivity at court after the St. Bartholmew's Day Massacre, the young king of Navarre cut quite a figure at the Valois court, hunting in St. Germaine and dancing in the

[37]AD-PA, B26, B33.

Table 4.4 Expenditures on Food and Drink—Servant vs. Seigneurial Repasts

Dates/Participants	Bread (%)	Wines (%)	Meats & Fish (%)	Fruits & Spices (%)
4-28 February 1576 King's train	22.4	35.2	40.1	2.3
7-28 February 1576 King separate from train	10.1	22.5	63.3	4.1
1-31 July 1586 King's train	17.9	20.6	57.9	3.6
1-31 July 1586 King separate from train	10.6	20.1	60.9	8.4
AD-PA Source, respectively by year: B26, B26, B101, B101				

Louvre. Living in the midst of courtly excess and mimicking many of its rituals, Navarre's expenditures on food and drink remained consistently low. In January 1576, while on a round of balls and hunts, Henri's ordinary expenditures amounted to slightly over 5,000 livres. A year later, when on countless little campaigns and skirmishes against rival Catholics in the southwest, his treasurers routinely disbursed 6,000 to 7,000 livres monthly for basic necessities. Indeed, as tables 4.5a and 4.5b make clear, summer campaigning often put a greater strain on the household treasury than life at court. Henri's ordinary expenditures invariably increased during the summer, which remained the traditional season for military campaigning, especially during the tumultuous and often unpredictable decades of the Religious Wars. During these months, the company of gentlemen who dined at Navarre's tables and enjoyed the rare privileges of fodder for their horses swelled the ranks of the household retainers on record, and expenditures on food and drink increased as much as 20 percent. By contrast, food expenses in the household headed by Jeanne d'Albret and later in the household headed by Catherine de Bourbon, customarily declined in summer when it was no longer important to eat heavily to stave off the effects of cold.[38]

---

[38]For Catherine de Bourbon's ordinary expenditures, see the general household accounts, beginning with AD-PA, B22. No specialized ordinary accounts exist for her household.

142 • The Economics of Power

Table 4.5a Summer Food Costs in the Ordinary Accounts: 1571–1589 (in livres tournois)

Item	July 1571	%	July 1576	%	July 1583	%	July 1586	%	July 1589	%
Bread	359	18.6	610	14.9	789	15.9	790	10.7	1702	17.1
Wine	495	25.9	933	22.8	758	15.3	1389	18.9	3558	35.8
Meats & Fish	958	50.9	2367	57.9	2999	60.5	4266	58.1	3894	39.4
Fruit & Spices	97	5.1	178	4.4	409	8.3	901	12.3	792	8.0
TOTAL[a]	1909		4088		4955		7346		9946	

AD-PA Source, respectively by year: B8, B26, B72, B101, B130

[a]Stable expenses and lodging which normally appear in the ordinary accounts have been omitted.

Table 4.5 Winter Food Costs in the Ordinary Accounts: 1571–1589 (in livres tournois)

Item	January 1572	%	January 1576	%	January 1583	%	January 1586b	%
Bread	652	16.1	590	13.1	743	16.6	835	14.2
Wine	469	11.5	1236	27.9	620	13.8	809	13.8
Meats & Fish	2761	67.9	2403	54.2	2699	60.3	3668	62.6
Fruit & Spices	183	4.5	201	4.5	418	9.3	550	9.4
TOTAL[a]	4065		4430		4480		5862	

AD-PA Source, respectively by year: B23, B26, B72, B100

[a]Stable expenses and lodging have been omitted.
[b]There is a 1.8% error factor in the July 1586 accounts.

The steadily escalating costs of feeding Navarre's household certainly did not escape the notice of his household officials. Between 1576 and 1586, Navarre's summer food costs increased by almost 80 percent; by 1589 they had increased another 30 percent. Thus by the 1570s, Navarre's expenditures on food and drink comprised around 55 percent of his total household expenditures, in contrast to the 35 to 45 percent expended by his mother and sister. (see table 4.6) While there are difficulties calculating percentages from the general or household treasury, since treasurers also recorded funds transferred to other accounts as "expenditures," the percentage of money spent on daily necessities is significantly lower than the 65 to 75 percent that Kristen Neuschel has suggested her Picard nobels spent on food and drink.[39] Equally striking

Table 4.6 Accounts of Treasurers of the Royal Household

Year[a]	Total Payments[b]	Ordinary Food Expenditure[b]	Percent of Expenses
1556	64,879	30,340	46.8%
1559	100,672	30,714	30.5%
1565	124,870	56,758	45.5%
1569	92,871	31,523	33.9%
1570	—[c]	40,072	—
1574	51,990	28,266	54.4%
1579d	75,522	34,522	45.7%
1579e	—[c]	80,768	—
1582e	—[c]	70,490	—
1583e	59,751	34,429	57.6%
1587e	210,382	115,582	55.0%
1595e	120,576	44,555	37.0%
AD-PA Source, respectively by year: B6, B144, B13, B15, B16, B24, B48bis, B154, B157, B83, B160, B139			

[a]The fiscal year was from January 1 to December 31.
[b]All payments and expenses are given in livres tournois. Included in this figure are charges for lodging and heating costs, which were calculated as part of the basic necessities of the household.
[c]Some pages are missing from the manuscript, including those with total payments.
[d]Accounts for Catherine de Bourbon.

[39]This percentage is somewhat lower than the figures of 65 to 75 percent suggested by Neuschel, *Word of Honor*, 165; and in certain years could be even lower. The explanation for such declines in percentages are many, including increased expenditures on luxuries, decreased household size, or a large transfer of money to another treasurer. See also Major, "Noble Income," 36–39.

[e]Accounts for the household of Henry de Navarre.

is the general consistency in actual expenditures on food and drink in Jeanne d'Albret's and Catherine de Bourbon's households between 1556 and 1595. Only three times in this thirty-year sample did their food costs exceed 35,000 livres.[40]

Not all food costs were recorded in the ordinary accounts. Certain officers on mission for the Albrets were reimbursed for their journey and the food and drink they consumed; these and other expenses were paid for from the extraordinary accounts or general treasury. While such expenditures are an important indication of the activity of the household, they rarely comprised more than 5 percent of all expenses. Many officers and servants within the household who held positions which entailed frequent travel, were provided money allowances which were factored into the ordinary accounts. Grooms and stable hands, for example, were often given allowances.

While food expenditures were clearly a significant part of the Albrets' total annual outlay, their generally conservative patterns of feasting and their observation of hierarchical patterns of dining checked excessive expenditures. Most important, their use of the purveyorship system gave a measure of stability to the overall structure of their household finances and expenditures which was very important to the achievement of some kind of economic equilibrium. It is to this intriguing system, that we turn next.

II. The Purveyorship System

The quest for refinement, the desire for variety, the difficulty of finding supplies in a nascent market economy, all explain why procuring food for noble households increasingly became a matter for professional middlemen, known as merchant-purveyors. By the sixteenth century, any French aristocrat with a pretension to greatness, and a retinue to match, enlisted the services of the merchant-purveyor in order to regularize the provision of goods to the household.[41] The association between the merchant-purveyor and his noble clients was no casual matter. The terms of the relationship—the responsibilities and duties of each party—were laboriously hammered out before a notary,

---

[40]On the difficulty of establishing percentages from general totals and the subtleties of the accounting system, see Neuschel, *Word of Honor*, 165; and Major, "Noble Income," 25–31.

[41]The majority of these contracts can be found in the Minutier Central des notaires de Paris. See, for example, Baron d'Andouins' contract with Etienne Dubyé, MC CXXII, 1375; Jean, Comte de Soissons with Jean Sergeant, MC VII, 78; Maréchal de Retz with

who witnessed and sealed the agreement, which could run from several paragraphs to several pages.

Several features of these purveyorship contracts make them of critical importance to any discussion of the social and economic fortunes of the great nobility. First and foremost, purveyorship contracts fixed the price at which goods were furnished to noble households. Merchant-purveyors pledged to provide their wares without any augmentation in price for the duration of the contract, an agreement which in theory offered great nobles the same freedom from the day-to-day, season-to-season fluctuations in the marketplace as their country cousins. Second, by guaranteeing and stabilizing household prices purveyorship contracts reinforced the Albrets' traditional seigneurial role as the arbiters and guarantors of the moral economy, and more generally, moral order and social stability. Instead of daily haggling over prices with merchants, it was their responsibility to adjudicate disputes between merchants and producers. Before the Estates, they regularly entertained grievances from local people as well as from merchants complaining that the Albrets' own agents had violated the moral economy. Thus, purveyorship contracts reinforced the Albrets' seigneurial and moral right to regulate the marketplace and protected them from its worst excesses and fluctuations.

Purveyorship contracts regulated the purchase of nearly all foodstuffs and necessities for the Albrets and their household. The fortunate survival of contracts and household accounts for the house of Foix-Navarre-Albret for the period between 1538 and 1595 makes it possible to reexamine the problems of noble expenditure and food prices during a crucial half century of French history.[42] Merchant-purveyors provided meat, bread, fruits, vegetables, spices, and linens at prices, and sometimes in quantities, stipulated in advance.[43] Although it is not always easy to penetrate the legal formalism that often obscures the main text of these agreements, one point emerges clearly; the scions of the house

---

Jean Delastre, MC IX, 144; la duchesse de Nevers with Claude Dubyé, MC XI, 146. I am indebted to Béatrice Véniel, who generously shared the results of her voluminous research on purveyorship and who identified a number of contracts negotiated before Parisian notaries by members of the house of Foix-Navarre-Albret. Béatrice Véniel, "Les marchands pouvoyeurs au XVIe siècle," Thèse, troisième cycle, Université de Paris IV, 1972.

[42] Two of these contracts and household accounts are housed in the Archives Départementales des Pyrénées-Atlantiques, but the majority of contracts can be found in the Minutier Central in Paris.

[43] Purveyorship contracts for fruits, vegetables, spices, and linens no longer exist, but their terms can be deduced from figures and comments in the ordinary and extraordinary accounts of the household.

of Foix-Navarre-Albret were as hard-headed and aggressive in procuring foods and basic necessities as they were in managing land, rents, and royal offices.

The earliest evidence that we have that suggests that the Albrets were using merchant purveyors is a contract between Henri d'Albret and Adam Monnyer, a merchant in meat and fish.[44] Notarized in Pau in 1538, the contract served as the prototype for all future agreements between the Albrets and their merchant purveyors. In the opening clause, Monnyer agreed to follow Albret and his household throughout France and all of the estates and domains of the Albret family. The body of the contract listed the goods that Monnyer agreed to furnish and their prices. The list of goods was, by and large, the longest part of any purveyorship contract because every item was carefully described to ensure that no dispute over weight, quality, or size could arise. And finally any advances, fringe benefits, or pay schedules to which the noble client had agreed were stipulated in careful detail.

Not surprisingly, the 1538 contract bears the imprint of Henri d'Albret's obsession with detail and his dogged pursuit of the smallest financial advantage. Perhaps most notable to the modern mind was the sheer scope of Monnyer's undertaking. By the terms of the contract, the Palois merchant agreed to furnish 187 different kinds of meat and fish upon request throughout the length and breadth of the kingdom of France. A less notable, but arguably more important, feature of the contract was that Albret agreed to make payment for the goods only after they had been furnished to the household. Extant contracts for other court nobles in Paris show that purveyors traditionally demanded substantial advances from their noble clients, in large part because it proved so difficult to collect payment after the fact.[45] Monnyer's willingness to forgo the customary advance speaks both to his faith in his client's fortunes and to some tough bargaining on Albret's part. In any case, it was a privilege that the Albrets would successfully defend in future contracts. The terms of the contract specifically prohibited "any augmentation in prices" for its duration, although Monnyer was granted an escape clause of sorts. A final proviso stipulated his right to renegotiate prices in case of war, when inevitably requisitioning goods would become difficult and prices would rise.

This first contract is a fastidiously tight legal document, written over several pages in a scribbled notarial hand. Yet it is a rude affair

---

[44]AD-PA, B2038.

[45]For example, see A. De Lamothe, "Marché passé entre le prince de Condé et le sieur Dubyé," *Revue des sociétés savantes*, 7 (1874):495–505.

when compared with a contract Jeanne d'Albret negotiated two decades later.[46] Jeanne's 1564 agreement with two Béarnais meat merchants, Nicholas Garnereau and Jacques Rouer, is even longer, tighter, and tougher—a more comprehensive document in every way. First, Garnereau and Rouer pledged to provide their goods and services for four years instead of one—a provision which theoretically protected Jeanne against yearly as well as seasonal price increases. Secondly, vast powers of arbitration were extended to Jeanne's household officers in their daily dealings with the purveyors. By the terms of the contract, they could reject provisions in less than "good and reasonable state," buy better quality goods at the expense of the purveyor, or pay less than contract prices for what they judged to be inferior merchandise. In short, they could claim the right to act as quality inspectors for their mistress. Finally, the contract stipulated, with a vehemency missing in 1538, that provisions were to be available upon request, "without excuse whatever the hour or season."[47] It is difficult to imagine a modern contract that could have delineated the duties of a vendor and the privileges of a buyer any more clearly or specifically.

One rather open-ended clause at the end of the agreement provided the purveyors a measure of flexibility in their association with Jeanne d'Albret. Garnereau and Rouer reserved the right to petition for compensation "if it [were] found that they suffered great, evident or notorious losses."[48] It is important that we not make too much of this clause, and yet not too little. As should be obvious by now, the Albrets attempted to leave their merchant-purveyors as few escape routes as possible, and invariably stipulated somewhere in their contracts that no impediment of time, distance, or season could ever justify late supplies, increased prices, or inferior provisions. These stipulations, they insisted, were the risks of purveyorship. In practice, however, the Albrets could not always enforce such rigorous conditions, especially during the Religious Wars. The first hint of things to come was this "compensation" clause. Little by little, the Albrets began to acknowledge that their purveyors faced potentially crippling difficulties in times of war or crisis, and they consented to consider—at the very least—demands for compensation. Henri d'Albret had agreed to renegotiate with Monnyer in case of war; the 1564 contract provides us with the first suggestion that the disorders and disturbances that plagued

---

[46]AD-PA, E1998.
[47]Ibid.
[48]Ibid.

France by the middle of the sixteenth century might lead to additional changes in the purveyorship contracts.

The vague promise to entertain purveyors' requests for compensation did not mean all such petitions were granted out of hand. When conflicts of interest did arise, purveyors petitioned the maîtres d'hôtel and comptrollers as their first recourse. The obvious bias of these officers, who ultimately depended on the Albrets' good grace for their own advancement, was certainly never open to question.[49] Their main function, after all, was to protect their patrons' interests. But we will never know just how many petitions never made it past the hands of the comptroller. Even after a request was deemed worthy, it had to be forwarded to the Albrets' personal council, which could also withhold approval on one trumped-up pretext or another.[50] The Albrets' officers rarely conceded payments hastily or injudiciously to even the most importunate purveyor.

While the suits were pending, either in the Albrets' personal council or in the great law courts of the land, merchant-purveyors were expected to assume the loss themselves or pass it on to some less suspecting or less powerful farmer or tradesman. Complaints registered by angry farmers and local merchants at the meeting of the Estates of Béarn suggest that purveyors sometimes did try to cut their losses or to circumvent the marketplace altogether by requisitioning their supplies at cut-rate prices.[51] In 1563, one year before Jeanne negotiated with Rouer and Garnereau, farmers around Pau complained vociferously that royal purveyors had used veiled references to their connections, as well as outright threats and intimidation, to commandeer supplies at prices well below the market value.[52] In general, the Albrets greeted such complaints with equanimity. Promises to reprimand their overzealous employees were always tendered, but no move was ever made to settle the claims personally.[53] In the complicated matrix of relationships established directly and indirectly by the purveyorship contracts,

---

[49]Ibid.
[50]Ibid.
[51]AD-PA, C684, fo. 119.
[52]Ibid. Among the complainants was Arnaud d'Andouins of Gan, who testified to the Estates that royal grooms—who often served as purveyors as well as in the stables—were using their position to purchase hay at less than half the asking price in the market. According to Andouins, the grooms had taken 77 *quintaux* of hay from him and paid only 22 *ardits* (5 sols, 6 deniers) instead of the market price of 8 *sols jacques* (11 sols, 6 deniers).
[53]Ibid.

the Albrets were always the last party to experience any effect from rising prices.

It would be easy to argue from the evidence of the purveyorship contracts alone that the Albrets were in an enviable position throughout even the most crisis-filled decades of the sixteenth century. While food prices in the markets at large more than tripled over the course of the century, food prices cited in the Albrets' purveyorship contracts remained remarkably stable. Purveyorship contracts for meat, game, and fish provide the clearest example of this startling phenomenon. From 1538 to 1584—that is, for three generations—purveyors continued to furnish their wares to their Albret clients at roughly the same prices. (see table 4.1) This price stability contrasts sharply with the image of the sixteenth-century seigneur slowly losing purchasing power as grain and food prices rose. Not until 1595 did merchant-purveyors begin to charge prices which reflected the changing conditions in the marketplace. In that year, Catherine de Bourbon contracted with one Georges Seillatz to provide meat and fish to her household at prices three times higher than those paid by her grandfather in 1538—or for that matter, her brother in 1584.[54]

What provoked this sudden and intriguing shift in custom? Unfortunately, the contract itself offers no clear explanation, but a number of plausible answers quickly come to mind. Catherine's recent move to Paris and her intimate activities with the court no doubt prompted the increase in prices, at least in part. In Paris, then as now, everything from personal services to basic necessities generally cost more. Moreover, prices, particularly for food and grain, were not nearly so erratic as was once thought until after 1585, or even as late as the 1590s.[55] Catherine's move to Paris, then, also coincided with one of the periods of greatest economic crisis in sixteenth-century France. More important than these possible explanations, however, is the fact that Catherine's fortunes, had markedly improved by 1595 and easily offset the threefold increase in prices.[56] In fact, the treasurer's account shows Catherine's expenditures for food and other basic necessities represented less of a charge proportionally on the household budget in 1595 than in any year since 1569, when Jeanne d'Albret had initiated her austerity program.

[54]MC XC, 159.
[55]For Parisian prices, see Micheline Baulant and Jean Meuvret, *Prix des céréales extraits de la mercuriale de Paris, 1520–1698*, 2 vols. (Paris: S.E.V.P.E.N., 1960–1962); for the southwest, where prices were generally lower, see Georges and Geneviève Frêche, *Les Prix des grains, des vins, et des légumes à Toulouse, 1468–1868* (Paris: Presses Universitaires de France, 1967).
[56]Major, "Noble Income," 25–40.

III. The Evolution of Purveyorship Contracts during the Religious Wars

The Religious Wars complicated the relationship between merchant-purveyors and their noble clients. While the contracts that the Albrets made with their merchant-purveyors, in general, still ran the length of their terms without renegotiation, the uncertainties of wartime commerce intensified the merchant-purveyors' desire to keep profit margins as high as possible. The apparent price ceiling that appears particularly in meat and fish contracts belies the very real emotion and conflict that often attended settling a contract. Merchant-purveyors clearly did try to increase their prices long before 1595. An extant draft of a contract from 1572, for example, shows that one of the Albrets' most reputable purveyors in meat and fish, Pierre Huart, had every intention of doubling his prices and demanding additional compensation besides.[57] Indeed, Huart proposed a wide range of changes—a three-year contract, a hefty increase in per diem provisions for his aides, and a magnanimous dinner plan for himself including the right to share banqueting honors with Catherine de Bourbon—scarcely any of which were honored in the final contract. On the other hand, Huart did not leave the bargaining table empty-handed. The contract he signed was almost a carbon copy of the very first agreement he had concluded with Catherine's mother, Jeanne d'Albret, with one small, but important difference: the addition of a 4,500-livre bonus, granted to the importunate merchant "out of respect of the expensiveness of provisions and in order to relieve [his] losses."[58]

As the preceding award should make clear, the Albrets had no intention of meeting their purveyors' demands in full, but neither were they anxious to alienate good and faithful servants and creditors. Their aggressive pursuit of the advantage at the bargaining table did not blind them to the fact that generosity, under the right circumstances, was good business; and the Religious Wars provided them with repeated opportunities to demonstrate their largess. Presented with increasingly desperate petitions from merchant-purveyors, who predicted all sorts of grim fates unless their demands were met, the Albrets consented to entertain the demands for some form of compensation with a more open hand. In a recent study of purveyorship in sixteenth-century Paris, Béatrice Véniel has argued that there was a veritable exodus from the purveyorship business in the 1580s and 1590s.[59] By her reckoning, some of the most established purveyors in France simply chose to close up shop rather than risk the very real

[57]MC XXVI, 23–10
[58]Ibid.
[59]Véniel, "Les marchands pourvoyeurs,"146.

physical and financial dangers of purveyorship during wartime. The Albrets' efforts to respond to the inflamatory pressures facing their purveyors tempered the worst effects of the economic crisis and helped preserve patron-client relations.

Broadly speaking, the Albrets adopted three methods of compensation to satisfy their purveyors. The most popular and traditional was the extraordinary bonus which we have already had occasion to consider. The precedent for such awards was established by 1564, and Jeanne d'Albret used this method to compensate several of her merchant-purveyors for their losses during the second and third Religious Wars.[60] By the 1570s and 1580s, however, the Albrets preferred to grant compensation to their merchant-purveyors through a convention known as *le parisis*.[61] In technical terms, this meant that while food prices were figured in *livres tournois* the merchant was paid in *livres parisis*, worth fifteen deniers to the sol instead of twelve.[62] One obvious advantage of this system was that it provided a very rational way of assessing the purveyor's bonus at the end of any given month, or, indeed, for any given day.[63] Eventually, the process was streamlined even further, and it became commonplace to commute the payment to a fixed sum which was supposed to approximate the payment of *le parisis* (or *double parisis* during wartime) for the entire year.[64] Such practice, was the genesis of the 4,500 livres which Catherine de Bourbon agreed to pay Huart in 1572.[65] Besides the ease with which payment could be calculated, the convention of *le parisis* was an appealing method of compensation because it meant no more than a 20 percent addition, except during war, when payment of the *parisis* could be increased to 50 percent of each day's expenditures.[66]

---

[60]For example, see AD-PA, B16, for compensatory payments promised to Nicholas Garnereau in 1569; AD-PA, B19, for bonuses made to Pierre Huart and Authier Joachim Authier, merchants in meat and fish in 1570 and 1571. Short of funds, Jeanne d'Albret made payment on Garnereau's bonus nearly nine months after his death—a fact which probably explains why Garnereau's sole surviving heir so willingly ceded his position as purveyor to Huart and Authier. These two were slightly more fortunate. At one point in their careers, their bonus payments reached 1,200 livres monthly. Altogether, these awards added roughly a 25 (24.5) percent charge on the ordinary expenses of the household in the fall of 1571.

[61]See for example, AD-PA, B84, B2485; MC XXXVI, 23–10.

[62]This eventually became a standard bonus exacted by purveyors throughout France. See, for example, a purveyorship contract for Catherine de Medici, MC XIX, 319.

[63]In the ordinary accounts kept by the kitchen stewards and maîtres d'hôtel, the payment in *le parisis* was always added in daily. See AD-PA, B18.

[64]MC XXXVI, 23–10; AD-PA, B84.

[65]MC XXXVI, 23–10.

Finally, there was a third, less material form of compensation which the Albrets tendered to all of their merchant-purveyors and which reveals even more clearly the Albrets' interest in keeping their purveyors as clients rather than treating them as autonomous market actors. They extended to purveyors the privileges of household service and its attendant perquisites. In legal terms, merchant-purveyors were often considered members of the household; they were frequently enrolled on the civil lists and given an honorific salary.[67] As a result of these measures, they enjoyed all the financial benefits of royal service, including exemption from the taille, forced loans, and contributions, as well as numerous opportunities for social advancement.[68] Like many enterprising place-seekers, purveyors used their positions to advance their social as well as their financial fortunes. The meteoric rise of purveyors like Pierre Huart, who after only two years in service could safely style himself the seigneur de Gravier in legal documents, testifies to some of the more elusive compensations of service.[69] Even more impressive is the career of Henri Mocet, who began as one of Huart's servant-accountants in 1572. By 1600, Mocet found himself in a prominent position in the royal court in Paris, saw family members in prestigious positions in the royal household, and eventually lived to see a great nephew marry the daughter of a minor noble.[70]

Despite the protestations of concern and promises of compensation that were issued by the Albrets during the Religious Wars, there is very little to suggest that the position of the merchant-purveyors changed significantly for the better. The Albrets continued to insist on certain privileges, including, most importantly, the right to furnish payment and compensation only after the provisions had been purchased. In theory, they agreed to pay for their provisions at the end of each month, at which time compensatory bonuses, such as *le parisis*, were also doled out. In reality, it was sometimes years before the purveyors were paid in full. And the constant financial drain of the Religious Wars did nothing to improve this state of affairs. By the 1570s, a steady flurry of decrees, promissory notes, and letters were issued from the comptrol-

---

[66]See the ordinary accounts of the maîtres d'hôtel.

[67]See AD-PA, B16, B48bis, B91, B144, B154, B157, B160, etc. Salaries that were obviously an honorific flourish began at 5 livres early in the sixteenth century and gradually increased to 12 livres. In 1593, those merchants who followed Henri to Paris enjoyed a substantial increase to 200 livres. But initially, salaries were the least significant part of the benefits merchant-purveyors derived from household service.

[68]BN, Collection Clairambault, 360, fo. 261.

[69]MC XC, 121, August 1, 1572.

[70]MC XC, 121; AD-PA, B2561; BN Carrés d'Hozier, Mocet.

ler's officers.[71] Most correspondence promised prompt payment from the first available sources of income. Some went so far as to assign the revenues from certain seigneuries to cover a particular debt to a purveyor.[72] Yet even with such expedients, many payments were made on debts years overdue.[73] Not surprisingly, such practices could create tremendous tensions between the Albrets and their purveyors. The ill-feeling that lack of payment could engender sometimes led purveyors to take legal action, which ironically often dragged out the payment process even longer.

As Lawrence Stone has pointed out, the litigious behavior of members of the English nobility depleted many a patrimonial fortune.[74] But it is difficult to assess the impact of lawsuits on the Albret fortune. It is doubtful that the Albrets welcomed legal entanglements, particularly ones not of their own design. On the other hand, all available evidence suggests that legal fees were almost always a very insignificant part of their total expenditures and that legal action rarely intimidated the Albrets into making payment.[75]

The checkered careers of Jean and Etienne Choisné, who served as merchant-bakers to Navarre for nearly a decade, illustrates the tremendous difficulties and frustrations that purveyors could face in trying to collect payment from their highly placed clients. Both Jean and Etienne, brothers and merchants from the Vendômois, entered Navarre's service in 1574.[76] The details of the very first contract that they signed with Navarre can only be deduced from the household records and from later contracts which still exist.[77] No doubt, as in later contracts, they agreed to furnish both *pain blanc* for Navarre and the household officers and *pain commun* for the menial servants, with a promise to demand no augmentation in price or compensation "except *le parisis*...if the King [Navarre] goes to war." They predictably agreed to supply only the finest quality bread, free of any cheap fillers, with the certain promise that any reductions in quality would mean a concomitant reduction in price. For his part, Navarre understandably

---

[71]For evidence of the increasing difficulties of purveyorship and the Albrets' attempts to satisfy the demands of their creditors, see AD-PA, B16, B2289, B2318, B2350, B2388, B2549.

[72]See, for example, AD-PA, B2388.

[73]AD-PA, B2289, B2549. As one purveyor complained, the coffers of the general treasurer were chronically "short of funds," AD-PA, B2350.

[74]Stone, *Crisis of the Aristocracy*, 240–42.

[75]Fees for legal suits, for example, are rarely recorded in the general treasuries.

[76]AD-PA, B2388.

[77]For examples of the contracts the Albrets negotiated with their merchant-bakers, see AD-PA, B2485, B2530; and MC XXIV, 38.

promised steady monthly payments. Within a few months of the signing of the contract, however, the Huguenot leader had begun to default on payments. In all fairness, the Choisnés were paid more frequently and regularly than most merchant-purveyors in Navarre's employ. In 1576, for instance, the maître d'hôtel recorded thirty-five separate installment payments to Jean Choisné. Even so, by the end of that year, Navarre still owed the merchant more than 1,000 livres for provisions and another 1,500 livres for miscellaneous loans to the household.[78] That Choisné could make impromptu loans to household officers suggests that the merchant was hardly cash-poor, but that did not lessen his desire to recover what was owed him, particularly as payments in arrears were mounting. By 1578, Choisné held promissory notes worth 13,480 livres, a figure which represented nearly two years' provisions.[79]

The Choisné brothers doggedly pursued every opportunity to collect the outstanding sums, including confronting the individual *fermiers* whose revenues had been assigned to their account. In 1577, for instance, Jean Choisné journeyed to Agen to claim payment from the fabled Huguenot Toulousain merchant, Pierre Assezat, who, as farmer-general of the Albret estates in Navarre, had been named paymaster for part of his patron's debt.[80] During the highly-charged encounter that followed, Assezat insisted that the Navarre treasury was empty, denied that he bore any personal responsibility as farmer-general of Navarre for the private debts of his master, and refused to honor the 2,000-livre promissory note that Choisné had carried with him. Exasperated, the merchant-baker appealed to the Agenois seneschal, who commanded Assezat to pay up in three days.[81] Even so, the wily Toulousain again refused to make payment and eventually his obdurate demeanor forced Choisné into a higher court of appeal. In October, Choisné took his case to Navarre, who refused to take sides against either of his employees or acknowledge the debt as his responsibility any longer.[82] Instead, he ordered Choisné to take the whole suit to the Parlement of Bordeaux. Two years later, the 2,000 livres was still outstanding on the Choisnés' accounts.[83] In other words, Jean Choisné had been given a first-rate runaround.

This embarrassing debacle did not end the Choisné brothers' determination to go to any lengths to recover outstanding payments from

[78]AD-PA, B2388.
[79]Ibid.
[80]AD-PA, B2318.
[81]Ibid.
[82]Ibid.
[83]AD-PA, B2388.

the house of Foix-Navarre-Albret. In 1582, in an effort to resolve an unpaid account worth 1,015 livres, Jean Choisné once again took his grievances to the Parlement of Bordeaux.[84] But as the events of 1582 reveal, he elected to attack the problem from a different angle. The man he sued was none other than Louis La Fons, the general treasurer for the entire fortunes of the house of Foix-Navarre-Albret. In private, La Fons joked that if every treasurer in France were held personally responsible for the private debts of his master, "there would never be anyone to take the position."[85] But in a moving deposition before the court, the Choisnés' lawyer claimed that La Fons, as chief minister to Navarre, was ultimately responsible for the private debts of his patron, who as a member of the royal house of Navarre, clearly could not be legally pressed to settle. The Choisnés' lawyer took La Fons to task because the treasurer had paid other household servants, dispensed with other minor debts, and exhausted the treasury before attempting to pay the large sums owed to merchant-purveyors. In his closing statement, he warned that unless purveyors were paid more regularly the entire system would fold. "If they are not paid," he remarked pragmatically, "they will not be able to continue."[86] Despite this grim prediction, the Choisnés' second attempt to win a judgment in their favor ended no more conclusively than the first. Disgruntled and frustrated, the Choisné brothers left Navarre's employ in 1583.[87] In the dense judicial maze of the Old Regime, wronged purveyors often had little recourse before the law.

The rapidly changing roster of merchant-bakers who served the Albret households in the 1580s and 1590s suggests the particular difficulties these purveyors faced during the last two decades of the Religious Wars.[88] In some parts of France, troop movements impeded the smooth transport of grain; in others, "rebels" of either party razed and burned harvest fields and created grave shortages.[89] The spate of

---

[84] AD-PA, B2350.
[85] Ibid.
[86] Ibid.
[87] I cannot determine the exact date of their departure. However, the ordinary accounts for Catherine's household show that a new merchant-baker, Pierre Seillatz, was furnishing bread to the household in 1584. Seillatz continued to serve as purveyor to the household of Catherine de Bourbon in one capacity or another for the next two decades and was rewarded for his loyal service with an extraordinary donation of 600 livres in 1598. See AD-PA, B111, B142. For his contract to supply meat and fish to Catherine in 1598, see Le Blant, "Marché de viande et de poisson pour Catherine de Bourbon," *126–41*.
[88] For a partial list of the purveyors who furnished bread to Catherine's household, see AD-PA, B22, B111, B136, B2350, and MC XXIV, 38; for those who serviced Navarre,
[89] AD–Haute-Garonne, B107, B144, B152, B160, B162.

decrees issued by the Parlement of Toulouse proscribing the exportation of grain from Languedoc to Béarn under threat of death testifies to the seriousness of the grain shortage in the southwest in the 1580s.[90] In temporary retreat in La Rochelle in the fall of 1586, even Navarre was pressed to interject a note of grim realism in an otherwise pretty billet-doux to his belle Corisande: "Consider the plight of Champagne and Burgundy," he wrote, "where a horseload of wheat is worth fifty livres to Paris' thirty."[91] Indeed over much of France, rising grain prices produced panic in 1586 and reports circulated concerning half-starved vagrants who in desperation ate unripened wheat in the fields and "threatened to eat [the owners] too, if they would not allow them to eat grain."[92]

In the face of such chronic market instability during the Religious Wars, merchant-purveyors of bread were reluctant to commit to a prix fixe for several years and yearly contracts became the rule rather than the exception.[93] With greater and greater frequency, merchants followed the Choisnés' lead and left the Albrets' employ to pursue more lucrative ventures. Contracts of short duration, however, not only benefited the merchant-purveyor; they could also serve the advantage of the noble patron if prices declined.[94] In 1586 and 1587, for example, the strict efforts of the *parlementaires* of Toulouse to fend off crisis and protect the grain harvest succeeded in keeping grain and bread prices lower around Toulouse than in much of the rest of France.[95] Perhaps as a result, Navarre was able to negotiate a contract with his merchant-bakers in which the prix fixe actually declined almost 10 percent.[96]

Of all the purveyorship contracts that were negotiated by the Albrets, the most perceptible rise in prices took place in those for fruit,

---

see AD-PA, B100, B113, B118, B130, and B2350; for purposes of comparison, note the long terms of service that marked the careers of Jeanne d'Albret's merchant-bankers, AD-PA, B6, B18, B22, B23, B144.

[90]Ibid.
[91]*Recueil des lettres missives de Henri IV*, I: 224–25.
[92]Pierre de L'Estoile, *Mémoires journaux de Pierre de L'Estoile*, 12 vols. (Paris: Lemerk, 1878), 2:353.
[93]See, for example, AD-PA, B2485.
[94]Such was the case when Catherine de Bourbon renewed her contract with Romcay and de la Haye at 8 sols deniers instead of the nine sols that she had paid in 1575, MC XXIV, 38.
[95]Frêche, *Les Prix de grains*, 1: 224–25.
[96]AD-PA, B42, B72, B100.

vegetables, and linens. (see table 4.7) Bread prices, by comparison, look almost stable. We must be careful, however, to attribute price changes, both increases and decreases, to the proper causes. Greengrocers and launderers contracted to supply their wares annually in fixed quantities for one lump sum, which the household accountants then divided and added daily to the kitchen accounts.[97] Consequently, the costs cited in the ordinary accounts were not the price paid per item, but the price paid per diem. Between 1571 and 1589, per diem costs for fruits, greens, and bath linens doubled. In the same period, the complement of servants, officers, and *fidèles* that the Albrets employed on the civil lists also increased dramatically.[98] Thus, per diem costs rose in part because of the increase in household size, which in turn can be attributed to the political designs and social maneuverings discussed earlier.

IV. Wine and Other Bacchanalian Pleasures

Of all the basic necessities furnished to the household, only wine was exempt from the price protection of the purveyorship contracts. For reasons that are not clear, the Albrets preferred to buy directly from local wine merchants and noble *vignerons* at the established market rate (*suivant le taxe*) in each locality where they set up court. Supplementary rolls, kept by the wine stewards to aid the comptrollers who reconciled the ordinary accounts at the end of each month, noted the contribution of each local merchant, who, in theory, received satisfaction before the royal household moved on.[99] As the survival of numerous promissory notes issued to local merchants testifies, theory rarely coincided with practice.

In the absence of contractual arrangements, merchants could haggle with household comptrollers and stewards about the proper price for their precious product. Notable is the unctuous 1581 petition of a Palois merchant, Arnaud Guilhem. Having furnished three *barriques* and two *barricots* of wine at the set rate of 27 livres per *barrique* for Navarre's service in June 1581, Guilhem claimed he was entitled to additional compensation because the barrels of Jurançon that he had furnished were bigger ("according to the custom of Jurançon") and better than those furnished by his local fellow merchants. In relatively quick order, the comptroller agreed that Guilhem's barrel had contained more wine and a supplementary payment was granted within

---

[97]See, for example, AD-PA, B18, B26, B42, B72, B100.
[98]AD-PA, B16, B2374.
[99]See, for example, the demand for payment by Arnauld Guilhem for wine furnished to Henry and household in Pau and Eaux Chaudes during a 1581 sojourn, AD-PA, B2390.

Table 4.7 *Marchés De Pourvoirie* House of Foix-Navarre-Albret: 1571-1589

Item Provided	1571	1575[a]	1576[a]	1576	1579	1583	1586	1589
Bread per dozen	6s[b]	9s[c]	8s 6d[c]	8s[b]	8s[b]	8s[b]	7s 6d[b]	9s[b]
Greens per day	22s 6d	—	—	42s 6d	42s 6d	33s	33s	35s
Fruit per day	39s	—	—	75s	75s	75s	75s	80s
table linens per day	30s	—	—	43s	37s 6d	6£ 11s 6d	6£ 11s 6d	6£ 17s
Bath linens per day	30s	—	—	60s	70s	55s	55s	55s
Total[d]	5£ 7s 6d	—	—	11£ 8s 6d	15£ 13s	15£ 2s 6d	15£ 2s 6d	15£ 7s

Source, respectively by year: AD-PA,B18; MCXXIV,38; MCXXIV,38; AD-PA,B26; AD-PA,B42; AD-PA,B72; AD-PA,B100; AD-PA,B130.

[a] Figures from a contract for the provision of bread to the household of Catherine de Bourbon
[b] The weight of each loaf was regulated at 9 ounces
[c] The weight of each loaf was regulated at 8 ounces
[d] All figures are in livre tournois, sols tournois, and derniers

two months of the request.[100] Not all petitions for additional payment, though, were settled as quickly as Guilhem's.

As Guilhem's case suggests, the prices which the Albrets paid for wine varied enormously not only from region to region, but even within the same locality. Quality and quantity could be used by merchants to increase their price and circumvent established market rates. Certainly, variation in price in one locale must be attributed to difference in quality and quantity. The hearty Chalosse that Navarre drank in Pau cost less (10.5s. per *setier*) than the more delicate and prized Jurançon (16s.8d. per *setier*).[101]

Beyond the qualitative differences in wine we could certainly expect to find, there were vast regional differences in price to which the household budget was adjusted, whether for better or worse, in the absence of a purveyor's contract. Extracts from the expense accounts and extant wine lists compiled by stewards show as much as a threefold increase in one year in prices paid for ordinary red wine. In January 1582, for example, the maîtres d'hôtel paid 8£.10s. for one barrel of red wine at Casteljaloux. One month later in Saint Jean d'Angely a barrel of claret cost 13£. 10s. Five months later Sieur de Berthonie furnished several barrels of red wine to Navarre and his household and charged only 5£.10s. per barrel. (see table 4.8) As a wine list from Agen indicates, sometimes a bargain was struck with wine producers and merchants in one locality, who furnished drink at a fixed price (once harvest prices had stabilized) from late fall until the next harvest in September or October, making for some stability in wine prices.[102]

Records indicate that the Albrets continued to draw on the same pool of merchants and nobles to provide drink to the household. When Navarre sojourned at the court in Paris in 1576, he employed the services of Henri Meslée and Jean de la Pelonnier, styled "merchants of Paris who followed the court."[103] But he was not truly pressed to mimic royal practice in this matter until sometime after he became king of France. Ordinary accounts show that Navarre continued to commandeer wine from local merchants on his travels through France until sometime after 1589. The earliest extant purveyorship contract for wine for Henri's household dates from 1608.[104]

[100]AD-PA, B2390, B2561.

[101]AD-PA, B2341.
[102]AD-PA, B2424.
[103]AD-PA, B26.

Table 4.8 Wines Furnished to the King of Navarre, 1582 (in *livres tournois*)

Wine Type	Source	Month	Place	Price per barrique
Claret	de Legle	January	Casteljaloux	8£ 10s
Blanc	de Legle	January	Casteljaloux	9£ 10s
Claret/Blanc	de Nouveau	February	Creon	10£
Claret	—	February	Coutras	5£ 10s
Claret	Thomas	February	Jarnac	6£
Claret	—	February	St. Jean d'Angely	13£ 10s
Blanc	—	April	Surgeres	8£
Blanc	—	April	La Rochelle	12£
Claret	—	April	La Rochelle	7£
Blanc de bouche	—	May	Pau	8£ 2s
Claret	de Berthonie	June	St. Jean d'Angely	5£ 10s
Blanc	Bonnet	June	St. Jean d'Angely	5£ 10s
Claret	—	October	Nérac	10£
Blanc	—	October	Nérac	10£
Claret	—	October	Nérac	11£ 12s
Claret	—	October	Nérac	13£ 4s
Claret	—	November	Nérac	7£ 10s
Blanc	—	November	Nérac	7£ 10s
Source: AD-PA, B56				

Apart from the wine purchased from local merchants and consumed on location by the household, the Albrets sometimes drank from their own stores when in residence at one of their many châteaux, a practice which the maîtres d'hôtel scrupulously noted in the ordinary accounts. This *vin du cave*, however, accounted for only a small portion of total household consumption. In January 1572, for example, while holding court in Nérac, Jeanne d'Albret and her household drank no wine from the castle cellars.[105] In January and February 1576 at

[104] MC XC, 167, December 27, 1607. By the terms of this contract, Vincent Toituer, merchant in wine, living on Rue St. Denys in Paris, agreed to furnish wine for one year at 96 livres for *vin de table* and 48 livres for *vin commun*.

[105] AD-PA, B23.

Nérac, Navarre's wine stewards provided drink for the table by purchasing wine from the usual suppliers—local merchants and nobles—but they also used wine from the castle cellar. Nonetheless, wine stores in the château cellar used at no daily cost to Navarre and household came to only 9.9 percent of the total wine consumption of the household for the months of January and February.[106] Later, in June 1579, Navarre and his train sojourned in Pau for seventeen days and drank 700 *setiers* of claret and white wine from his cellars out of a total 1,282 *setiers* consumed. More than half (54.6 percent) of the drink then came from the royal cellars free of immediate cost.[107] This large consumption of household wine supplies, however, was unusual. In the fall of 1579, Henri spent another long period at Nérac. Of the more than 5,000 *setiers* of claret that slaked his thirst and that of his attendants and servants, only 66 *setiers,* or 1.6 percent, came from the castle stores.[108] In September 1582, another 1,625 *setiers* of choice Jurançon and Chalosse were consumed—all of it purchased from the vineyards of Béarnais notables and nobles.[109] Clearly, wine from the castle stores amounted to only a small percentage of total consumption during sojourns in Pau and Nérac and an infinitesimal percentage of total consumption annually.

It is tempting to assume that the wine from the cellars came from the domanial vineyards, and occasionally designations in the ordinary accounts—*clairet de la vigne*—support this contention.[110] Other wine not so designated may in fact have been purchased from merchants, stored in castle cellars for later use, and entered on the household accounts much later. For example, an extant contract with François Cauterac, a merchant from Calignac, notes the provision of seventy-two barrels of wine put in the cellar of the castle at Nérac in 1579.[111] Less problematic are the gifts of wine made to the royal family. During a stay in Lectoure, Jeanne and her train drank barrels of wine at the behest of her host. In Layarc, Petit Paire from Agen gave a barrel of white wine to the Queen to celebrate her ceremonial entry into the city. In Périgueux, La Dame de Chaluz also made a lavish gift of two barrels of wine to the Queen of Navarre.[112] Although these gifts indicate one of

[106] AD-PA, B26.
[107] AD-PA, B42.
[108] AD-PA, B43.
[109] AD-PA, B65.
[110] AD-PA, B42, June 16, 1579.
[111] AD-PA, B2561.
[112] AD-PA, B23.

the interesting prerogatives of nobility, they account for a negligible portion of the total consumption of the household.

Both in symbolic and economic terms, wine played a significant role in the Albrets' fortunes. Within Henri de Navarre's own lifetime, the charming story circulated that his first taste of wine was the Jurançon his grandfather, Henri d'Albret, dribbled on his infant lips at birth. And thus, the Jurançon of Béarn, like the viscounty itself, became identified with the house of Foix-Navarre-Albret in the popular imagination. Wine was often exchanged as gifts between nobles, too. Both its sacramental use and its pleasurable effect made wine a prized commodity and a significant charge on the Albrets' food budget. In financial terms, wine was the second heaviest food charge after meat on the monthly journals. In the absence of purveyorship contracts, seasonal and regional price fluctuations significantly affected the Albrets' wine expenditures. Regardless of price, wine, like bread, considered one of the staples of human life, continued to be purchased and drunk in great quantities.

V. Conclusion

In 1548, Henri d'Albret's total annual expenditure came to 94,636£. 13s. 1d.[113] Forty years later, Navarre's expense for food and other basic necessities alone exceeded this by over 20,000 livres, amounting to 115,582 livres.[114] Rising prices explain this heavy food charge, but only in part, as the contained costs of the purveyorship contracts show. We need simply to look at the household rolls to find the other reason for the increasingly large figures that food charges represented on the annual budget: Navarre, with a household of 300 plus servants, soldiers, and dignitaries, was routinely feeding and entertaining three times as many people as his grandfather had done, with a household numbering 117 at midcentury. During periods of crisis, the Albrets were not above reducing their complement of servants to reduce expenses, and other efforts were made to keep food expenses in check, including the designation of cheaper bread and wine for menial servants and lesser officers in the household.[115] Even the small daily stipend some officers received in lieu of *bouche à court*, actually decreased for a time during the 1580s when campaigning left Navarre in difficult straits.[116]

---

[113] AD-PA, B160.
[114] AD-PA, E300.
[115] See Flandrin, *Families in Former Times*, 105.
[116] AD-PA B113, B118.

Until the 1590s, purveyorship contracts protected the family fortunes from the volatile swings and inflationary trends of the sixteenth-century economy. However the demand of war, the militarization of Navarre's household, and the inflationary swings of the last decade of the sixteenth century produced strains on the family finances that even purveyorship contracts could not contain. In addition, the Albrets continued to observe the traditional Catholic rituals of feast and fast abandoned by their poorer confreres because the fish proscribed by the Catholic Church was such a delicacy. The pull of convention thus also compromised the Albrets' efforts toward solvency as we will see more fully in the next chapter.

Five

The Burden of Status

"All aristocratic life in the later Middle Ages," observed Johann Huizinga, "was a wholesale attempt to act the vision of a dream. In cloaking itself in the fanciful brilliance of heroism and the probity of a past age, the life of nobles elevated itself toward the sublime."[1] Sixteenth-century noblemen, like their medieval counterparts, recognized the intimate interplay between power and conspicuous display. Indeed many historians recently have argued that magnificence and display became an even more crucial source of noble identity and distinction from the sixteenth century onward as many of the familiar touchstones and bonds of feudal society vanished beneath the pressures of civil and religious disorder.[2] Most great noblemen subscribed to the principle that "power required magnificence in order to achieve its objectives of assent and respect,"[3] and they spared no expense in order to convince their vassals and aristocratic rivals of the power that they claimed to possess. In an era when priests taught their illiterate parishioners the incontrovertible verities of the Gospels with the aid of statuary, stained glass, and richly embroidered tapestries, nobles conveyed potent visual messages of power and prestige to their followers through extravagant ceremony and display.[4]

---

[1] Huizinga, *The Waning of the Middle Ages*, 41.
[2] Harding, *Anatomy of a Power Elite*, 21–31.
[3] Bergin, *Cardinal Richelieu*, 6.
[4] On the function of ceremony and ritual in the creation of political power, see Ralph Giesey, *The Royal Funeral Ceremony in Renaissance France* (Geneva: Librairie Droz, 1962) and *Cérémonial et puissance souveraine, France, Xe-XVIIe siècles* (Paris: Armand Colin, 1987); also Lawrence Bryant, *The King and the City in the Parisian Royal Entry Ceremony: Politics, Ritual, and Art in the Renaissance* (Geneva: Librairie Droz, 1986).

Magnificence and display may also have fulfilled another crucial political function in the sixteenth century. Joseph Bergin and Daniel Dessert have both recently argued that the conspicuous extravagance of Cardinal Richelieu and Nicholas Fouquet, Louis XIV's ill-fated superintendent of finance, served to assure their creditors and those of the Crown that the monarchy was a sound credit risk in the seventeenth century.[5] In much the same way that modern economists assess the recovery of a recessionary economy by analyzing the strength of consumer confidence, early modern bureaucrats, who often loaned much of their own money to the royal treasurer, spent money prodigiously in order to convince royal creditors of their own personal solvency, and by extension, the stability of royal finances. In other words, they spent money in order to attract more. It is reasonable to suspect that similar motives may have inspired the French aristocrats of the sixteenth century, who were also scrambling around the courts and great banking houses of Europe for funds to support either the Huguenot cause or the Catholic League. Frequently pledging their own wealth as collateral, they no doubt wanted quite literally to appear worth the investment. Renaissance exuberance, then, may have been more than the sign of a boorish and profligate nobility at play; it was often a shrewd confidence game played by nobles to attract creditors and therefore a reasonable credit policy.

Conspicuous display may well have been a necessary complement to power in the early modern period, but it also posed one of the greatest threats to the maintenance of that power and influence. According to contemporaries, it was this love of magnificence which more than anything else ruined many venerable old families in France. In 1567, the Venetian ambassador, Jerome Lippomano, penned a scathing indictment of French aristocrats at court, who not only spent their own wealth, "but that of others," on foolish fripperies, gluttonous banquets, and horses.[6] More recently, Denis Crouzet, backed by a dazzling array of statistics, has offered a similar analysis of the French aristocracy of the sixteenth century. According to Crouzet, "the exuberance of the French Renaissance, the taste for objets d'art, and the desire to cut the appropriate figure in a court society fascinated by external prestige" was the single most important reason for the paralyzing indebtedness of the aristocracy on the eve of the Wars of Religion.[7] Like the Nevers family whom Crouzet has studied, the Albrets

---

[5]Daniel Dessert, "L'Affaire Fouquet," *L'Histoire* 32 (1981):46; Bergin, *Cardinal Richelieu*, 6.
[6]As quoted in Crouzet, "Recherches sur la crise," 11.
[7]Ibid.

provide an interesting case study of the relationships among power, consumption, and indebtedness. Drawn into the very center of religious politics and court life in sixteenth-century France, the Albrets engaged in the traditional noble patterns of conspicuous consumption against a background of conflicting tensions and changing values. While it would be much too simplistic to argue that there was an inverse relationship between the growing intensity of the Albrets' commitment to the Huguenot party and the extent of their indulgence in the cultural and material conventions of the Valois court, religious sensibilities did shape the Albrets' expenditures on material goods and luxuries in important ways. Male- and female-headed households also produced different structural patterns of conspicuous expenditure which are particularly meaningful for the discussion of the escalation of courtly refinement and the love of luxury among the nobility. Thus, beyond asking what percentage of the Albrets' total capital outlay went for luxuries, and whether they experienced a crisis of indebtedness, we must also examine the purpose and design of their spending habits. Did expenditures on luxuries fluctuate during the sixteenth century and why? How did they express their status and rank while on the road or at court, far from any obvious territorial expression of their sovereign and seigneurial power? And did they significantly vary their show of status and wealth when on their estates?

I. Adorning the Body

According to Achille Luchaire, it was the love of luxury and sartorial splendor which "devoured" the feudal revenues of the house of Foix-Navarre-Albret in the fifteenth century.[8] The extent to which clothing, jewelry, and other accoutrements of personal adornment absorbed a major share of the Albrets' medieval fortunes reflects their tremendous importance as markers of social status. Sumptuary laws had long linked certain materials, colors, and cuts of clothing with nobility and rank; as well, the medieval church had drawn potent associations between rank and color. Sixteenth-century nobles exploited such associations to enhance their own personal status and to delineate the extent of their power and influence over the human community over which they exercised lordship. Gifts of clothing and jewelry were among the most common means of recognizing and publicizing personal ties in noble society. Nobles routinely bestowed gifts of clothing on their friends; they noted significant events in the lives of their

---

[8]Luchaire, *Alain le Grand*, 53.

officers and servants by giving clothing as well; and they marked their control over the young nobles in their household by dressing them in livery, often emblazoned with their family crest.[9] Even horses and dogs wore livery, thus identifying them with their master.[10]

As Kristen Neuschel has argued, personal adornment became an even more significant indicator of noble identity in early modern France as other claims of noble status—office, pensions, and clientage—were challenged and as patterns of courtly culture and consumption changed.[11] Clothes, jewelry, horses, and carriages magnified the physical stature and, thus, the political standing of nobles, transforming otherwise ordinary-looking men and women into mythic heroes whose magnificence commanded obedience and respect. On the occasion of Jeanne d'Albret and Antoine de Bourbon's first ceremonial entry into the city of Limoges as the duke and duchess of Périgord, the civic recorder rhapsodized that

> [Bourbon arrived] dressed in a rich tunic with sleeves of cloth of silver and gold buttons....he rode a beautiful white horse, the handsomest ever seen...[while] the Queen of Navarre, dressed in a cloth of gold trimmed in ermine...[was] also riding on a white horse.[12]

The ability to dress in the finest clothes, trimmed in the rarest material, also testified to the economic power wielded by the great nobility. And clothes, unlike châteaux, were easily portable symbols of a noble's status. Even so, over the course of the sixteenth century, a surprisingly small portion of Albrets' wealth went to clothes and other "dead-end" wealth; much more significant were their investments in jewels and jewelry, which could be sold, pawned, or used as collateral far more easily than could land.

In many ways, Henri d'Albret's habits and patterns of consumption during his early years at court reveal a young man caught between the military passions of the Middle Ages and the courtly refinements of the Renaissance. Achille Luchaire's projection of Henri d'Albret's expenditures at court for the year 1518, for example, suggests that a remarkably small percentage of his total income was devoted to clothing and other courtly refinements. According to Luchaire's calculations, Henri's

---

[9]See Neuschel, *Word of Honor*, 168.
[10]Jacques Laprade, ed., "Un inventaire des tentures et des meubles transportés de Pau à Nérac en 1578," *Bibliothèque d'humanisme et Renaissance: Travaux et documents* 24 (1962):413–30.
[11]Neuschel, *Word of Honor*, 168; idem, "Noble households," 621.
[12]Roelker, *Queen of Navarre*, 112.

annual expenditures amounted to slightly over 30,000 livres, but of this total sum, only 3,000 livres was earmarked for clothes, horses, and other "extraordinary" expenses.[13] Thus, he expended slightly less than 10 percent of his entire budget on goods which contemporary observers and recent historians have argued were at the root of the aristocratic crisis of the sixteenth century.

Over the course of the sixteenth century, the Albrets permitted themselves more luxuries as the family fortunes increased. Household officials recorded expenditures on clothes, jewelry, horses, and other special purchases and activities in "extraordinary accounts," to distinguish such purchases from the basic daily necessities recorded in the ordinary accounts.[14] Jeanne d'Albret (1556–1572) steadily increased her spending on luxuries. (see table 5) From 1556 to 1565, expenses recorded on the extraordinary rolls rose from 10,000 livres to over 30,000 livres annually, accounting for almost 30 percent of her total capital outlay. But as we have seen already, Jeanne was never reluctant to scale down expenditures in order to remain financially solvent. Thus in 1569, facing rebellion in her viscounty of Béarn and among various French fiefs, Jeanne ordered her officials to make budgetary cuts across the board, including staff and food expenditures. But it was Jeanne's efforts to eliminate luxury spending that produced the most dramatic results. Extraordinary expenditures plummeted from an all-time high of 36,382 livres in 1565 to just 8,872 livres in 1569 accounting for less than 10 percent of her total capital outlay, comparable to the outlay of Henri d'Albret in 1518.

For much of 1570 and 1571 Jeanne remained in La Rochelle and its environs, presiding over the brilliant assembly of Huguenot nobles who had taken refuge in the Protestant port at the outbreak of the third Religious War. The extraordinary rolls list numerous expenses which might be considered frivolous, particularly in the midst of a bitter war: a watch of gold, studded with diamonds and rubies, and imported from

---

[13] AD-PA, E561.

[14] The care with which the household officer, who kept the accounts, scrupulously detailed and described the goods purchased, down to the last button and thread, also reflects the value attached to material things and the human services that provided them. The description of materials purchased for one dress or doublet could run for several pages and conveyed not only a sense of the commodities purchased, but also the labor involved in producing the final product. See, for example, AD-PA, B21, fos. 14–18, where materials purchased for dresses and doublets furnished to chambermaids and pages were described. For a discussion of the relationship between value and labor in preindustrial economies, see the collection of essays in Arjun Appadurai, ed., *The Social Lofe of Things: Commodities in Cultural Perspective* (Cambridge: Cambridge University Press, 1986); also Neuschel, *Word of Honor*, 162–73; and idem, "Noble Households," 608–9.

Table 5 Extraordinary Expenditures in the Treasurer's Accounts[a]

Year[b]	Total Payments	Extraordinary	Percentage Expenses
1518	30,404	3,000	9.9
1556	64,879	10,211	15.7
1559	100,672	21,792[c]	21.6
1565	124,870	36,682	29.4
1569	92,871	8,872	9.6
1572[d]	206,205	83,866	40.7
1576	66,021	20,641[e]	31.3
1579	75,522	22,728	30.1
1582[f]	447,146	40,587	9.1
1587[f]	615,199	37,600	6.1
1584	58,054	6,619	11.4
1590	92,922	14,207	15.3
1595*	363,139	38,718[g]	10.7
AD-PA Source, respectively by year: E561, B6, B144, B13, B15, B35, B32, B48bis, B157, B160, B111, B135, B137			

[a]in livres tournois.
[b]Fiscal year in most accounts ran from January 1 to December 31.
[c]Includes Henri de Navarre's extraordinary expenses, which are calculated separately.
[d]Account runs only for six months; Jeanne d'Albret died May 1572.
[e]Includes extraordinary expenses: *argenterie et menus plaisirs*.
[f]Henri de Navarre's accounts; the rest following Jeanne d'Albret's death are for Catherine de Bourbon.
[g]Not included in the quarterly extraordinary rolls were 12,424 livres spent to purchase furniture for Catherine's Parisian apartment.
*Account originally in écus, translated into livres at the rate of 1:3.

Paris; a silver cage; and a Spanish horse. Equally interesting is an entry for 493 livres paid to one Michel Beranger, the treasurer general of Henri's household, "for having brought and conducted from the city of Paris to the city of La Rochelle a certain quantity of silverplate."[15] There is little question that some of these purchases were fripperies with which to wile away time within the sturdy ramparts of La Rochelle, but the silverplate, undoubtedly, served a more practical purpose. For generations the Albrets had hocked their silverplate or melted it down in order to fund their forays into and around Haute-

---

[15]Raymond, "Notes extraites des comptes de Jeanne d'Albret," 12(1867):178–80.

Navarre, and there is little question that this purpose was the fate of the silverplate Henri requested from his apartments in Paris.[16] The extraordinary accounts from 1571 also bear testimony to Jeanne's efforts to settle long outstanding debts to creditors. Notable is the payment of 780 livres to Henri de Vous, for "certain large books and tomes on portraiture which were delivered to the deceased King Henri, father of the Queen, without having been paid for."[17] Numerous war-related charges—soldiers' pensions and salaries—also measurably increased expenditures.

Two or three years of economizing could not resolve the enormous debts which had accumulated from years of conspicuous consumption—some dating back to the time of Alain le Grand and which frequently amounted to well over 20 percent of expenditures. (see table 5) Calculations of Jeanne's total net worth on the eve of marriage negotiations with the house of Valois in 1571 reveal a rather somber picture of indebtedness. Interest payments on permanent rentes constituted a charge of 30,356 livres on annual revenues, but these debts were not among Jeanne's most pressing obligations. With net revenues expected to reach nearly 300,000 livres in 1572, these rente charges were well within acceptable limits. On the other hand, the register of debts included 243,643 livres not constituted as perpetual rente and a large number of outstanding payments to purveyors of luxury goods. Outstanding debts on clothing alone amounted to 17,000 livres, while nearly ten times that amount, 150,000 livres, was owed to merchants "furnishing silverplate."[18] Thus, roughly 30 percent of Jeanne's indebtedness after the third Religious War was due to purchases of specifically luxury goods. This figure is only slightly smaller than those calculated by Crouzet for the dukes of Nevers who, between 1565 and 1578, amassed a debt estimated at 178,151 livres, almost 40 percent of which was due to the purchase of what Crouzet calls "merchandise." Here, however, the similarity between the two houses ends, for Crouzet shows that over 50 percent of the Nevers' credit was taken out on jewelry, watches, and expensively wrought trinkets, while another 35 percent was owed to tailors, furriers, and tapestry artisans. While jewelry and gold trinkets could be fairly easily converted into liquid capital,

---

[16]See, for example, the discussion of Alain le Grand's attempts to finance the expedition into Spain in 1520 by selling his silverplate, in Jacques Laprade, ed., "Inventaire de la vaiselle que Monseigneur (Alain d'Albret) veut engaiger ou vendre...pour recouvrir agent pour le bailler à Roy Navarre pour lui aider à recouvrir son royaume," *Bulletin de la société des sciences, lettres et arts de Pau* (1961): 83–87.

[17]Raymond, "Notes extraites des comptes de Jeanne d'Albret," 12(1867): 179.

[18]BN FF 3948.

much of the Nevers' purchases were "dead-end" wealth.[19] The same cannot be said for the Albrets; the silverplate which comprised such a heavy charge on Jeanne's debt lists could be, and was, converted into ready cash to pay hungry troops in the field and to secure loans for the Huguenot party.

Debts notwithstanding, Jeanne was able to find creditors in the winter and spring of 1572 willing to finance the frenzied spending that attended her efforts to negotiate a suitable marriage contract for Henri. In the sixteenth century the union of two noble houses was a complex affair of state and private ambition which contributed to the social synthesis of noble elites while consolidating family fortunes and prestige.[20] The elaborate negotiations which preceded the actual solemnization of the marriage in church provided ample occasion for ceremony and ritual which could ruin many a family fortune before the marriage was consummated. In addition to dowries, the contracting parties spent money lavishly on gifts, clothes, and expensive entertainments which showcased family wealth and influence. The potential alliance of two royal families only heightened the expense involved in such public displays of dynastic pride. Thus in 1572, even though Jeanne was still heavily in debt, she decided to spare no expense in order to secure further Henri's rightful position as a prince of the blood and as potential heir to the crown of France with the fortuitous Valois marriage. Records suggest that Jeanne found some of her creditors among a number of professional financiers, who served as creditors for the royal court; but she also borrowed extensively from a number of friends and private individuals, including a number of prominent officials in her household, who offered her loans at reasonable rates.[21] Several months before arriving at court to negotiate the final draft of the marriage contract, Jeanne's expenses rose dramatically; food and transport for the cumbersome train that snaked its way toward Blois topped 7,000 livres in February.[22] Once in Blois, Jeanne indulged in a round of entertaining and diplomatic maneuvering which drove ordinary expenses even higher, while expenditures on clothing, jewels, and other luxuries reached 28,438 livres in the month of March alone.[23]

In a letter penned to Henri on March 8, however, Jeanne made it clear that she disdained the profligate living she found at court, even if

---

[19]Crouzet, "Recherches sur la crise," 17–20.

[20]See Robert Muchembled, "Famille, amour et mariage: Mentalités et comportements des nobles artésiens à l'époque de Phillipe II," *Révue historique* 247 (1972): 247–55.

[21]Raymond, "Notes extraites des comptes de Jeanne d'Albret," 12(1867): 182–83. AD-PA, A4.

[22]AD-PA, B35.

[23]Ibid.

she was temporarily forced to engage in it for political purposes. Moreover, she had no desire to see Henri ensconced in such a den of iniquity after his marriage and urged him to seek asylum apart from court after the nuptials. As she wrote:

> Not for anything on earth would I have you come and live here.... Here women make advances to men rather than the other way around.... And the men cover themselves in jewels. The king recently spent 100,000 écus on gems and buys more everyday.[24]

Yet despite all her disdain for the effeminate habits at court, Jeanne recognized that jewelry represented a good investment. In a budgetary system in which expenditures frequently preceded receipts, jewels and silverplate functioned as more than decorative luxuries. They were mortgaged, put up as collateral for loans, and in extreme emergencies melted down to be struck into coinage, which is perhaps why jewels and silver figured so prominently in aristocratic marriage contracts and were so frequently given as gifts to favorites. Jeanne's jewels had served her well as collateral for loans from England during the third Religious War. Accordingly, she chose to bestow jewelry upon Henri as one of her wedding gifts. Indeed, once a suitable marriage contract was signed in early April, Jeanne threw herself into an orgy of spending in order to prepare for the wedding. A postscript on the extraordinary accounts notes that Jeanne, even in failing health, managed to expend 26,262 livres "from her arrival in Paris on 16 May 1572 to her death on gold jewelry, trinkets, precious stones, and jewels...for the marriage of the King."[25] Returning from one of her many spending sprees on June 4, Jeanne was suddenly struck down with a fever from which she died a week later. An inventory taken in 1583 of jewels, silverplate, and intricately fashioned ornamental pieces, stored for safekeeping in the fortified citadel of Navarrenx, reveals the wisdom of Jeanne's investments. Henri's officers counted literally dozens of chests filled with necklaces, brooches, silver goblets, and salt cellars encrusted with baroque pearls and rubies—a seemingly endless treasure store of easily convertible wealth with which to finance the Huguenot party and army.[26]

Extraordinary expenditures never again quite reached the peak of 83,866 livres achieved in 1572. (see table 5) Charles IX forced Catherine de Bourbon and Henri de Navarre to economize, and appointed

---

[24]Roelker, *Queen of Navarre*, 313.
[25]AD-PA, B35.
[26]AD-PA, A4.

Henri de Mesmes, a financial officer in his own household, to oversee the perilous fortunes of the house of Foix-Navarre-Albret. Mesmes lasted only two years as trustee, but during his sojourn in the household he imposed strictures which reduced the charges on Catherine's extraordinary rolls. Almost immediately upon Mesmes' departure from the household, however, Catherine began spending 20,000 livres annually on clothing and other luxuries. With an income, largely derived from pensions and gifts, which only amounted to 60,000 to 70,000 livres annually, such expenditures represented a sizable portion of her budget. She could, though, be pressed to economize during tight periods, and by 1584 her expenditures on luxuries had dropped to 6,619 livres.[27]

The fact that a male now headed the house of Foix-Navarre-Albret increased extraordinary expenditures accordingly in the 1580s. Household accounts show that Henri's extraordinary rolls carried charges of nearly 40,000 livres; to these expenditures, which accounted for less than 10 percent of his total outlay, should be added moneys spent on horses, hunting, and other masculine pleasures, most of which were recorded on separate rolls kept by the chief squire in the stables.[28] Stable charges comprised an increasingly heavy burden on the Albret fortunes after 1572, a function of the masculine and military character of Henri de Navarre's household. Under Jeanne d'Albret the stables and their expenditures had remained fairly modest. The accounts testify to numerous modest charges for Jeanne's *petite écurie*, so-called because it contained mostly pack and carriage horses, rather than the great Spanish stallions which were favored by her son for military and ceremonial purposes. Jeanne's stables rarely numbered over twenty-five horses, of which only two to three were suitable for her personal use.[29] Until her death, stable charges were never significant enough to merit a separate account and were always included on the ordinary accounts—a practice which Catherine de Bourbon continued in her own household after her mother's death.

Masculine society, however, centered around horses in the sixteenth century. Horses remained a potent symbol of aristocratic power and status. Sixteenth-century nobles still idealized themselves and their ancestors with great equestrian statues, where they were represented like Renaissance condottieri forcing their will upon subordinate urban populations. Nobles still contrived to impress their vassals and

---

[27] AD-PA, B83, B91.
[28] For some of these, see AD-PA, B28, B34, B38, etc.
[29] AD-PA, B18, B19.

rivals by moving around the countryside mounted on great horses and attended by a number of gentlemen clients.[30] Jeanne herself cultivated Henri's love of horses and frequently bestowed them upon him as gifts: a Spanish stallion costing 250 livres in 1562, a beautiful bay worth 271 livres, and a black charger worth 297 livres in 1571.[31] These prized horses formed the nucleus of what became Henri's stables, which eventually rivaled those of other great aristocrats in France. By the time Henri had reached his early twenties, he kept more than fifty horses in his stables, eleven of which were prize Spanish stallions, where only two decades earlier, his father Antoine de Bourbon at the height of his military career had kept only thirty-eight.[32]

Following established convention, Henri kept and staffed two separate stables.[33] In the *petite écurie* were found the ordinary horses used for draft purposes and routine travel. In the second stables, the *grande écurie,* were the splendid steeds which Henri and his men mounted for military exercises and parades. Until his flight from court in 1576, Henri kept only a modest number of horses in the great stables, as suited his life as a courtier. Fewer than a dozen mounts in all appear on the stable accounts before 1572; after 1576 his role as one of the leaders of the Protestant party required a radical reorganization of the stables. By 1577 Henri could count twenty great chargers in the *grande écurie*, and in 1578, this number swelled to twenty-eight. For the next decade, acquisitions continued apace, as Henri tried, despite the misfortunes of war and civil turmoil, to keep a reasonable number of mounts available for his men and armed entourage.[34] In 1582, for example, he spent more than 10,000 livres on horses in order to replace those lost, killed, or taken as part of the spoils of war.[35] Part of that 10,000 livres Henri spent to build up the *petite écurie,* which in 1582 had forty-six horses. Grooms primped and curried an average of seventy horses in Henri's stables during the Religious Wars, and accordingly, his stable expenses created an increasingly heavy burden on his annual budgets. In one notable year, 1585, 49,298 livres were discharged from Henri's personal accounts for the stables.[36]

---

[30] See Harding, *Anatomy of a Power Elite*, 175.
[31] AD-PA, B8, B17.
[32] Pierre Gutton, *Domestiques et serviteurs*, 250.
[33] For extensive discussion of Henri's stables, see Jean Robert, "Les grande et petite écuries d'Henri III de Navarre," *Bulletin de la société des amis du Château de Pau*, n.s. 88 (1983):3–39.
[34] For some examples of purchases, see AD-PA, B157, B159, B160.
[35] AD-PA, B157.
[36] AD-PA, B159.

After 1574 the increasing artificiality of Henri III's court also imposed additional charges on Henri de Navarre's personal budget. The truly elegant male no longer wore simply long hose—perhaps embroidered or striped, and attached by points to an underjacket or doublet (referred to as a *pourpoint* in French)—which had been the dress at midcentury. Increasingly, men sported both upper and lower stockings (*chausse* and *bas de chausse*), which were in effect breeches and stockings. Moreover, as the doublet gradually grew shorter to reveal these enticing innovations, trunkhose or breeches took on a variety of shapes, each more fantastic than the last, and requiring reams and reams of material. Silks, velvets, and fine linens were used in abundance, as material was plumped and padded around the human form. Most breeches required at least three contrasting layers of materials in addition to several bands of piping, braiding, and lace that garnished the outside of the garment. The first layer—usually a fairly light fitted base around which the padding was arranged—was constructed of linen. Onto this linen shell an inner lining of richer material was sewn, usually requiring three to four times as much yardage as the base. And onto these two layers, a third layer of material was sewn, which was generally split into panes or pinked, so that the inner lining would show through. The textural richness and opulence of such garments—sometimes requiring eight to ten *aulnes* of material—conveyed the obvious wealth and well-being of its wearer as well as the power to command the services of skilled artisans who could fashion such exquisite pieces. If that were not enough, it became the fashion in the 1570s to further garnish men's breeches with great swirls of contrasting material, called *canions*, which extended from the bottom of the trunk hose to the knees or just below. As a final flourish, sash garters, usually of silk, were tied below the knees. Doublets and jerkings were less fanciful than breeches, but still sported great puffed, slashed sleeves, and a myriad of buttons, bands, and lace. And, of course, a richly lined cloak and a plumed or tufted toque was de rigueur.[37]

It is clear from the extraordinary accounts that Henri followed the capricious dictates of fashion; the private tailors who dressed the lackeys in the stables and the valets in the chamber were just as scrupulously loyal to fashion as were the tailors in Paris. Henri spent well over 10,500 livres outfitting the thirty-three pages and lackeys in his stables and the young men in his bedchamber in 1577.[38] His tailors

---

[37] Joan Nunn, *Fashion in Costume, 1200–1980* (New York: Schocken, 1984); for examples of these described in the extraordinary rolls, see AD-PA, B20, B21, B36.
[38] AD-PA, B36.

provided exquisite liveries for the pages: cloaks of blue "English cloth" lined in grey velvet; a grey doublet embroidered with gold thread; and long knee breeches of violet and shot through with silver thread. Shoes were provided almost biweekly, a testimony to the energetic activities of the pages as well as the flimsiness of the slippers-cum-shoes worn by courtiers. The quarterly roll from January to March 1577, for example, shows that the fifteen pages in the small stables were provided with ten pairs of shoes each.[39] By 1583 Henri had reduced his extraordinary expenditures by more than half, but clothing for his household servants and the young noblemen in his charge still received top priority. More than 20,000 livres was still spent on outfitting the household,[40] although, to their credit, careful calculations reveal that the household tailors costumed the pages for roughly the same prices they had demanded from Jeanne d'Albret twelve years earlier, a product of the relative price stability of both wages and many luxury goods in the sixteenth century.

In spite of these heavy expenditures, records of Henri's indebtedness upon his accession to the throne of France reveal that very few purveyors of luxury goods still figured among his creditors. The overwhelming charges on his accounts were outstanding debts to financiers, such as the brothers Balbany, who lent money "for the affairs of war," and to financial officers in his army and household, who had covered deficits in the treasury for years and hoped finally to be repaid. These were slowly acquitted over nearly ten years with receipts from the *Epargne*.[41]

Catherine de Bourbon restrained her spending for only one year after Henri's de facto reign as king of France. By 1591 she was spending well over 30,000 livres on the extraordinary accounts. Perhaps as part of her role as both regent of Béarn and princess of France, she began to bestow liberalities in a manner befitting a sovereign.[42] Once at court she was drawn into an even more dazzling spectacle and competitive pace. To help meet the expenses of these costly court entertainments, Henri granted her ever-increasing extraordinary pensions, which tripled her revenues. After Henri finally won Paris and installed himself in his capital in 1594, Catherine followed in April with eight carriages and wagons in train.[43] While in Paris she occupied large

---

[39]Ibid.
[40]AD-PA, B79 through B82.
[41]AN, KK146.
[42]AD-PA, B135, B136.
[43]Roelker, *The Paris of Henry of Navarre*, 278.

apartments on the Rue Deux Écus, from which she began to scandalize the Parisian populace with her rather overt attempts to proselytize for the Reformed faith.[44] Yet even Catherine's sober Protestantism did not restrain her from indulging in her well-cultivated passion for fine clothes, carriages, horses, and court festivities. In 1594, the expenses listed on her extraordinary rolls actually represented a slight decline from expenditures during her regency in Béarn, but omitted from these accounts were significant purchases made on furniture, horses, and the other accoutrements of court life. In spite of the fact that Catherine had gradually stripped the château in Pau of most of its fine tapestries and treasures, which now adorned her Parisian apartments, she still managed to spend 12,423 livres on apartment furnishings. Another 1,311 livres was spent refurbishing the château d'Olinville, a gift from her doting brother.[45] By 1598, Catherine had also fallen prey to the new Parisian passion for horse-drawn, closed carriages. Accounts show that she had at least two and spent over 1,000 livres for four grey horses to convey her carriage in style. And eventually she purchased two additional greys to add to the line. The final horse was evidently a magnificent steed, for which she was willing to pay 162 écus. There were apparently other equipage expenses as well—enough to occasion a loan of 1,200 écus from merchants in Paris at 8 percent interest.[46]

A cursory glance at Catherine's accounts after 1595 suggests that in principle she had more than enough income to acquit her debts to purveyors of luxury goods. But as already noted, collecting the extraordinary pensions that Henri had granted was a long and drawn-out process. In 1595 projected receipts fell short by more than 100,000 livres, leaving Catherine's treasurer with debts amounting to over 90,000 livres to pay out of his own pocket and creditors to fob off with promissory notes on other revenues.[47] And the situation was not likely to improve for the next few years. As L'Estoile noted in his journal, by February 1596 "the King was so constrained by the need of money to reestablish the intendant of finances who had been abolished a month before."[48] By 1598 Henri's grants to Catherine had increased yet again, but 190,636 livres were still outstanding according to the treasurer's register—a sum made all the more onerous by the fact that Catherine's court expenses continued to mount unabated. By far the greatest drain

[44]Ibid., 283, 285.
[45]AD-PA, B138.
[46]AD-PA, B142.
[47]AD-PA, B139.
[48]Roelker, *The Paris of Henry of Navarre*, 278.

on her accounts were moneys spent on food, salaries, and gifts—which would later be judged extortionary by the Conseil du Roi, but extraordinary expenditures, which continued to rise, still amounted to only 42,813 livres.[49]

II. Palaces and Gardens

By the sixteenth century, nobles not only transformed their physical bodies through dress into dazzling and heroic images of sovereignty, they also shaped their physical environment in ways which enhanced their dynastic identities. Humanist treatises which equated the public display of wealth with personal magnificence and morality, Francis I's energetic efforts to build and remodel royal residences in Paris and the Loire Valley in the latest Italianate styles, and the development of military artillery which rendered the massive fortifications of medieval châteaux essentially defenseless all encouraged a kind of building mania among sixteenth-century French nobles which continued, and in certain cases even escalated, during the Religious Wars.[50] From Paris to the provinces, great aristocrats and provincial nobles alike indulged in the desire to create permanent and personal monuments to their family's power. The enormous cost of construction meant that most nobles satisfied their desire to achieve immortality through monumentality by adding Renaissance-style features to the exterior and interior of the old château rather than razing it entirely and starting anew.[51] But even minor cosmetic changes, such as the addition of classical bas-reliefs, motifs, and windows, often resulted in a dramatic restatement of the meaning and function of patriarchal authority in Renaissance society.

Treasurers' accounts, château rolls, and inventories testify to the Albrets' vigorous participation in the building craze of the sixteenth century. Altogether, they owned or controlled more than twenty châteaux-forts, most of which were strategically located in their southern domains. To judge from surviving inventories and accounts, most of these were still essentially medieval fortresses, with more crenelated towers and parapets than windows, and sparse furnishings designed to meet the needs of the garrison soldiers who typically resided within

---

[49]AD-PA, B142.

[50]For an analysis of the impact of humanist philosophy on the Renaissance building boom, see Richard A. Goldthwaite, "The Florentine Palace as Domestic Architecture," *American Historical Review* 77 (1972):977–1,012.

[51]See, for example, Neuschel, "Noble Households," 599–601; also Dewald, *Pont-St-Pierre*, 199–201, 214; Harding, *Anatomy of a Power Elite*, 173–74.

them. Swords, lances, barrels of saltpeter, and canons were more plentiful than tapestries and paintings.[52] Captained by local nobles, who were salaried officials of the house of Foix-Navarre-Albret, these châteaux symbolized the Albrets' patriarchal authority over local elites and were crucial to their efforts to strengthen their ties with these elites. Given the strategic importance of these châteaux, it should come as no surprise that they were carefully maintained and repaired. Of all the châteaux in the Albrets' possession, however, only those in Nérac and Pau were extensively remodeled and richly appointed with Renaissance furnishings and objets d'art. The loss of Haute-Navarre to Ferdinand of Aragon in 1512 underscored, in particular, the importance of the château of Pau, located in the viscounty of Béarn, where the Albrets could claim sovereign privileges similar to those they had exercised over Navarre.

In the decade and a half after Ferdinand's victory, the Albrets systematically transferred the principal administrative offices of their extensive domains to their château in Pau in an effort to create a new ceremonial center for expression of their sovereign powers. In 1513 Catherine de Foix ordered the seneschal of Béarn to hold audiences in the *basse-chambre* of the château of Pau instead of the eleventh-century stronghold of Orthez, which had served as the ceremonial site for the counts of Foix in the fourteenth century. Catherine's efforts were followed in 1520 by Henri d'Albret's creation of the Chambre des comptes, which he situated in Pau. Four years later, he also transferred the royal mint from the château-fort of La Forquie, where the viscounts of Béarn had been minting coins in their own image since the tenth century, to the public square just below the château of Pau. The château, which had been the meeting site for the Estates of Béarn, Foix, Bigorre, Marsan, and Nébouzan since the end of the fifteenth century, and the city of Pau itself, thus became even more fully identified with the Albrets' political, and later religious agenda.

Modern scholars of Renaissance Italy have detailed the efforts of elite families to dominate their urban environments, and thus city-state politics, through carefully conceived domestic building programs. In like manner, the Albrets' administrative reforms in the early sixteenth century were accompanied by a building program which reflected their desire to place a proprietary mark on the urban landscape. From 1512 onward the Albrets lavished money and labor on their château in Pau. In the process, they dramatically enlarged the

---

[52]C. Barrière Flay, "Le capitaine Jean Le Comte: gouverneur du château et de la ville de Foix, 1584–1600," *Bulletin périodique de la société ariègeoise* 5 (1906): 1–95.

size and shape of the château and its grounds and emphasized their collective powers in Béarn and their other domains. (see figure 5.1) Sometime around 1550 Henri commissioned the construction of a mill and atelier to house the royal mint and the Chambre des comptes. Located on the south side of the château, the buildings, aptly dubbed the *Tour de la Monnaie*, dominated the largest public square in Pau, which also served as the principal site for public executions. Against the protest of local residents, who found themselves displaced in the process, the Albrets annexed the private dwelling of their maître d'hôtel to the east of the château in order to provide lodging for foreign ambassadors, clients, and local nobles who could not be accommodated in the cramped quarters of the château proper.[53] Communicating walkways were constructed to link these new additions to the older château, thus creating a kind of palace compound which, in turn, was surrounded by the private residences of family officers whose responsibilities confined them to a relatively narrow base of operations. Thus, by 1555, the surface area of the château grounds had more than doubled and much of the western end of the city of Pau had been transformed into a princely enclave. The frequent presence of one family member or another at the château furthered an almost mythic association, later embellished by seventeenth-century chroniclers, between place and power.[54] Henri d'Albret's decision late in life to end his wandering and reside in Pau, his insistence that Jeanne give birth to the future scion of the house of Foix-Navarre-Albret within its hallowed walls, and Henri de Navarre's birth in there in 1553 guaranteed the prominence of the château in family lore.

Until the 1530s, the main edifice of the château itself was remarkable for its forbidding austerity. In spite of intensive remodeling and construction in the fourteenth century under Gaston Fébus, contemporary chroniclers still likened the château to a Moorish fortress. In total area, the château was impressive: 480 feet long and 300 feet wide.[55] Five towers and an outer wall of fortifications thirty feet high, sur-

---

[53]AM-PA, DD7.

[54]While Marguerite d'Angoulême showed an almost immediate preference for Henri's ancestral stronghold of Nérac, she was often in residence in Pau on her way to take the healing waters of Eaux Chaudes in the Pyrénées; Dartigue-Peyrou, *Vicomté*, 240. Until her death in 1532, Henri's older sister, Anne, lived in almost constant residence in the chateau and served as lieutenant general of Béarn during her brother's frequent absences; AD-PA, E596.

[55]By comparison, the new château built by Louis de Roncherolles, baron of Pont St Pierre, around 1520 was about 106 feet long and 31 feet wide. See Dewald, *Pont-St-Pierre*, 200.

1. Grand Stairway
2. Lower Great Hall
3. Vaulted Salon
4. Ovens
5. Vaulted Kitchens
6. Vaulted Salon
7. Stairway
8. Hall
9. Cabinet of Queen Jeanne (doubtful attribution)

a. Donjon
b. Mazères
c. Billère Tower
d. Montauser Tower
e. Tour de la Monnaie

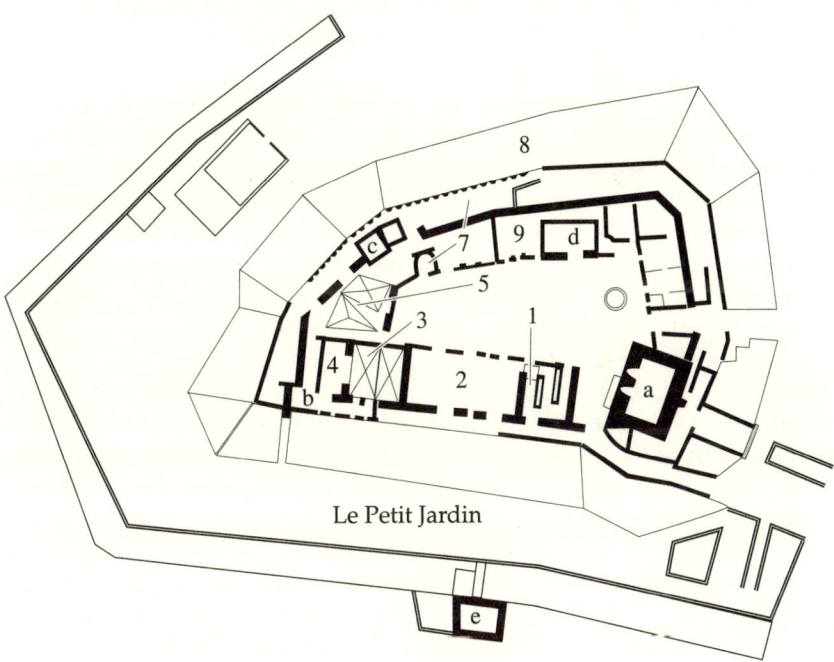

Figure 5.1 Château of Pau

Source: Ritter, *Le Château de Pau* (Paris, 1919).

rounded by natural moats twenty-seven feet wide, protected the château from invaders.[56] Henri d'Albret's decision to refurbish the castle in the new Renaissance style followed closely and not coincidentally upon his marriage to Marguerite d'Angoulême. The royal marriage, and the lucrative settlement and stipends that it brought, provided the means and the motive to undertake costly renovations.[57] Francis I's own conspicuous efforts to style himself a Renaissance prince upon his return from Italy by commissioning the massive renovation of royal residences around Paris and in the Loire valley contributed in large measure to Henri's decision to remodel his ancestral home.[58] Just one year after Francis had announced his intention to remodel the Louvre, Fontainebleau, and Madrid, Henri contracted with three master architects from Bourges with proven records of royal service to make significant alterations on the château.

In an effort to create a residence worthy of an enlightened Christian prince, the architects added ornate, cruciform windows decorated with classical motifs and armorial crests to lighten the somber facade and minimize the closed, defensive effect of the older château-fort. The result was, according to one traveler's account, a château that seemed to have "as many windows as there were days." Other features of the Renaissance style, such as the extensive use of classical bas-reliefs incised into the masonry itself, added a gracious and refined texture to the exterior of the château and its windows. The use of Henri's and Marguerite's initials, elaborately sculpted into the facade and into the archway of a new marble staircase leading to the great hall on the second floor, reflected the exuberant glorification of self which appears frequently in humanist writings; it also called attention, as did the widespread use of personal motifs on Italian Renaissance palazzi, to the dynastic ambitions of the Albrets, now linked by marriage to the royal house of France.[59] The only jarring note was the brick donjon flanking the east side of the château, which was left virtually untouched. By all artistic measures, the juxtaposition of the donjon against the highly ornamented exterior of the residential wings of the château proper spoiled the grace and sophistication of the Renaissance additions; to Henri's contemporaries, however, it symbolized the multiple and varied nature of the Albrets' power.[60]

---

[56]G. Bacle de LaGrèze, *Le château de Pau* (Paris: Didier, 1854), 25.

[57]For the marriage settlement, see chap. 2.

[58]R. J. Knecht, *Francis I*, 253–64.

[59]Goldthwaite, "The Florentine Palace," 992.

[60]Leopold Chalenay, ed., *Vie de Jacques Esprinchard, rochelais et journal de ses voyages au XVIe siècle* (Paris: S.E.V.P.E.N., 1957), 269.

In recent years, early modern historians have argued that the frenzied efforts of the nobility to exhibit wealth and power through the construction of dazzling dwellings contributed to its political and economic demise.[61] Regrettably, the paucity of detailed castle records for the first three quarters of the sixteenth century makes it difficult to assess the full impact of Henri's capital improvements on his private fortunes. The accounts of the domanial treasurers, who usually took responsibility for the repairs and renovations, rarely recorded all of their expenditures under separate chapter headings until the 1570s, when the pressure of a burgeoning household and burgeoning military expenses mandated greater order in their accounts. More problematic, however, are the deliberations of the Estates of Béarn which indicate that donations beyond the purview of family treasurers were occasionally advanced by the Estates themselves to pay for capital improvements deemed to be in the community interest. Limited as these sources are, they can reveal the pattern and magnitude of the Albrets' personal investment in architecture, which appears conservative when compared with the efforts of their royal Valois cousins.

Estimates of Francis I's expenditures on the masonry alone of his château de Madrid, for example, run to 174,000 livres,[62] but nothing in the Albrets' domanial accounts ever even approximates such a grand sum. Expenditures for reparations in the accounts of the treasurers of Béarn in 1531, for example, reached barely over 800 écus (2,400 livres).[63] And for the next twenty years, repairs to the château mentioned in the domanial accounts rarely run over 1,000 livres, at a time when gross receipts could reach as high as 127,000 livres.[64] Most important, two patterns do emerge which suggest that Henri d'Albret and his daughter, Jeanne, were eager to make capital improvements that brought in real material profits, at the same time following cultural conventions. Repairs for mills, a lucrative source of rental income, almost always exceeded funds advanced to embellish their private dwellings.[65] The Albrets also shrewdly played on popular fears of Spanish and marauding royalist troops and brigands to raise large donations from their estates to cover the cost of building schemes and

---

[61]See, for example, Lawrence Stone, *Family and Fortune: Studies in Aristocratic Finance in the Sixteenth and Seventeenth Century* (Oxford: Clarendon Press, 1973), 62–91; idem, *Crisis of the Aristocracy*, 549–55, 710–12; Neuschel, "Noble Households," 600-601.

[62]Knecht, *Francis I*, 256.
[63]AD-PA, B225.
[64]AD-PA, B252, B263.
[65]AD-PA, B226, B238, B242, B251, B252, B257.

repairs that could be subsumed under the heading of military expenditures. In 1538 Henri d'Albret used the growing antagonism between Charles V and Francis I to raise the specter of a Spanish invasion, and thus pried 10,000 écus (30,000 livres) out of the Estates to build massive new defense works at Navarrenx.[66] Later, on the eve of the baron Terride's invasion of Béarn in 1569, the Estates voted 17,000 écus to shore up the fortifications at Navarrenx which engineers had declared "imperfect."[67] Apart from the reconstruction of a tennis court destroyed by occupying troops in 1569, Jeanne d'Albret made few contributions out of pocket to renovate the château structurally. Between 1560 and 1572 the biggest construction project undertaken on the château grounds was largely underwritten by the Estates of Béarn. In 1572 the auditors of the Chambre des comptes in Pau earmarked 4,000 écus from the donation by the Estates for the construction of a special archival tower to protect precious family charters and financial records from royalist troops.[68] Next to these sums, the 67 livres paid out from the domanial treasury to the master carpenter, Arnauld de la Teulère, to fortify the castle in Pau against the possible depredations of royal troops seems minuscule.[69]

In 1610, the *Mercure français* eulogized the many achievements of Henri IV, noting that "as soon as he was master of Paris, you saw masons at work everywhere."[70] Henri's confinement at court between 1572 and 1576 hindered his plans to put a definite mark on his birthplace until the 1580s, but his desire to reshape the physical landscape around the château manifested itself almost immediately upon his arrival in Pau in 1576. In contrast to the Albrets' building projects earlier in the century, Henri's remodeling designs spanned two decades and taxed the reserves of the family treasury. In 1581 work on the gardens alone cost over 5,000 écus, while total expenditures on repairs in Béarn reached well over 10,000 écus.[71] The next year expenditures climbed even further, reaching 12,997 écus.[72] By 1600 expenditures on reparation and remodeling projects in Béarn alone peaked at a staggering 16,831 écus.[73] Between 1579 and 1600 the treasurers of Béarn disbursed 3,000 écus yearly just to cover the building costs of master

---

[66]Dartigue-Peyrou, *La Vicomté*, 138. See also AD-PA, C681.
[67]Raymond Ritter, *Le château de Pau* (Paris: Champion, 1919) 108ff.
[68]AD-PA, C692, a quote in Ritter, *Le château de Pau*, 115.
[69]AD-PA, B250.
[70]David Buisseret, *Henri IV*, 131.
[71]Ritter, *Le château de Pau*, 118.
[72]AD-PA, B268.
[73]AD-PA, B293, B294.

architect, Hervé Boullard. His salary—and the salaries of master artisans under his employ—added another 1,000 écus to the budget.[74]

Rumors of Navarre's prodigious expenditures spread far and wide, no doubt fanned by the king himself. A young Protestant visitor, Jacques Esprinchard, marveled in 1598 that Henri was purported to spend 10,000 livres a year on the upkeep of his garden.[75] To Esprinchard, such abstract sums implied far more than great wealth. Behind these figures was the labor of dozens of human beings, employed at a mere 3 to 4 sols a day, scurrying to carry out Henri's designs and commands. Château rolls dating from 1587 suggest courtyards, gardens, and corridors buzzed with activity the year round as carpenters, masons, glaziers, carters, locksmiths, and gardeners went about their business.[76] In 1589, for example, workers planted 1,270 trees in Le Petit Parq. Day laborers, sometimes as many as 150 men and women at a time, filled the gardens planting trees, clearing ditches, clipping hedges, and in short, maintaining a tight control over the natural world.[77] Their presence testified to the power and sovereignty of Henri's will.

By 1598 the château gardens stretched roughly fifteen miles to the west of the château and were considered to be one of Henri de Navarre's greatest achievements. (see figure 5.2) The splendid order of the gardens offered testimony to Henri's ability to achieve stability in the tumultuous political world of the sixteenth century as well as to exert control over the natural world. Indeed, according to Roy Strong, the sixteenth century witnessed the emergence of great noble and royal gardens, whose beautifully sculpted parterres and topiaries were "the adjunct of monarchy, the expression of the post-Reformation assertion of royal power and omnipotence."[78] While the gardens and parks at Pau helped fulfill a variety of human needs—pleasure, amusement, repose, and love—they also fulfilled an explicitly political purpose.[79] Jacques Esprinchard's descriptions of the gardens in the château of Pau in 1598 reveal a well-designed and articulated political agenda. In

---

[74]AD-PA, B268, B269, B293, B498, B504, B509–511, B514–518, B531, B536, B546.

[75]Chalenay, *Vie de Jacques Esprinchard*, 272.

[76]See Neuschel's discussion of the relationship between human labor and power in *Word of Honor*, 170–71; AD-PA, B511, B516, B531, B532.

[77]AD-PA, B268, B514, B516, B517.

[78]Roy Strong, *The Renaissance Garden in England* (London: Thames and Hudson, 1979), 25.

[79]On Jeanne's fondness for the parks surrounding the château of Pau and the playhouse she built Catherine, see Roelker, *Queen of Navarre*, 411; on Henri de Navarre's love of gardens see Raymond Ritter, "Les jardins du château de Pau sous Henri IV," *Pyrénées* 37 (1957):41–45.

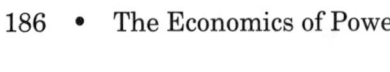

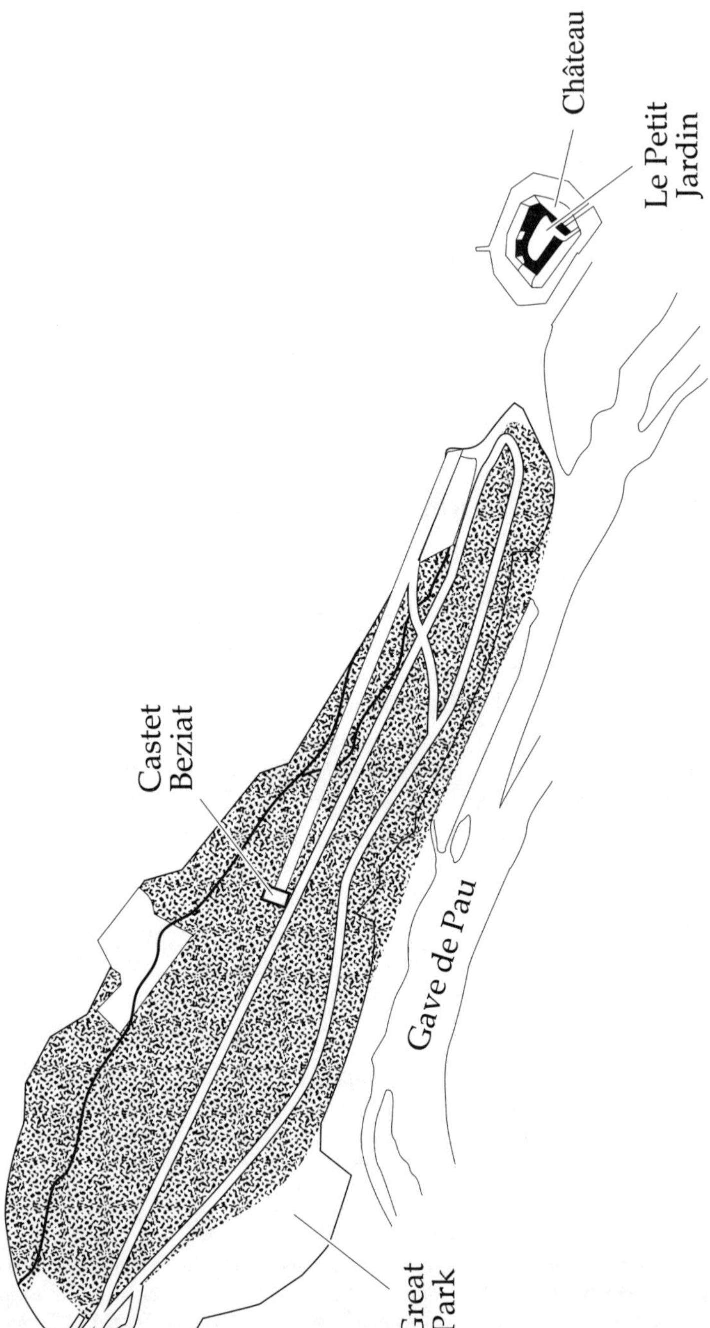

Figure 5.2 Château of Pau and its Gardens (18th c)
Source: Ritter, *Le Château de Pau* (Paris, 1919).

addition to the usual menagerie of beasts that filled Renaissance gardens were two detailed renditions of Biblical stories. Like a carefully orchestrated Lenten sermon, there was an Old Testament theme—the story of Jonah and the whale—and a new Testament image—the great angel of Revelations with the seven glowing lampstands in her hand.[80] Simon Schama has recently argued that the story of Jonah and his inexorable journey toward the recognition of the sovereignty of God was rarely part of a popular preacher's repertoire, except in the Netherlands.[81] Yet here in Henri de Navarre's gardens was a representation of Jonah, a particularly suitable image for the Bourbon monarchy in 1598. Both Jonah and the angel stand as powerful reminders of the sovereignty of God and the prophetic destiny of his servants. Both functioned as cautionary tales to the Christian—or Christian subject—tempted to question the curious wisdom of God's divine will and divine choices.

III. The Use of Space and Furnishing

Within their châteaux and on the road the Albrets created around themselves a level of material elegance which reinforced their dynastic claims and signaled subtle gradations of rank and privilege among their followers. The peripatetic lifestyle of great nobles like the Albrets placed a premium on furnishings which could be easily transported, quickly installed, and yet still conferred the requisite message of power and permanence.[82] Intricately embroidered silks, velvets, and linens which could be draped from poles to create temporary pavilions, canopies, and thrones in even the rudest surroundings provided the most practical solution to the problem of establishing rank while on the road, in the battlefield, or in rented lodgings in Paris. Huge woollen tapestries also accompanied the Albrets on their seemingly endless journeys from one château to another and to court. Tapestries adorned dank walls and covered crudely finished tables, benches, and camp beds, lending an air of warmth and richness to otherwise often somber surroundings. Draped behind places of honor at the dinner table or in the *grande salle*, they signaled important gradations of rank within the Albrets' household and entourage.

---

[80]Chalenay, *Vie de Jacques Esprinchard*, 270–71.
[81]Simon Schama, *The Embarrassment of Riches: An Interpretation of Dutch Culture in the Golden Age* (New York: Alfred A. Knopf, 1988), 130–44.
[82]For a fuller discussion of the importance of portability in the sixteenth century, see Neuschel, "Noble Households," 615.

By 1555 the Albrets' impressive collection of largely Flemish woolen tapestries, ceremonial canopies, and curtains represented a significant investment of resources and labor. Two tapestry artisans were employed full-time to guard, clean, and repair the collection, which included more than forty complete tapestry cycles, some composed of more than a dozen separate pieces each.[83] Many of these tapestries had been in the family for generations and were described in inventories as "old" or "worn," but others, judging from the themes represented, were clearly recent purchases. In addition to portraying classical images, such as the Gallic Hercules, which by the mid-sixteenth century had become an almost hackneyed iconographic reference to French royal authority, a number of tapestries also presented Old Testament themes, such as the destruction of Jerusalem, the rebellion of Reheboem, the life of Esther, and the reign of Nebuchadnezzar, which had achieved a certain popularity among Calvinist preachers and printers because they depicted the dire consequences of tyranny, the certain redemption of God's chosen people, and the necessary resistance of evil.[84] Heraldic motifs, which traced the genealogy of the illustrious political and military alliances of the house of Foix-Navarre-Albret, were enormously popular because they permitted an unabashed demonstration of dynastic ambition. Of the 135 tapestries and curtains inventoried by Navarre's tapestry maker, Bertrand Gontelle, in Nérac in 1578, at least a dozen were silk, embroidered with the heraldic symbols, crests, and mottoes of the houses of Foix-Navarre-Albret, Valois, and Bourbon.[85] Typical of these was the cloth referred to as the "lit de Melusine," emblazoned with the family crest of the house of Bourbon, which was probably modeled after the ceremonial throne, the so-called *lit de justice*, used by Valois monarchs to stage their appearances before the often intractable Parlement of Paris.[86] Not surprisingly, in the spring of 1579 Navarre ordered the transport of several armorial draperies, including the "lit de Melusine" from Pau to Nérac, where he entertained Marguerite de Valois, Catherine de Medici, and the entire royal cortège.[87]

[83]Pierre Bayaud and Jacques de Laprade, eds., "Un inventaire du château de Nérac (1555)," *Bulletin des amis du château de Pau* 12 (1962):11–16.

[84]On the symbolic significance and political uses of the Gallic Hercules in sixteenth-century France, see Bryant, *The King and the City*, 130–35, 164–67, 172; see also Marc René Jung, *Hercule dans la littérature française du XVIe siècle* (Librairie Droz: Geneva, 1966).

[85]Laprade, ed., "Un inventaire, 1578," 413–30.

[86]See, for example, Sarah Hanley, *The "Lit de Justice" of the Kings of France: Constitutional Ideology in Legend, Ritual and Discourse* (Princeton: Princeton University Press, 1983).

[87]For an evocative description of the château of Nérac in March 1579, see Babelon, *Henri IV*, 260–269.

For a fraction of the cost of a Flemish woolen tapestry or a silken drapery embroidered with gold thread, the Albrets commissioned paintings of themselves, their forbears, and their royal cousins and wives, directed toward the same political end as the tapestries. Court painters were kept busy creating flattering likenesses which were sent as inexpensive mementos to heads of state all over Europe or were hung in chambers and corridors in the Albrets' private residences. Forty-two portraits of royal relatives and diplomatic allies graced the foyer of Catherine of Bourbon's Paris apartments on the Rue des Deux Ecus and served as a powerful reminder of Catherine's long and illustrious lineage even before visitors entered her presence.[88] Portraits also served as a powerful reminder of the extent of the Albrets' influence and the disastrous consequences that could befall those who attempted to thwart it. In 1595 Catherine de Bourbon paid Claude Mailhet, the concierge and court painter in residence at the château of Foix, 2 écus for having painted the gruesome image of three rebels hanged for treason.[89]

As Robert Harding has suggested, the tapestry and painting collections of great French nobles reinforced as well as reflected the patriarchal structure of private and public politics in early modern France.[90] Their tapestries and paintings highlighted illustrious marriages, ancestors, and heroic deeds. At the same time, the mélange of styles, the old and the new, served as much as reminders of the family's accumulation of power over generations as the rows of ancestral portraits hanging in the great hall.

IV. Cultural Values

Nobles' libraries were also a mixture of the old and the new in the sixteenth century. The growth of print culture broadened nobles' book collections and their patronage of humanists and printers. The transformation of the Albrets' manuscript and book collections over the course of the sixteenth century testifies to their growing attraction to the courtly, humanist culture of the Renaissance as well as their keen sensitivity to the political uses of print.

The library that Henri d'Albret inherited in 1517 reflected the chivalric tastes of the fifteenth century. In a 1519 inventory of the furnish-

---

[88]Pierre Bayaud and Jacques de Laprade, eds., "Inventaire après décès des meubles de Catherine de Bourbon contenus en son Hôtel de la rue Deux-Écus à Paris," *Bulletin des amis du Château de Pau* 21 (1969):11–19.
[89]AD-PA, B140.
[90]Harding, *Anatomy of a Provincial Elite*, 171.

ings of the château of Pau, Henri's maître d'hôtel, Orrias Bourguignon, listed a total of thirty-seven books stuffed away in a chest in one of the ground floor rooms just off the cavernous kitchen.[91] All but three of these books were manuscripts on parchment rather than printed on paper. Histories, chivalric romances in French and Catalan, practical medical manuals, and devotional literature comprised the bulk of Henri's library. There is no reference in Bourguignon's inventory to other furnishings, to the writing tables and chairs, terrestrial globes, or painted mottoes which typically graced the libraries of parlementaires-cum-humanists, such as Michel Montaigne.[92] An inventory taken a few years after Henri's marriage to Marguerite d'Angoulême showed little change in Henri's library or reading tastes. *Lancelot du Lac, The Romance of Aymery de Narbonne, The Chronicles of Narbonne, The Chronicles of Froissart*, and *Remedies for Wounds*, all the classic texts of chivalric literature parodied by Cervantes, still figured prominently in Henri's library of forty-four books.[93]

By 1555, however, Marguerite's humanist inclinations and the spread of print culture had transformed the Albrets' literary collection. Regrettably, the five officers who inventoried the château of Nérac, which Marguerite favored over Henri's isolate Béarnais domains, listed very few titles for the 197 books they found "in the chamber of the library," which makes it difficult to analyze the Albrets' changing intellectual taste in detail. Even so, the sheer number of books, their precious bindings, which are described while the titles are not, and their setting suggest the bibliophilic passions of Renaissance humanist collectors. We are not quite in the presence of Montaigne's private library painted with Latin mottoes to provoke studious reflection, but rather in a small, private wardrobe furnished with a small table, a game of

---

[91]L. Soulice, *Catalogue de la Bibliothèque de la ville de Pau: histoire locale* (Pau: Imprimerie Véronèse, 1886), iv–vi.

[92]For the transformation of the library, Roger Chartier, "The Practical Impact of Writing," in *A History of Private Life: Passions of the Renaissance*, ed. Roger Chartier (Cambridge: The Belknap Press of Harvard University Press, 1989), 134–42. In England, most books were kept in the hall rather than in a study or bedroom until the sixteenth century and thus were more likely valued as objects conveying social prestige rather than intellectual stimulation. See Peter Clark, "The Ownership of Books in England, 1560–1640: The Example of Some Kentish Townfolk," in Lawrence Stone, ed., *Schooling and Society: Studies in the History of Education* (Baltimore: Johns Hopkins University Press, 1976), 95–111.

[93]Pierre Bayaud and Jacques de Laprade, eds., "Inventaire des meubles du Chateau de Pau estarés en mains de Orryas Bourguignon Me d'Ostel du Roy...le XXVIe jour de septembre 1533," *Bulletin des amis du Château de Pau* 10 (1961):10–15. For a comparison to the libraries of other military nobles, see Harding, *Anatomy of a Power Elite*, 174.

draughts, finely wrought paintings, and relics. The bas-relief of St. Jerome, patron saint of melancholic scholars, the small emblems, and the historic scene on linen and wood, as well as the religious relics located throughout the château also reveal the pietistic nature of Marguerite's humanist learning. In a cabinet, decorated in blue cloth, coffers filled with fifty-seven pieces of embroidery, many with explicitly religious themes dominated, including a crucifix, worked in gold and silver thread, a veronica (face of Christ) in gold and silk thread, and a "little round *Ecco Homo*." Elsewhere in the château, so clearly devoted to humanist pleasures and female pastimes, there were also halberds, corselets, and helmets for a legion of sixty to seventy soldiers and forty crossbows.[94]

By the 1550s the Albrets were not only purchasing books; they were also commissioning them in a conscious effort to bolster their sovereign power in Béarn and elsewhere. Keenly aware of the political uses of the printing press, Henri d'Albret sponsored the first printing press in the viscounty of Béarn. In 1552 he encouraged two printers, Jonah de Vingles from the venerable printing center of Lyons and Henri Pouvre of Toulouse, to settle in Béarn, and engaged them to print two thousand copies of the newly redacted customary laws, *fors*, of Béarn which highlighted and encouraged the tradition of political and cultural separatism in the region and formally delineated the extent of the Albrets' sovereign powers. Henri's actions clearly reflect the Renaissance fascination with the written law as a tool of monarchical power. As a formal expression of the regional particularism and quasi-independence of Béarn, the printing of the *fors* of Béarn also drew the enthusiastic support of the local estates, which bankrolled the printers' efforts and sold the broadsheets at ten sols a piece to the local municipalities.[95]

The establishment of a printing press and print culture in Béarn, beyond the reach of royal censors in France, was particularly convenient after 1560 when royal edicts became increasingly specific and linked "all production of placards, hand bills and pamphlets that could tend to move people to seduction" to the cries of lèse-majesté.[96] In Béarn Jeanne d'Albret increasingly used the printing press to perpetuate her religious policies and dynastic strategies. In 1571, for example, she commissioned Nicolas Bordenave to write a didactic and

---

[94]Bayaud and Laprade, eds., "Un inventaire (1555)," 11–16.
[95]AD-PA, C681. See also Louis Desgraves, *Etudes sur l'imprimerie dans le sud-ouest de la France aux XVe, XVIe et XVIIe siècles* (Amsterdam: Erasmus, 1968), 17–29.
[96]As quoted in Jeffrey Sawyer, *Printed Poison: Pamphlet Propaganda, Faction Politics, and the Public Sphere in Early Seventeenth-Century France* (Berkeley: University of California Press, 1991), 24.

moralistic history of recent events in Béarn and Navarre, and employed him to edit her own memoirs.[97]

The Albrets' patronage of Protestant printers and poets extended beyond Béarn. Among Jeanne's most important protégés were the Rochelais brothers, Pierre and Jerome Haultin, who published more than two hundred pamphlets between 1570 and 1587. Jeanne's patronage of Pierre Haultin established the two brothers as the Protestant printing house par excellence and gave the Haultins a virtual monopoly on Protestant literature and propaganda for half a century. Under the protection of the Albrets, Pierre and Jerome Haultin flourished and published political broadsides, religious devotionals, and music which celebrated Calvinist doctrines, theologians, and Huguenot party leaders. Between 1570 and 1585 the Haultins published four editions of Clement Marot's *Psalms*, translated into glorious French, an edition of the New Testament in Basque, commissioned by Jeanne in 1571, along with an alphabet of Matthew, a New Testament in French, and a seventy-two page pamphlet defending the revival of Huguenot hostilities in 1577. They also published many pamphlets commissioned directly by the Albrets and their inner circles of confidants, clients, and Protestant apologists who publicized the Bourbon cause. Between 1585 and 1589, the Haultins published seven pro-Bourbon pamphlets by Philippe Duplessis du Mornay, Simon Goulart's *Histoire du Present*, a thinly veiled attack on Ligueur activities in France, and a satiric work on death.[98]

However, evidence can be detected in the extraordinary accounts. Printers' costs and book purchases were still a very insignificant part of the Albrets' total expenditures on luxuries. In July 1571, for example, Jeanne d'Albret paid a Rochelais bookseller, Marin Villepoux, 34 livres for four classical histories and two Bibles for Henri's edification. Several years later, Haultin furnished fifteen hundred volumes of the pro-Bourbon pamphlet, *La Loi Salique*, and one hundred copies of *La Vie des Bourbon* to Henri de Navarre, at a cost of four sols per volume.[99] While the cost of such printed treatises and propaganda pieces, even when purchased in bulk, was quite small, the Albrets recognized that the political benefits could be enormous.

---

[97]Raymond, "Notes extraites des comptes de Jeanne d'Albret," 11(1866):129.

[98]For an overview of the careers of the Haultin brothers, see Louis Desgraves, *Les Haultin, 1571–1623* (Geneva: Librairie Droz, 1960); idem, *Etudes sur l'imprimerie*, 12–29.

[99]Raymond, "Notes extraites des comptes de Jeanne d'Albret," 11(1866):129; ibid., 12(1866):424.

V. Conclusion

Inspired by political necessity and courtly convention, the Albrets engaged in traditional aristocratic patterns of conspicuous consumption. Drawn by familial politics to the very center of court life, where they were influenced as well by the Renaissance courtly culture of the Valois monarchs of France, the Albrets directed a greater and greater share of their spending toward the luxury goods and artistic and literary pursuits so praised by Renaissance humanists and so favored by their peers. Beyond the spread of the new courtly culture of the Renaissance that reshaped the politics of consumption in aristocratic circles, the politics of gender also dramatically altered the general pattern of investment in luxury goods. The higher political profile of aristocratic males and their continued participation in the equestrian military habits of the feudal past generally increased total expenditures on luxuries in male-headed households. Thus, by the 1570s the combined impact of the growing refinement of the French royal court under Henri III and Henri de Navarre's assumption of his adult duties and the control of the family fortune after Jeanne's death drove up total capital outlay on luxury goods. At the same time, the greater access that noble males were accorded to royal pensions, gifts, and military offices also often meant greater incomes, which offset the impact of their increased expenditures on conspicuous luxuries.

The Albrets' conversion to Calvinism also affected their investment in luxury goods. Expenditures on serious artifacts of the faith, especially the printed word, became routine in the treasurer's accounts along with the patronage of Calvinist artists and printers. Moreover, the necessity of creating an image of sufficient strength and power to hold together the Huguenot alliance in the face of royal opposition compelled both Jeanne and Henri to engage in beautification and building projects and propaganda efforts which increased expenditures. By the 1570s, the wisdom of purchasing luxury items like jewelry and silverware that could be easily converted into cash or offered as collateral was more evident than ever. Jewelry comprised an increasingly important cache of wealth upon which the Albrets based their bid for political and religious dominance of the Huguenot party and France more generally. After 1570, extraordinary expenditures remained an important share of total expenditures, but were gradually supplanted by the costs of war-making. Military expenditures and war-related expenses constituted a far greater burden on family resources in the 1580s and 1590s.

Six

Financing the Faith

I cannot believe that there are some so ungrateful, so cold or so stupid that they would refuse to offer aid according to the means that God has given them."[1] So wrote an impassioned Henri de Navarre to the recalcitrant consuls of Nîmes in November 1587, hoping to persuade these Languedocian officials to raise 20,000 écus for the German and Swiss mercenaries, who, after months of negotiation, had finally entered France to fight for the Huguenot party. "I alone cannot satisfy them," Navarre went on to explain, "not only because it is not reasonable, but also because of the great and extraordinary expenditures that I have made and supported, for which I have spared neither the sale nor engagement of my lands, nor any credit that I could garner and find in or outside the kingdom [of France]."[2]

Navarre's strong words paint a poignant picture of the financial plight of the Huguenot noble during the civil wars in France. Time and time again Huguenot notables and princes delved deep into their own treasuries for funds to sustain the fight against the enemies of the Reformed faith. As a result, the finances of the Huguenot party in France were inextricably connected with the household finances of its aristocratic leaders,[3] and nowhere was this more true than with the finances of the "party protectors" Jeanne d'Albret and her son, Henri de Navarre. Family lands and jewels were put up as collateral for party loans negotiated in London, Paris, and Geneva. Household officers and

---

[1] Berger de Xivrey, ed., *Lettres missives*, 2:314.
[2] Ibid.
[3] Harding, *Anatomy of a Power Elite*, 176.

servitors served simultaneously as financial officials in the household and as treasurers of war for the Huguenot party. Soldiers' pay, accoutrements, provisions, ammunition, and other war-related expenses comprised an increasingly significant charge on the family accounts during the last three decades of the century. During the Religious Wars, the militarization of noble households and household economies further blurred the fine, often indistinguishable, line between the public and private finances in early modern France, and seriously taxed the resources of even the fullest purses and richest fortunes, including those of the house of Foix-Navarre-Albret.

I. Military Finance

Tracing military expenditures during the Wars of Religion is not an easy task because the Albrets disbursed funds for the war effort from several different accounts. No one account under the jurisdiction of the Chambre des comptes at Pau or Nérac summarized all the money spent for military enterprises. Domanial accounts recorded sums used to fortify strategic points of local interest—a castle, town wall, or tower—and to pay minor *capitaines de ville* and governors of small towns.[4] More exhaustive were the accounts of the general treasurers, who administered all the household finances and discharged the debts incurred by family members. Here, during Jeanne's reign, we find the payments made to the Swiss guards and to the companies stationed in the permanently fortified city of Navarrenx in Béarn. On the pension lists appear the names of certain captains of war and the occasional indemnity paid to a wounded soldier or war widow. In the 1570s and 1580s, as the wars virtually transformed Navarre's household into a standing *compagnie d'ordonnance*, treasurers made entries for funds spent to garrison Huguenot strongholds along the Garonne River, to outfit pages for the Huguenot army, and to send ambassadors to the courts of Europe to negotiate for aid.[5] Yet even these seemingly complete accounts, which often run to hundred of pages, do not include some important military payments, most notably those made to troops, native and foreign, in the field. For these expenditures, the Albrets named special or "extraordinary" treasurers of war, who received and dispensed revenues raised especially for the war effort. Unfortunately, very few of these extraordinary accounts have survived the ravages of

---

[4]See, for example, the domanial accounts of Armagnac and Fézenzaguet, AD-PA, B1588, for local defense during the first three civil wars.

[5]For example, AD-PA, B154, B157, B159.

war.[6] Those accounts still extant often cover the expenses of only two or three companies at most, in part because many commanders assumed the responsibility of paying their troops themselves by contract or by commission to circumvent the inherent danger of transporting money during war. Moreover, many commanders often paid their troops by imposing a tax or a ransom on a captured town in return for not pillaging it and thereby avoided the cumbersome bureaucracy of the extraordinary war treasury system all together. Thus, much of the financing of the Huguenot party armies (like the financing of early modern armies in general) was ad hoc and carried out by public displays of force. At the same time, efforts to attract loans from sympathetic Europeans were often conducted in great secrecy and with all the Byzantine twists and turns of high diplomacy. Since much of the financing of the Huguenot party was conducted in great secrecy, there are only intimations in the margins of the household accounts, in family letters, and in diplomatic dispatches of funds secretly advanced for party use. Yet even these cryptic references, together with other sources, can reveal the magnitude of Jeanne d'Albret's and Henri de Navarre's personal involvement in war financing in the late sixteenth century, although the numbers we arrive at must be considered approximations of their total efforts to finance the faith.

II. A Reluctant Beginning

The first of the Religious Wars erupted in March 1562 and lasted for only one year, during which Jeanne d'Albret carefully avoided any financial entanglement in the affairs of her coreligionists. Even the special expenditures that she was forced to initiate for her own safety and the security of her subjects in Béarn were covered in part by extraordinary donations from the estates in that viscounty.

The first salvos of the conflict coincided with Jeanne's banishment from court by her husband, Antoine. Even Jeanne's formal claims of neutrality, however, did not appease Catholic sympathizers, who knew that her religious passions and proclivities were more Reformed than Roman. Accordingly, the Queen of Navarre took refuge at her husband's Vendômois estates in the late spring of 1562. Soon after, accompanied by an escort of over three hundred Béarnais soldiers and captains of war, Jeanne began the slow and surreptitious journey back to the relative freedom and security of the viscounty of Béarn. With funds pro-

---

[6]Note, in the preface to the household account, AD-PA, B160, Mace DuPerray's account of the damages inflicted upon his papers by enemy troops after the battle of Coutras in October 1587.

vided by the Estates of Béarn, the seigneur d'Andaux and his company of men squired Jeanne and her train through the Catholic territories of Limoges and Périgord.[7] In August 1562, the entourage finally reached Béarn, where Jeanne remained ensconced in her château at Pau until the end of the war. From there, she authorized numerous expenditures for the defense of her realm, threatened to the north and east by vigorous fighting. Garrisons were reinforced and two members of her privy council were commissioned to stockpile the chief citadel of Navarrenx with supplies necessary to withstand a siege. The principal towns of Béarn supplied wheat and salt for the munitions stores at the fort, while the Estates voted a larger-than-normal donation in 1563 to help Jeanne reimburse her subjects for their contributions.[8]

Jeanne was too late to protect her lands and subjects in Armagnac and Fézenzaguet, where many Catholic troops were stationed and fighting was probably the fiercest. War also ravaged her territories in Albret and Mont-de-Marsan. In a letter penned in the winter of 1563, Jeanne complained that Blaise de Monluc, the Catholic commander of troops in Gascony, was "creating all the disturbances he can, such as seizing all my property at Nérac, Mont-de-Marsan, Lectoure, and Casteljaloux."[9] Nonetheless, the accounts of the domanial treasurers show that Monluc's campaigns did little to damage irreparably the flow of rents from these properties into Jeanne's coffers. In the duchy of Albret, where the seigneuries of Nérac and Casteljaloux were located, treasurers actually registered an increase in revenues only a year after the war. In Lectoure, estate officials managed to collect 2,666 livres from beleaguered renters in 1563, which represented a 7 percent increase in revenue over antebellum figures. Indeed, only Jeanne's estates in Mont-de-Marsan registered a marked decline in revenues at the end of the year.[10]

With the publication of the Peace of Amboise in Paris in March 1563, a precarious order was restored to Jeanne's territories in the southwest. Catholic leagues, sworn to continue hostilities, formed in Toulouse, Agen, and Cadillac. The parlement in Toulouse, dominated by Catholics, refused to register the edict of pacification.[11] Given this

---

[7]Roelker, *Queen of Navarre*, 195, 313.

[8]Charles Dartigue-Peyrou, *Jeanne d'Albret et le Béarn d'après les délibérations des Etats et les registres du Conseil Souverain, 1555–1572* (Mont-de-Marsan: Imprimerie Jean-Jacoste, 1934), 55.

[9]Roelker, *Queen of Navarre*, 300.

[10]Ad-PA, B1581 and B1584. See also Major, "Noble Income," 29.

[11]Janine Garrisson-Estèbe, *Protestants du Midi, 1559–1598* (Toulouse: Privat, 1980), 166–73.

state of affairs, the arming of Béarn continued. At the convocation of the Estates in January 1564, discussion centered on the defense of Navarrenx. Members of the first estate urged immediate refortification of city walls and repair of the trenches, proposing an extraordinary donation of 2,000 écus for the project. Other delegates claimed that the sum was not enough. At the final vote, 3,000 écus were accorded by the Estates of Béarn for repairs at Navarrenx.[12]

In the aftermath of the first Religious War, creditors from as far away as Italy presented Jeanne with the unsettled military debts of her late husband, Antoine, who had been mortally wounded at the siege of Rouen while fighting for the royalist cause. Many were not bills which Jeanne could expect her subjects to shoulder, since they derived in large part from Antoine's extravagant lifestyle at court and his love of gambling and fine clothes. But Jeanne privately settled even the promissory notes presented to her by munitions merchants and other purveyors of military supplies which undoubtedly derived from Antoine's service as commander of royal troops.[13] Acquitting the household of lavish debts accrued over several years taxed the limits of Jeanne's annual revenues. Most revenues were already promised to creditors or earmarked for normal household expenditures, which burgeoned in the 1560s in direct relation to Jeanne's increasing influence and power.

To resolve the liquidity problem created by the disturbances of war, mounting debts, and an expanding household, Jeanne authorized the sale of properties in Périgord, including the seigneurie of Peysac, for 10,000 livres cash.[14] As a sign of just how desperate she was for liquid wealth, Jeanne implored a household official, in her large, scrawling hand, to "search for the money that the late King had hidden in the lower room of the château of Nérac, whose keys had been lost,"[15] a revealing indication of how unwieldy even the Albrets' financial administration was becoming. All of Jeanne's efforts still left some of Antoine's creditors unpaid until long after his death.[16]

---

[12]Dartigue-Peyrou, *Jeanne d'Albret et le Béarn*, 41; for the original deliberations, see AD-PA, C682.

[13]For evidence of Antoine's prodigality, see an extant account of his extraordinary expenses, AD-PA, B7. For his participation in the wars, see A. de Ruble, *Jeanne d'Albret et la guerre civile*, and Marquis de Rochambeau, *Lettres d'Antoine de Bourbon et de Jehanne d'Albret* (Paris: Librairie Renouard, 1877).

[14]AD-PA, B1843.

[15]AD-PA, E586.

[16]AD-PA, E566. A promissory note issued by Navarre in 1575 pledged an outstanding payment to two Milanais merchants for artillery purchased by the late king of Navarre, Antoine de Bourbon.

By 1564 Jeanne had renounced her neutrality. She aggressively pursued the task of implementing religious reform in the viscounty of Béarn and, in turn, made the necessary social and financial adjustments necessitated by religious change. To meet the material needs of the Reformed Church in Béarn, Jeanne and a newly organized ecclesiastical council authorized town magistrates throughout the viscounty to seize and sell all movable goods belonging to the Catholic confraternities and designated moneys from the sale of these religious goods for ministers' salaries, alms for the poor, and other pious works. In spite of the long tradition of Béarnais separatism, which had encouraged the growth of Calvinist sensibilities in the Pyrenean viscounty, Jeanne's actions sparked protests which compromised her efforts to raise money for the Reformed Church in Béarn. In the valley of Ossau, for example, Catholic magistrates refused to carry out their commission and vehemently demanded the restitution of the chalices, crosses, and other church ornaments that had been seized forcibly by Jean de Nogues, an enthusiastic henchman for the ecclesiastical council.[17]

In Navarre, where opposition to Jeanne's attempts to impose Calvinism upon a resolute Catholic majority eventually flared into open rebellion in 1567 and 1568, Jeanne could not count on military aid from the Estates of Navarre, which did not meet in 1568 to vote their annual donation.[18] Nor could tolls be collected from rebel strongholds. Arnaud d'Esquille, Jeanne's treasurer in Navarre, succeeded in collecting only 1,781 livres in revenue, instead of the usual 9,000 to 10,000 livres, and most went toward repairs and defense.[19] The revolt in Navarre constituted just one of many disturbances around France, generally referred to as the second Religious War. While the publication of the Edict of Longjumeau in March 1568 ended widespread warfare, beneath the patina of peace that reconciled Huguenot to Catholic in France, and Jeanne to her subjects in Navarre, few tempers had cooled. The Catholic commander, Blaise de Monluc, lay in wait, ready to begin the wars again, and many Navarrese Catholics were willing to help him. By August 1568, realizing that neutrality was no longer a viable option, Jeanne fled with Henri and Catherine to the Huguenot refuge of La Rochelle; there, for the first time, she took an overtly direct role in the affairs of the Huguenot party in contrast to her quasi-neutrality of earlier years.[20]

---

[17]Dartigue-Peyrou, *Jeanne d'Albret et le Béarn*, 56.
[18]Major, "Noble Income," 29.
[19]Ibid.
[20]Roelker, *Queen of Navarre*, 270–308.

Jeanne proved to be a boon to the party. She organized members of her own household and privy council into a supervisory body responsible for handling party funds and financing the war effort.[21] The *Conseil près de La Royne de Navarre*, as it was entitled in official parlance, negotiated loans with English merchants in return for certain customs concessions in La Rochelle. French wood merchants were pressed to lend their services and supplies to mount cannons along the parapets of the fort at La Rochelle. Extraordinary taxes of 84,000 livres were levied upon the four hundred most prominent citizens in the Atlantic port city, but only after a larger levy of 184,000 livres had been stoutly rejected by the Rochellais.[22]

To allay the fears of prospective creditors to the Huguenot cause, Jeanne and other leading members of the Huguenot party mortgaged their own estates and jewels as a guarantee against sums borrowed.[23] In July 1569, at the height of Montgomery's Huguenot campaigns in Béarn, for example, Jeanne presented her jewels to Elizabeth of England as collateral for a loan. Twenty thousand English pounds poured into Huguenot war chests as a result.[24] Later the same year Jeanne's agents negotiated an even more impressive loan from Elizabeth and used two magnificent rings valued at 90,000 écus as collateral. With these precious effects in hand, the English queen agreed to furnish 66,000 écus to the Huguenot party, which was in desperate need of ready cash to pay the German mercenary troops in its service. Jeanne later reclaimed the rings in the spring of 1570 when she repaid the English loans with moneys derived from the sale of ecclesiastical lands and effects in her duchy of Albret.[25]

In Béarn, the confiscation of land belonging to the Church and rebel leaders after Montgomery's victory over them in August 1569 brought over 80,000 livres annually into a special treasury. Jeanne used much of this money to provide salaries for her Calvinist ministers, fellowships for the training of future pastors in Geneva, and funds for the Protestant academy she established in Lescar in Béarn. Only after the money earmarked for religious education was spent did Jeanne consider using funds from the special treasury on more explicitly military purposes: to shore up defenses at Navarrenx; to pay soldiers' salaries; and to repay citizens' loans.

---

[21]Ibid., 312.
[22]Ibid., 312; see also Jeanne's sale of her viscounty of Bruilhois Armagnac, AD-PA, B1588; Major, "Noble Income," 30.
[23]AD-PA, B1588; Major, "Noble Income," 30.
[24]Roelker, *Queen of Navarre*, 310.
[25]AD-PA, B16.

On August 8, 1570, the Peace of Saint Germain was signed, ending the third round of warfare between Catholics and Protestants. Among the many concessions granted by the Crown to the rebels was the promise to pay the balance still owing to German *reiters* for their services.[26] This generous provision, however, did little to relieve Jeanne of the many other debts and charges she had incurred on behalf of the Huguenot cause. Where would the money come from? The domanial treasuries were dangerously depleted of funds. Rents from the stricken territories of Béarn, Albret, and Armagnac were difficult to collect, and the little money that was coaxed out of cash-strapped renters could be transported only with great difficulty and expense over roads swarming with soldiers-cum-bandits.[27] Once again, certain expedients were adopted: Jeanne reduced numbers in her household and suspended the salaries of many of those remaining in service in order to have money available for her more anxious creditors. Officers in the household fortunate enough to have resources of their own were tapped for low interest loans with which Jeanne paid the daily expenses of the household.[28] Money was thus freed from her general treasury to pay some of her war debts.

Nonetheless, the Queen of Navarre was still so besieged by creditors by the end of 1570 that she was forced to more drastic measures. Letters dispatched to estate officials in the spring of 1571 all mentioned "the necessity to raise princely sums immediately to avoid total ruin … because of the losses during the recent troubles."[29] To do so, Jeanne proposed alienating some of her most profitable lands and the seigneurial privileges they carried. Jeanne issued a number of decrees to Jean Alespée and Bertrand de La Valade, councilors in the Chambre des comptes in Nérac, concerning the domain in Périgord, where a lively trade in land, predating the third civil war, was already characteristic Albret policy.[30] She authorized her officials to sell her rights of high justice in the parishes of Saint Orse, Atur, Sablon, and Saint-Pierre de Clignac. Saint Orse alone brought in 2,250 livres to the general treasury, while Jean Foucauld, seigneur de Lardimalie, purchased the rights of justice in Saint Pierre de Clignac for 1,000 livres. The entire parish of Saint-Joulet in Périgord was sold to Pierre de Mar-

---

[26]Roelker, *Queen of Navarre*, 310.
[27]AD-PA, B16 and B17.
[28]See, for example, the 4,400 livres borrowed from the seigneur de Vigneau in February 1569 and paid back in 1570 without interest, AD-PA, B16. For a discussion of rentes, see B. Schnapper, *Les Rentes au XVIe siècle* (Paris: S.E.V.P.E.N., 1957).
[29]Roelker, *Queen of Navarre*, 289.
[30]AD-PA, B1843 through B1852.

quessac for 5,500 livres.[31] Jeanne also ordered the repurchase of the Périgordian parish of Thonac, only to turn around and immediately resell it to the seigneur de Losse for 12,000 livres profit.[32] In all, Jeanne garnered more than 20,000 livres from alienations in her county of Périgord in 1571.[33] Another 30,000 livres were added to the general treasury from the sale or alienation of important seigneuries in the duchy of Albret.[34] Finally, to reward Count Montgomery for his brilliant campaign on her behalf in Béarn, Jeanne bestowed upon the Huguenot captain the estate of Saint-Geniès, worth about 700 to 800 livres annually in rent.[35]

As a result of this mad land trade, payments to the general treasury in 1571 compared favorably with those of peacetime years and permitted Jeanne to pay off some of her debts. According to a financial report prepared by Henri de Mesmes, the Royal Master of Requests, during marriage negotiations between Henri de Navarre and Marguerite de Valois, revenues from the estates administered by the house of Foix-Navarre-Albret reached 188,564 livres only one year after the Peace of Saint Germain, as compared to 170,000 livres annually during the 1560s.[36] As the Master of Requests hastened to point out, however, Henri's fortunes as King of Navarre were also encumbered by annual expenses and debts of over 500,000 livres. Furthermore, lands alienated by his parents would only be redeemed at a total cost of 169,021 livres. For Mesmes, the long-term prognosis for the house was not particularly positive.[37]

Indeed, one year later, in 1572, revenues fell disastrously to 104,053 livres.[38] The jurisdictions of Albret, Périgord, and Armagnac, all sites of extensive alienations during the civil wars, suffered marked declines in rent receipts. Thus, Jeanne's attempts to save her house from financial ruin by alienating part of her domain left her more deeply in debt than ever. Elsewhere, the Estates of Foix and of Béarn failed to meet to vote their customary donations of 9,000 livres and 19,000 livres respectively.[39] With creditors still to pay and only enough money in her treasury to cover household expenses, pensions, and sala-

---

[31] AD-PA, B1856; AD-PA, B1855; and BN FF3948.
[32] AD-PA, B1854.
[33] BN FF3948.
[34] Ibid. In most cases, Jeanne retained her right of repurchase.
[35] Ibid.
[36] Ibid.
[37] Ibid.
[38] AD-PA, B148.
[39] Ibid.

ries, Jeanne borrowed money and negotiated loans from loyal servitors in the spring of 1572 to cover the cost of journeying to Paris to celebrate her son's marriage. From her loyal lady-in-waiting, DuVerger, for example, Jeanne borrowed 2,000 livres to pay the expenses of her sojourn in Tours.[40] Two months later, the lady Renée lent Jeanne 3,000 livres for her household and travel expenses from the Bourbon estates in Vendômois to Paris.[41]

Once in Paris, there were lavish expenditures made on the eve of Henri's marriage. To help cover these purchases, Jeanne authorized her maître d'hôtel, Sieur de Juscourt, "to find some good sum of money, either rente or otherwise ... in order to support the great expense that she was obliged to make for the marriage of the king." From merchants in Tours, Juscourt raised 2,400 livres which he brought to Paris in early June. From the accounts, it is clear that these loans were intended to resolve a cash-flow problem created by the enormous sums of money Jeanne was spending to finance the festivities and gift-giving surrounding Henri's imminent marriage. Juscourt, in fact, hoped to repay the loans to his Touraine creditors within the month to avoid any but the most minimal interest charges. Jeanne's untimely death on June 9, 1572, however, prohibited such a measure of economy. Juscourt was constrained by Jeanne's chancellors and secretary of finance to leave the money with the household treasurer who had several large medical fees to acquit, as well as funeral expenses. To pay for the illustrious funeral worthy of a queen of Navarre, members of the privy council had to borrow 6,000 livres from a Parisian *parlementaire*.[42] Jeanne's legacy, then, to her son and heir, Henri de Navarre, was a treasury rich in convertible wealth but drained of ready cash.

III. The St. Bartholomew's Day Massacre and Its Aftermath

Henri's expenses in the first months after his mother's death are terribly difficult to delineate. Peace and his impending marriage momentarily stopped the drain of military expenses on his dwindling revenues, although prenuptial festivities must have been costly, unless Jeanne had arranged for the Valois court to assume most of these expenses. With great pomp and circumstance, Henri de Navarre married Marguerite de Valois on August 18, 1572; six days later Paris was

---

[40]Raymond, "Notes extraites des comptes de Jeanne d'Albret," 12(1869):182. By 1572 Jeanne's ordinary expenditures were running around 7,000 livres monthly or 84,000 livres yearly.
[41]Ibid., 183.
[42]Ibid., 183, 184.

convulsed by the Saint Bartholomew's Day Massacre. Under orders from the prefect of Paris, city officials ransacked the house of Navarre's personal treasurer, Jean Bernard, and seized his papers. The notarial inventory prepared afterwards revealed that Bernard was serving as war treasurer for the Calvinist party in France in addition to his post in Navarre's household. Among his effects were numerous receipts for loans from German and English creditors amounting to 7.5 million livres, receipts for taxes levied upon the population of La Rochelle (192,753 livres), and a promissory note for 854,153 livres still due to Prince Casimir of the Palatinate for German *reiters*. But to what extent his activities jeopardized his master's personal fortunes, or to what extent Navarre backed these loans, is difficult to ascertain.[43]

What is certain is that Charles IX considered the financial fortunes of his new brother-in-law so precarious that he dispatched one of his own financial officers, Henri de Mesmes, to reorganize and supervise Navarre's household finances.[44] Mesmes bitterly contested his forced appointment as superintendent of finance of the house of Foix-Navarre-Albret, charging that the task of making this noble house solvent was "beyond the power of mortal men."[45] Moreover, as the superintendent of finance Mesmes assumed personal responsibility for Navarre's debts, which were mounting dangerously and quickly. By 1574 Mesmes had used over 40,000 livres of his own money to satisfy Navarre's anxious creditors. In the spring of 1574 he argued that he needed to go to Paris to put his personal affairs in order; Mesmes noted in his memoirs that "he took this pretext to retire (from service) little by little."[46] By 1575 Mesmes' salary was dramatically crossed out on Catherine de Bourbon's civil tolls and the treasurer scrawled in the margins, "for lack of service."[47]

For much of Mesmes' term of service, Henri was held in custody at court, where he made good use of the pleasures available—hawking, hunting, pursuing amorous adventures, gambling, and even courting his most dangerous rivals, the Guises. But by January 1576, tensions were so thick at court between rival factions that Navarre wrote to his childhood companion and lieutenant general in Béarn, Miossens, that he feared an attack on his life by members of the Catholic Holy League:

---

[43]MC III, 433.
[44]Harding, *Anatomy of a Power Elite*, 159.
[45]Mesmes, *Mémoires*, 182–84. According to Mesmes' calculations, annual expenditures outstripped annual revenue by a factor of two.
[46]Ibid., 184.
[47]AD-PA, B25.

> The court is more strange than I have ever seen it. We carry daggers, wear jackets of mail and often a breastplate under our cloaks. We are always ready to cut each others' throats. They say that they will kill me but I want to be one jump head of them.[48]

Less than a month later, Henri left court with three or four close friends, ostensibly on a hunting expedition, and rode southward for refuge. Hoping to rejoin the Huguenots in their fight for recognition, Henri only had time to reestablish his authenticity as a supporter of the Huguenot cause (after four years of cavorting with the Guises) before a new edict of toleration was issued. Early in May, Henri patched together his relations with Alençon, Condé, and other partisans of Huguenot Party resistance by agreeing to the terms of the Edict of Beaulieu. Highly favorable to Calvinism and its leadership, the Edict of Beaulieu confirmed Alençon as governor of Anjou, Condé as governor of Picardy, and Navarre as governor of Guyenne.[49]

As governor of Guyenne, Henri was quick to urge those under his charge, town leaders and captains of war, to follow the *politique* spirit of the Edict of Beaulieu, often called the "Peace of Monsieur."[50] But calming passions, stabilizing relations between Catholics and Protestants in the countryside, and restoring order proved to be nearly an impossible task. Troops whose wages were still in arrears could not be disbanded for fear of widespread brigandage. Those companies that remained intact, ostensibly to preserve and impose the tenuous balance achieved at Beaulieu, were not always nonpartisan. And everywhere city magistrates were unwilling to forget the indignities suffered during the troubles at the hands of one side or the other and stood ready to perceive partisanship in the slightest infringement on their resources or liberties. To appease the Catholic contingency in Bordeaux, for example, Henri ordered the seigneur de Bayaumont to return artillery and ammunition stolen from that city's stockpiles during the wars for use at the Huguenot stronghold in Agen.[51] Still, the city councilors and *parlementaires* in Bordeaux, capital city of the *gouvernement* of Guyenne, refused Henri entry in December 1576.[52] In dis-

---

[48]*Lettres missives*, 1:81–83.
[49]Buisseret, *Henry IV*, 9.
[50]See, for example, his letter to Vivans, governor in Périgueux, *Lettres missives*, 1:91–92.
[51]Ibid., 96.
[52]See Navarre's impassioned plea to the nobility, cities, and communities in Guyenne on December 21, 1576, to honor the edict of pacification and to show "to all an example of true reunion," notwithstanding the bad behavior of "five of six turbulent spirits in Bordeaux," *Lettres missives*, 1:113.

patches to commanders of peace-keeping companies, Henri constantly admonished them to behave with discretion in order to avoid aggravating conciliatory councils.[53]

In 1576 it required not only all of Henri's fabled charm and tact to hold onto his government of Guyenne, but also enormous sums of money. Indeed, peace could be nearly as expensive as war during the late sixteenth century. Troops charged with keeping the peace, garrisons guarding the Huguenots' *places de sûreté*, and Navarre's personal guard all had to be paid. By 1576 many of these expenses were paid by the French crown as one of the conditions of peace with the Huguenots. In practice, however, funds came from a number of public and private sources. In 1576, for example, the Crown's ordinary treasurers of war issued letters of credit from the *Epargne* to cover the wages of the forty soldiers and sixty archers who made up Navarre's personal company in 1576; but local treasurers of war, appointed by Navarre and under his control, continued to impose extraordinary taxes on the population at large in order to pay peacetime troops and garrisons.[54] Moreover, between 15,000 livres and 25,000 livres was disbursed from the domanial treasury of Béarn to pay the permanent garrison at Navarrenx and other garrisons established during the Religious Wars for the protection of the viscounty.[55] When these sources proved insufficient, Navarre paid troops out of his personal treasury.[56]

The worsening religious climate in the fall of 1576 compelled Navarre, as titular head of the Huguenot party in southern France, to write to the burgomasters of Zürich and Schaffhausen in Switzerland in search of even more military aid to counter "the design and enterprises that certain enemies of the reformed religion are making."[57] Navarre's fear that French Catholics were growing increasingly intransigent and bold and would provoke another round of hostilities was confirmed at the Estates General of Blois in 1576–77. Most Catholics in the assembly wanted no less than the reestablishment of Catholicism

---

[53]See Henri's order to La Réole in August 1576 concerning the movement of troops in the Agenais and particularly Villeneuve. Henri directed La Réole not to garrison troops in Villeneuve where the consuls had promised him "all service and obedience," *Lettres missives*, 1:98–100.

[54]See Robert Harding's lucid explanation of the extraordinary fiscal system which developed during the Religious Wars and enhanced the powers of the governors; *Anatomy of a Power Elite*; *Lettres missives*, 1:108.

[55]AD-PA, B151, B152. For moneys spent in the first years after Jeanne's death, see AD-PA, B148, which shows that around 15,000 livres were spent of the defense of Béarn in 1573, and B150, which reports that 23,000 livres were spent in 1575.

[56]*IAD, Basses-Pyrénées*, 182–86.

[57]*Lettres missives*, 1:109.

as the only religion in France; soon after the assembly was dismissed, war erupted again.[58]

In order to protect the practice of Calvinism in Guyenne, Henri mobilized troops with the aid of his new lieutenant general, the viscount of Turenne. To pay these new troops, Henri appointed extraordinary treasurers of war in towns throughout his province and ordered them to raise over 65,000 livres by imposing forced loans on the secular population and the Church.[59] In Mont-de-Marsan, where a company of thirty-nine men under the leadership of Sieur de Mesmes was established, Martin DuBoys, treasurer extraordinary, was authorized to levy a contribution of 11,625 livres upon the clerics of Aire. The bishop alone was to pay 1,515 livres. The clergy in the town of Dax were also assessed for 12,094 livres. A much smaller sum was levied on those associated with the cathedral in Bayonne. A subsidy was placed also on wine in hopes of raising 2,600 livres. For the rest of the money needed, Navarre's military treasurer counted on the secular population.[60]

In practice, treasurers very rarely collected the entire amount demanded. People were resistant—sometimes unable to pay, sometimes impossible to find. In the words of one frustrated official, "The village of [Vire] had been in part burned and put to ruin ... so much so that the inhabitants of the said town were far away from there ... and there was no way to recover anything from them." In Montaut, villagers were subject to the claims of the Catholic troops who occupied the town. In all, 11,939 livres for the 1577 Guyenne levy could not be collected because villages had been laid waste, abandoned, or occupied by opposing forces.[61] By late spring 1577, Navarre's war chest was nearly depleted. Expenses outpaced receipts, and contributions only slowly trickled in from the countryside.[62] Meanwhile, Catholic troops were making headway in Languedoc. Desperate for funds, Henri authorized his lieutenant general in Albret, André Meslon, to begin seizing ecclesiastical revenues in his hereditary duchy. Although all Catholic benefices and church lands were to be included on the rolls, Navarre stipulated that revenues would not be seized where ecclesiastical and

---

[58]Buisseret, *Henry IV*, 10–11.
[59]AD-PA, B2298, "Account of the expenses concerning the military in Guyenne."
[60]Ibid.
[61]Ibid.
[62]At the garrison in Mont-de-Marsan, for example, Mesmes received reinforcements in mid-April when Captain Scanebacque and his company of twenty-two men joined the garrison. Over the course of the next month, both commanders were busy recruiting new soldiers, and by mid-May, 135 soldiers were within the city. Partial payments almost immediately followed, and this situation lasted until the conclusion of the war.

monastic officials had not specifically declared themselves enemies of the Reformed religion.[63]

When this fifth Religious War concluded in September 1577, French Calvinists found themselves with few privileges, and sporadic violence characterized the lull between the wars. Henri spent the period after the Treaty of Bergerac trying to consolidate his control over the southwest. He complained repeatedly in his letters about the excesses and brutalities of troops who roamed the countryside and further set the people against his government; but sporadic, often disastrous, skirmishing remained the norm.[64] In 1579, Navarre spent over 11,000 livres from his personal treasury to maintain garrisons and governors at strategic points in Guyenne, while another 5,000 livres went for ammunition. To maintain morale, the governor of Guyenne doled out "peace" money to reward soldiers for their heroism in the past war and to provide for war widows. These miscellaneous awards amounted to 1,290 livres. (see table 6.1)

Respect for the compromise at Bergerac lasted but briefly, and the war resumed in early 1580. Scattered accounts show the various ways Navarre quickly mobilized funds for the Huguenot cause. The surest and swiftest method of raising the enormous amounts needed to recruit and outfit troops was to supply them from his own pocket. Consequently, in the winter of 1580, Henri alienated three of his most lucrative holdings in the duchy of Albret. On February 20, household officials sold Henri's properties in Puynormand and Villefranche for 48,033 livres. A little more than a month later, the sale of land in Vayre to Marie de Chaumont brought another 24,000 livres.[65] With more than 72,000 livres at his disposal, Henri waited for money to come in from other sources. Church lands and the wealth of recalcitrant Catholics provided moneys for new garrisons and companies. In April 1580, Navarre named the Count de La Rochefoucault his governor in the province of Saintonge and Angoulêmois and authorized this confirmed Huguenot to seize properties belonging to those of the "contrary party." In Pons, Jean Girault, a domanial receiver, was granted the authority

---

[63]*Lettres missives*, 1:140. Shortages of funds were especially serious in view of negotiations taking place with Cazimir in Germany. Just before the conclusion of the Treaty of Bergerac, this Protestant prince agreed to furnish 10,000 *reiter*, 10,000 foot soldiers, and 4,000 *arquebuziers* outfitted and armed at a cost of 120,000 écus, AN, K100, no. 18.

[64]See Henri's missives to Montmorency-Damville, governor of Languedoc in 1578, *Lettres missives*, 1:163–66, 194–97, 198–99, 214–15.

[65]AD-PA, B1473, B1522.

Table 6 Military Expenses Drawn from Navarre's Personal Treasury 1579-1587 (in *livres tournois*)

Year	1579	1582	1585	1587[e]
Garrisons	11,531	6,424	13,303	20,782
Gentlemen & War Captains	—	10,171	1,974	53,709
Pages[a]	810	1,560	3,330	3,363
Travel	—	25,108	17,300	26,940
Soldiers' Wages	—	—	—	4,062
Horses	—	10,107	10,217	23,425
Reparations	—	—	6,750	—
Ammunition	5,420	—	2,325	3,900
Miscellaneous[b]	1,290	—	9,970	11,316
Secret Expenses[c]	—	60,004	—	—
TOTAL	—[d]	—[d]	65,169	147,497

[a]Many young noblemen leaving their positions as pages in the household were equipped with arms specifically to "follow the King's service."

[b]Includes repaid loans, ransom money, awards for feats of bravery in the field, indemnities, alms, and "peace" money for soldiers wounded or unpaid in the Protestant forces.

[c]A curious chapter in these accounts denotes money paid out of the treasury for "purposes which the King does not want to specify."

[d]Some pages are missing in these accounts, including those with figures for total expenditures. No total of war-related expenses is possible.

[e]Account originally in écus. For purposes of uniformity, I have converted it into *livres tournois* at the rate of 3 livres to 1 écu.

to impose new taxes in order to further subsidize the troops under La Rochefoucault's command. Girault calculated that wages for the men in La Rochefoucault's personal company would come to 6,125 livres annually. To raise that sum, he assessed each of the 193 communes in the province 31£4s., and to provide supplies for the soldiers garrisoned around the province, Girault levied a surcharge on wine and auctioned off ecclesiastical benefices.[66] In Armagnac, church lands also provided funds for Huguenot forces where the military treasurer, Guillaume MaCary, was ordered to organize auctions in the ecclesiastical centers of Aire, Auch, Condom, and Lectoure.[67]

[66]AD-PA, B2468.
[67]AD-PA, B2470.

Catholic critics charged that Calvinist governors pocketed the money made from the sale of Church lands, but the accounts of military treasurers and receivers such as Girault and MaCary tell a different story. The money garnered from these confiscations in 1580 went almost exclusively to support Huguenot strongholds and to further the Huguenot religion in France. Funds from the sale of Church lands not only fed Huguenot troops and furthered the military efforts of the Huguenot party; they also fed struggling Huguenot ministers and furthered their religious ministry. In 1580 Navarre ordered that some of the revenues from benefices in Angoulêmois be used to pay the salaries of ministers in Jonzac, and he commanded MaCary to offer aid to the struggling congregation of Fleurance.[68]

The generous terms of the Treaty of Fleix, signed in November 1580, brought a measure of stability to France, and especially to the Midi, for almost five years. During this hiatus, Henri began the slow process of refinancing his treasury and redeeming his alienated domains. To finance the repurchases of the long-profitable seigneuries of Puynormand and Villefranche, Henri sought the aid of those subjects who had been protected during the recent troubles with moneys garnered from the sale of these possessions. In a letter dated 12 October 1581, Henri stated his desire to repurchase the parishes that he had been constrained to alienate in order to underwrite his military affairs, and he asked the inhabitants of Villefranche, Cazenave, and Puynormand to contribute 3,666 écus to the general treasury of Guyenne to that end.[69] After deliberations which took the better part of a month, representatives from nearly all the parishes in these three jurisdictions consented to the contributions. With uncommon finesse, however, delegates from Puynormand and Villefranche promised to pay their share of the levy—3,000 livres—only "according to their faculties, which were not great." What this bit of hedging meant was that moneys would not be raised until over a year later, and then only after Henri III of France and Navarre had promulgated numerous decrees urging the fair and equal levy of the sum.[70] Even with the levy, Navarre still had to find an additional 37,000 écus toward the repurchase of these seigneuries, a difficult task in view of his massive war debts. Domanial accounts show that Puynormand and Villefranche did not reappear on the rent rolls until 1586.[71]

---

[68]AD-PA, B2464, B1475.
[69]AD-PA, B1522.
[70]Ibid.
[71]AD-PA, B1478.

Thus, in spite of Henri's valiant and creative attempts to increase his income and recover his domain, the drain on his finances continued. Creditors obliged him to alienate additional properties, and these land sales more than offset any gains made to the treasury. In the duchy of Albret, for example, estate officials sold off three seigneuries in the fall of 1581 for a total of 60,000 livres.[72] The same year in Limousin, the seigneurie of Ayen was sold to the Bishop of Dax.[73] And in Bayonne, Henri tried to put the barony of Seignanx, including the city of Saint-Esprit, up for sale, hoping to garner 8,000 écus. The successful sale of this barony with its rights of justice to the inhabitants of Bayonne (who were endeavoring to expand their privilege to sell their wines and ciders in Saint-Esprit, where they had long been prohibited) was frustrated when estate officials appended the property of Gosse to the deal and asked a higher price. A compromise was reached only three years later when Henri agreed to let the people of Bayonne purchase the town of Saint-Esprit separately for 1,200 livres.[74]

Military expenses continued to be a heavy charge on Navarre's personal treasury, in spite of the Crown's promises to pay the considerable price of peace. Huguenot garrisons remained intact although reduced in personnel. Huguenot leaders had no intention of completely dismantling the military organization which guaranteed their freedom, nor were they required to do so by the terms of the peace. Nonetheless, funds from the governmental treasury in Bordeaux under the supervision of Matignon, whose Catholic proclivities served as a check on Navarre's activity, were disbursed with intentional slowness to company commanders. Tolls exacted from merchants shipping their goods along the Garonne paid only for those troops stationed in the châteaux-forts of Montségur and Figéac.[75] And, as usual, contributions levied on a war-weary populace rarely produced the expected returns. Consequently, Henri disbursed money out of his own coffers to calm discontented soldiers, many of whom served without pay for as long as eight months, in order to circumvent the dangers of rebellion.[76] In numerous letters to Henri III of France and others, Navarre catalogued the random violence which sent frissons of fear throughout the countryside and meant the establishment of minigarrisons in towns and châteaux

---

[72] AD-PA, B1473.
[73] AD-PA, B1472.
[74] Pierre Hourmat, "Henri de Navarre, gouverneur de Guyenne et la ville de Bayonne, 1576–1584," in *Henri de Navarre et le royaume de France 1572–1598* (Pau: Editions Marrimpouey, 1984), 137–39.
[75] *Lettres missives*, 1:414–16.
[76] Ibid., 1:399, 410–11.

until the alarms died down. Wages for these temporary *gardes de ville* frequently came from Henri's private treasury.[77]

We can sketch only in part the magnitude of Henri's military expenditures a year after the peace, but the figures are daunting. According to Julien Malet's 1582 accounts, Henri picked up the charges of the small garrisons guarding the cities of Tarascon, L'Ile Jourdain, Lectoure, Exideuil, Puymirol, and the châteaux at Puynormand, Montignac, and Merenx. Most "companies" in these towns numbered no more than ten soldiers, and charges for these troops came to only 6,424 livres—roughly one-third to one-half of the amount usually disbursed for this purpose during wartime. (see table 6.1) What is striking, however, is the number of *places de sûreté* on that roster whose charges Navarre was paying, in spite of assurances that these strongholds were the financial responsibility of the Crown. Henri also paid pensions to an ever-widening circle of gentlemen sympathizers and war captains who gathered about him in search of adventure and booty. Among them, by 1582, were six Scotsmen. The pay of these *gentilshommes en suite du roy* varied from the 3,000-livre bounty showered upon the Viscount de Meille to the 30 livres given to one Captain Perrichot. In all, 10,171 livres was shared among these opportunists and Huguenot warriors to encourage them to remain at Navarre's beck and call. By far, Henri's greatest expenditures on behalf of the party in 1582 were generated from his dealings with other Huguenot leaders in and beyond the kingdom of France. Couriers sent to Henri's companions in France and ambassadors sent to the Huguenot courts of Europe turned in a travel bill of 25,020 livres.[78]

Indeed, throughout the duration of the Treaty of Fleix, the travel expenses of Navarre's couriers and ambassadors comprised one of the more significant charges on his budget. "From infancy onwards," writes David Buisseret, "Henri had been signing letters to foreign princes— part of the perennial Huguenot effort to obtain foreign aid—now in 1583, he began to play that game with a vengeance, sending ambassadors from the Nérac court to virtually all the Huguenot courts in Europe."[79] The flurry of letters and diplomats dispatched to rulers sympathetic to the Huguenot cause eventually brought a strict repri-

---

[77]Ibid., 1:381–82.
[78]AD-PA, B157.
[79]Buisseret, *Henry IV*, 12. Also see Navarre's accompanying correspondence to the King of Sweden, John III; to the Elector of Saxony; to Lord Burgley; to Charles, Duke of Sudermain, presumptive heir to the crown of Sweden; to the King of Denmark, Frederick II; and to the Holy Roman Emperor, Rudolph II, *Lettres missives*, 1:535–43, 545–48, 557–64.

mand from Henri III of France in the winter of 1584, but it did little to dissuade Navarre from his actions.[80] He continued to elicit goodwill and aid from England and Germany, haranguing the king about the many ruptures in the conditions of the peace, and preparing for the resumption of war, which seemed only a matter of time.[81] In order to guarantee that his treasury would be full when war broke out again, Henri alienated more of his domain in Périgord and Albret in 1584 and 1585, and he borrowed large sums from creditors in Geneva and Paris.[82] Money from these land sales and creditors brought receipts to the general treasury up to 628,539 livres by 1585.[83]

Impressive as that figure was, Henri's prodigious spending still surpassed it. General treasurer Vincent de Pedesclaux dispensed 668,230 livres from his accounts in 1585. Much of this went to cover the rising costs of Henri's burgeoning household of military men as well as servants. Ordinary expenditures alone came to 104,924 livres; salaries accounted for another 82,023 livres. Specifically military expenditures came to only 65,169 livres, and so constituted but 10.4 percent of all funds disbursed from the general treasury. Enormous sums, totaling over 100,000 livres, however, were also funneled into the hands of two household treasurers, Mace DuPerray and Julien Malet, who coincidentally were serving as Navarre's treasurers of war. A hefty 30,917 livres had to be paid to cover annual interest charges on loans and rentes negotiated, at least in part, to finance the Huguenot army. Henri's commitment to Calvinism, it appears, pervaded nearly every aspect of his spending.[84]

Although hostilities were renewed in 1585, civil war recommenced in earnest in 1586. As the war escalated, so did Henri's military expenses. Henri was not above selling royal privileges and monopolies to interested parties willing to pay in ready cash. The difficulty of coercing moneys from reluctant royal officials "à court des fonds" increasingly prompted Henri, prodded by his own desperate treasurers, to farm out royal monopolies at a discount to interested parties who had the time and energy to assume the risks. It was a deal which could benefit both parties to the contract: Henri enjoyed an influx of needed cash, while the buyers could hope under the right circumstances to almost double their investments over time.[85] At a time when

---

[80] Ibid., 1:xli.
[81] Ibid., 1:633–34, 648–49, 653, 655–60.
[82] AD-PA, B1525, B1526, B1896, and AN, KK 146.
[83] Major, "Noble Income," 35.
[84] AD-PA, B159.
[85] AD-PA, B591.

the annual returns from investment in lands hovered between 3 to 5 percent, royal monopolies attracted a number of noble investors.[86] As a 1585 deal which Henri concluded with one of his loyal *serviteurs*, François de Bonne, seigneur de Lesdiguières, indicates, royal monopolies were often turned over to Henri's military officers at cut rates as compensation for service, and thus failed to generate sufficient revenues to cover escalating military expenses.[87]

By 1587, Henri found himself spending 149,526 livres from his own coffers to cover the cost of soldiers' wages, repairs, and ammunitions. Continued alienations in his northernmost estates kept receipts to the general treasury near 600,000 livres.[88] Simultaneously, citizens and peasants alike in Guyenne were being bled white by the soldiers garrisoned in the province. As the war dragged on, the contribution system faltered as communes grew too poor to meet their monthly payments. In Nérac, for example, contributions levied from the twenty-four communes surrounding the château yielded 537 écus 47 sols 17 deniers in November 1585 for the garrison established there. By May 1586, contributions began to decline alarmingly as commune after commune defaulted on its payment. By the end of 1587, Henri's commissioner in Nérac received contributions from only nine communities, most of which paid only a portion of their original assessment. Funds from this source yielded only 68 écus 22 sols 4 deniers for troops' wages in December 1587.[89] A similar situation prevailed around L'Ile Jourdain, where soldiers were paid in kind rather than specie. Here, wheat from Church lands and the estates of Catholic rebels was confiscated and put in the company munitions store to be distributed by the paymaster at proper intervals. However, these stores proved insufficient, and no more wheat could be found among the stipulated contributors. Accordingly, the desperate commander of the garrison appropriated 4,452 sacks of wheat from Navarre's own stores in the *moulin banier* to pay and provision his men.[90]

To cover the deficits that resulted when contribution quotas failed, Navarre relied increasingly on his war treasurers and commissioners, who were expected to balance their military accounts with their own private funds if need be. They were to be, in Robert Harding's words,

---

[86]Ibid.; for a discussion of returns on land investment, see Bergin, *Cardinal Richelieu*, 59.
[87]AD-PA, B591.
[88]AD-PA, B160.
[89]AD-PA, B1528. For other documents relating to the garrison at Nérac, see B1527, B1529, B1530.
[90]AD-PA, B1614.

"institutionalized on-going creditors."[91] The career of Adrian Auzère, valet de chambre in Navarre's household and commissioner of tolls along the Garonne, illustrates one of the ways in which Navarre financed his army with easily accessible, deferred-interest loans in the desperate years before his accession to the French throne.[92] Appointed commissioner in 1585, Auzère was cited in the original letter of commission for his "fidelity and loyalty and experience in the facts of finance," and guaranteed 1 sol per livre levied as wages.[93] Auzère served in the position for five years—apart from a brief illness in 1587. His accounts show steadily increasing revenues from just over 9,000 écus levied in 1585 to almost 60,000 écus between 1588 and 1589. Nonetheless, Auzère's burgeoning coffers failed to meet the growing demands of Henri's war treasurers and captains. In addition to paying the wages of garrisons guarding river traffic along the Garonne, Auzère was ordered to advance close to 30,000 écus to the war treasurers, Vincent de Pedesclaux and Simon Bellenger, between 1588 and 1589. According to Auzère's own reckoning, by 1590 he had paid 3,951 écus from his own pockets to cover military expenses and had yet to enjoy 1 sou of his salary.[94] After his accession to the throne of France, Henri ordered that Auzère be repaid (with interest) with receipts from the *Epargne*, but the final closing date on the Garonne River toll books indicates that Auzère was only fully reimbursed in 1609, just a year before Henri's death.[95]

The general assembly of the Huguenot party met at La Rochelle in the presence of Henri de Navarre in 1588. Since 1573 the military and political concerns of the Huguenot party had been deliberated and debated by this body, which performed many of the same functions for the rebel Huguenots as the Estates General did for the Kingdom of France. In 1588 the assembly confirmed Navarre's right to control the composition of the smaller provincial assemblies (local Estates) into which the Huguenot party was divided by recognizing his right to accept or reject candidates seeking office.[96] With many of the Huguenot military leaders—Fonterailles, Saint-Geniès, La Broue, Favas—in

---

[91]Harding, *Anatomy of a Power Elite*, 176.
[92]AD-PA, B1564 through B1568.
[93]AD-PA, B1564.
[94]AD-PA, B1567.
[95]AN, KK147, and AD-PA, B1567.
[96]For a discussion of the function of the General Assembly and the Huguenot party with its military and political focus, as opposed to the assemblies or national synods of the Reformed Church and their religious concerns, see Garrison-Estèbe, *Protestants du Midi*, 182–95, 339–48.

attendance, deliberations naturally turned to the army's finances and the progress of the war. It was clear to most that the war would have no easy conclusion, and that the time had come to reestablish some of the rules of war financing. The assembly reaffirmed the army's rights to levy ransoms for captive prisoners, provided the sums raised were used to compensate soldiers wounded in battle. Deputies confirmed Navarre's right to levy tolls for the support of the army, and warnings were issued to those commissioners who were too liberal with exemptions. Wages were established for the financial officers of the Huguenot army. And strict penalties were established for soldiers guilty of unrestrained pillaging, although booty was declared one of the just fortunes of war, so long as it was distributed fairly among the troops.[97]

To better plan for the upcoming year, Simon Bellenger supplied projections for the army's finances for 1589. Personal tailles, tolls, and surcharges on wine and salt clearly constituted the basis of the army's financing according to the war treasurer. The majority of the twenty-two garrisons listed in Bellenger's account also were expected to receive a good part of their wages from the lease of ecclesiastical domains and the sale of Catholic lands. Ransom and booty made up less than 1 percent of these projected finances. In all, Bellenger estimated that revenue from all these sources could provide over 1,043,947 livres for military use—certainly more than enough to provide the 858,090 livres needed for the salaries of officers and soldiers.[98] Were these projections realized? Receipts from Bellenger's 1589 accounts show that he advanced well over 150,000 livres of his private funds to cover military deficits that year.[99]

Henri de Navarre became Henri IV of France in August 1589, and one of his first acts as king was to order François Hotman, treasurer of the *Epargne* and author of the *Francogallia*, to pay off his enormous debts with receipts from the royal treasury.[100] As we have seen in Auzère's case, however, this was a process which took many years. And in fact, the new treasuries—public and private—that Henri took charge of in 1589 were as encumbered with debts as his own.[101] So as he waged war for religious peace in his kingdom from 1590 to 1598, Henri could not simply borrow from the treasuries of France; he also continued to support his officers and soldiers with revenues from his

[97]BM, MSS 2096.
[98]Ibid.
[99]AN, KK146.
[100]Ibid.
[101]See Martin Wolfe, *The Fiscal System of Renaissance France* (New Haven and London: Yale University Press, 1972).

private estates. In 1594, and again in 1595, he resorted to the alienation of part of his domanial patrimony so that he could meet the interest payments on many of his loans. Only with the restoration of peace in 1598 could Henri's treasurers truly turn to the task of recouping his lost domains and refinancing the treasury. With impressive swiftness, receipts in the general treasury of Béarn and Navarre had returned to levels comparable to, if not higher than, peacetime receipts half a century earlier.[102]

IV. Conclusion

The Albrets' involvement in the Religious Wars drew them into an elaborate system of military financing which depended as heavily upon the private fortunes and landed resources of the great nobility as upon public revenues. Neither the fiscal system devised by the Huguenot party nor the financial promises and pledges of the French monarchy were sufficient to meet the enormous demands of war and the equally exigent programs for peace. Contributions, forced and voluntary loans, tolls, and even the sale of Church lands, which had initially buoyed the Huguenots' military efforts, proved to be cumbersome mechanisms for raising funds and produced diminishing returns after 1585. Royal schemes to bail out troubled Huguenot nobles in return for promises of peace were hampered by the economic crisis which had gripped much of the French countryside by the 1580s. Thus, Huguenot nobles and their chief officers quickly became regarded as the surest sources of ready cash for party activities. Reared from birth to believe that the traditional military role of the nobility entailed committing both life and property to the defense of the realm, Huguenot nobles pledged their resources to the defense of the faith, only to be sadly disappointed when many of their nonnoble coreligionists were not willing to do the same.

The seemingly unending cycle of sectarian violence, brigandage, and social disorder, which continued even after peace was declared, created the need for defensive garrisons during peacetime, so that by 1569 the drain of war was nearly constant. The prolonged economic crisis that affected both noble and royal treasuries during the sixteenth century meant that even Navarre's accession to the throne in 1589 proved to be no easy panacea. However, decades of shrewd and careful handling of Albret landed resources and revenues facilitated the slow recovery of their private fortunes by 1605. By 1610, debts were being

---

[102]See the domanial treasurers of Armagnac and Fézenzaguet, AD-PA, B1676 through B1969, as an example of recovery in one of the most afflicted and war-torn areas. See also chap. 1.

repaid, alienated lands were being reclaimed, and rents were rising. Careful management, shrewd planning, and the demographic expansion of the early seventeenth century helped compensate for the terrible years of war. In 1587, Henri had pledged his lands and his life "entirely ... to the advancement of the glory and service of God and the deliverance of the Church."[103] In the end, he regained his lands, but lost his life.

---

[103]*Lettres missives*, 2:314.

Conclusion

The 'crisis of the aristocracy,'" wrote Charles Jago in 1979, "is firmly entrenched as one of the major themes in early modern European history."[1] Its literary origins lie deep in the past, in the murmurings and grumblings of the sixteenth-century nobles themselves, who felt threatened by the apparent effectiveness of the bourgeoisie, the encroaching arm of the state, and the depredations of war and social unrest. Contemporary accounts of a "crisis" influenced liberal nineteenth-century historians who, pressed to explain the triumph of the middle class and the capitalist ethos in their own day, argued that the decline of the aristocracy was rooted in the political, social, and economic disorders of the sixteenth and seventeenth centuries. In the twentieth century, social historians from Bloch to Braudel to Le Roy Ladurie have accepted these views and have even given them added luster with their compelling descriptions of the ways in which the rural and urban rich eroded noble power in the countryside. Only recently have historians begun to reexamine the "crisis" thesis, to balance literary accounts of decline with quantitative analysis, and to recast the nobility in a much more favorable light.

This study has focused solely on the fortunes of one noble family over the course of the sixteenth century. As such it has obvious limitations which are complicated by the fact that the Albrets cannot be considered in any way representatives of the nobility at large. Related by blood and marriage to the royal house of France, they had almost unrivaled opportunities to attract the financial resources and privileges of the Crown in their direction. Henri d'Albret used his marriage to Marguerite d'Angoulême to attract royal monopolies and offices his way and managed in the process to double the family fortunes. Even during the lean years of the Religious Wars, when Valois kings reputedly alien-

---

[1]Jago, "The 'Crisis of the Aristocracy' in Seventeenth-Century Castille," 60.

ated some of their greatest servants by withdrawing the privileges of patronage and office, the Albrets continued to receive royal favors with greater regularity than historians have suggested previously. And by 1595, it was gifts from the Crown and grants of royal perquisites, such as the *parties casuelles*, which accounted for the tremendous boon to Catherine de Bourbon's coffers. It would be an error, however, to argue that Catherine alone benefited from Henri's generosity, and as a result brought some semblance of order to her personal fortunes. In order to restore peace and stability to his war-torn kingdom, Henri IV paid out massive war indemnities and bribes to Catholic and Protestant nobles alike, compensating them for their losses and allowing many of the greatest nobles in France to rebuild their fortunes with royal funds.

Beyond royal patronage, the Albrets also capitalized on the economic currents of the sixteenth century to increase their fortunes. The theory that the great nobility lacked the enterprising spirit or flexibility to adjust to changing economic conditions turns out to be too simplistic. Instead of remaining the passive victims of the emerging capitalist economy and the inflationary trends of the sixteenth century, the Albrets profited from them. They leased their lands and developed their forests, as we have seen, with scrupulous attention to the limits and demands of the marketplace. At almost every turn, the Albrets attempted to maximize their returns from their estates, even when it meant recourse to apparently conservative measures, such as the revival and pursuit of seigneurial dues. Where the depredations of troops and warfare made it difficult to collect rents in the last decades of the century, the Albrets pushed their agents to adopt temporary expedients to lure lessees back to the land, while remaining careful always to balance short-term gains against long-term profits. All of these measures are far from the picture of aristocratic decline and failure that historians once proposed.

That the Albrets managed to increase their fortunes—indeed more than quintuple their revenues from land and office over the course of the century—is only part of the story. More problematic for the general shape of their fortune than unstable incomes were the ever-increasing demands on their revenues. First and foremost was the need to create and maintain the sprawling network of loyal followers and clients, kith and kin, whose presence confirmed the Albrets' claims to power and prestige. The partisan politics of the period offered the Albrets new channels through which to expand their influence and clientage connections; their chosen position as leaders of the Huguenot struggle for recognition required it. But the necessary generosity of patronage also placed tremendous pressures on their own personal fortunes. The amounts of money that the Albrets doled out for salaries, pensions, gifts, and other perquisites of service spiraled out of control in the last third of the sixteenth century. Even the ordinary accounts of the household were affected by this program of patronage. The sheer number of people—officers, servants, clients, and *fidèles*—who fed themselves every day at the Albrets' expense had as great an impact on the household budget as the price instabilities of the period which have inspired so much research. Indeed, careful calculation of the impact of price increases on the general contours of the Albrets' fortunes suggests that historians have been overly concerned with price lists.

As Joseph Bergin and Daniel Dessert have recently reminded us, the Albrets' contemporaries warned about the dangers of spending too little as well as too much. The belief that "power required magnificence to achieve its objectives" inspired spending habits we might call profligate, conspicuous display. But just as the patronage system fulfilled an essential political purpose in early modern France, so did conspicuous expenditure. It would be absurd, of course, to argue that Jeanne d'Albret bought jewels, Henri de Navarre indulged his passion for horses, and Catherine de Bourbon had herself escorted about Paris in coaches pulled by a team of six horses purely out of ideological conviction and political necessity. But it would be equally exaggerated to argue that all such expenditures reflected the dissolute passions of the aristocracy. The tales of unrestrained aristocratic exuberance and prodigality with which foreign agents and ambassadors regaled their sovereigns and with which *parlementaires* scandalized the public cannot be taken as entirely accurate depictions or as meaningful explanations of the uses and abuses of wealth and power. The intimate interplay between wealth, display, and power complicates any effort to assess economic intent and achievement in early modern France.

Much of what we have seen suggests that the Albrets made a valiant, if not always successful, effort to balance the demands of convention with the limits of their treasuries. It is clear that they readily diverted funds spent on fripperies toward war-related expenses and reduced expenditures on luxuries when necessary. Only in the last two decades of the Religious Wars did it become nearly impossible to make such a careful choice between convention and prosperity. As the Religious Wars waxed and waned, their finances became inextricably tied to the Calvinist cause. Navarre's household was virtually indistinguishable from his military regime; his personal fortunes sustained the fight against the enemies of the Reformed religion. There is little evidence to suggest that the Albrets used the wars to line their pockets as their contemporaries on both sides claimed. Rather, troop movements disturbed their ability to rent land, often destroyed the forests they had so carefully cultivated, and forced them to alienate land and mortgage their valuables in search of money to fund the Calvinist cause. Nonetheless, within a decade of the uneasy peace after Navarre's ascent to the throne and his arrival in Paris, estate agents were busy buying back lost domains, restoring properties devastated by war, and refinancing the family treasuries. The boon that befell the family fortunes when Navarre became Henri IV of France only partly explains this remarkable recovery. The Albrets were not suddenly saved from ruin by the treasure stores of France; close attention to the management of their resources over the entire course of the century spared them from some of the worst effects of the Religious Wars. Moreover, the changing economic and demographic conditions favored recovery at large. The restoration of the family estates cannot be attributed to private intentions alone. The demand for land and office—the growing throng of men willing to lease land, buy property, and invest in office—helped rebuild the estates and fortunes of the house of Foix-Navarre-Albret in the seventeenth century.

– Glossary of Measurements –

arpent	The principal measurement for land throughout France, equal to roughly one and a half acres.
aune	The principal measure for textiles in France. From the sixteenth to the eighteenth century, it was usually described in states as the length of 3 *pieds*, 7 *pouces*, 8 *lignes*, or slightly over a meter in length.
barrique	A standard measure of capacity used principally for wine, and considered synonymous with the demi-pipe. Measures vary from 50 to 66 gallons through France.
boisseau	The most common measure for wheat along with the *mine* (which was equal to six *boisseaux*). In the markets of the southwest, the *boisseau* equaled between 29 and 40 liters.
canne	Standard measurement for textiles in southern France, equivalent to 1.85 meters.
conque	Measurement used for dry products in southwestern France, particularly Bayonne. Varied from 3 to 4 decaliters throughout the region.
muid	A standard measure for liquids and grains. Capacity usually taken as an average wagon load.
sac	Measure used for grains and other dry products. Weight varied per commodity.
setier	Standard measure for liquids and dry products. Wine bought in *barriques* was usually subdivided into 36 *setiers*. In Paris, a *setier* contained 7.45 liters of liquid, but the volume varied throughout France.

Source: Ronald E. Zupko, *French Weights and Measures before the Revolution: A dictionary of provincial and local units* (Bloomington: Indiana University Press, 1978).

Bibliography

Manuscript Sources

Paris:

Archives Nationales
  Série KK (Comptes royaux): 100–101, 145–47, 150, 154, 159, 278

Bibliothèque Mazarine: 2096

Bibliothèque Nationale
  Fonds français: 3928, 20464, 21451, 21532, 21534–38, 32785
  Collection Dupuy: 322
  Collection Clairambault: 360
  Dossiers bleus: 375 (Labaig, Laffémas), 610 (Selve)
  Pièces originales: 1988 (Monceau), 2669 (Secondat)
  Carrés d'Hozier: 436 (Mocet), 438 (Monceau), 579 (Selve)
  Lorraine: 347

Bibliothèque Saint–Germain: 848

Minutier Central des notaires de Paris: III, 433; XIX, 319; XXIV, 38; XXXVI, 23; XC, 121, 147, 159, 167, 169

Pau:

Archives Départementales
  Série A: 4
  Série B: 4–9, 13, 15–29, 32–36, 38, 42–45, 48bis, 51–53, 60–69, 72–87, 91, 93–95, 100–11, 113–18, 125–30, 134–40, 142–44, 146, 148–57, 159–60, 63, 165, 225, 226, 238, 242, 246, 250, 251, 252, 257, 268, 268bis, 269, 293, 498, 504, 506, 509–11, 514–18, 524, 531, 532, 536, 542, 546, 559–60, 965, 999–1009, 1013, 1023, 1025, 1072–76, 1101, 1353–56, 1412, 1414, 1415, 1417, 1420–35, 1468, 1472–78, 1480, 1486, 1491–93, 1500, 1512–18, 1522, 1525–30, 1564–68, 1581–88, 1591–95, 1598, 1600, 1602, 1604, 1606–8, 1610, 1614, 1621–22, 1626, 1636, 1642, 1651–52, 1657, 1668, 1672–74, 1676, 1685–86, 1710, 1714, 1827, 1832, 1843–52, 1854–57, 1862, 1885, 1891, 1896, 1898, 1918, 1934–35, 1937–40, 1949–50, 1955–67, 1969, 2038, 2070, 2077, 2078, 2082–84, 2100, 2104, 2107, 2115, 2135, 2175, 2187, 2230, 2254, 2274, 2277, 2289, 2318, 2324, 2341, 2350, 2374, 2381, 2388, 2390, 2424, 2461, 2464, 2470, 2485, 2527, 2530, 2545, 2549, 2561, 2785, 3023
  Série C: 681, 682, 684, 692

Série E: 122, 300, 378, 382, 387, 558, 561, 566, 586–588, 596, 1495, 1520, 1998, 2005, 2008–9, 2012
Série F: 2

Archives Municipales
DD7

Nancy:

Archives Départementales
Série B: 1266, 1282

Toulouse:

Archives Départementales
Série B: 107, 144, 152, 160, 162

Published Primary Sources

Académie des sciences morales et politiques. *Catalogue des actes de François Ier.* 10 vols. Paris, 1887–1908.

Bayaud, Pierre and Jacques de Laprade, eds. "Un don d'Henry de Navarre à Robert Rémy." *Bulletin des amis du Château de Pau* 14 (1962):4–6.

———. "Inventaire après décès des meubles de Catherine de Bourbon contenus en son Hôtel de la rue Deux-Écus à Paris." *Bulletin des amis du Château de Pau* 21 (1969):11–19.

———. "Inventaire des biens meubles qui ont esté trouvés la dans le Château de Royne de Navarre, duchesse d'Albret, à Nérac, après que le cappitaine Rouzés est parti d'icceluy où il est demeure en garnison avec certain nombre de soldat … (14 juillet 1569)." *Bulletin des amis du Château de Pau* 15 (1962):5–10.

———. "Inventaire des joyaux et pierres qui étaient au cabinet de Navarrenx et qui ont portés en la ville de Paris selon la commission adressé au Sr du Pont (1601–1602)." *Bulletin des amis du Château de Pau* 5 (1960):11–18, 21–24.

———. "Inventaire des meubles du Château de Pau estarés en mains de Orryas Bourguignon Me d'Ostel du Roy … le XXVIe jour de septembre 1533." *Bulletin des amis du Château de Pau* 10 (1961):10–15.

———. "Un inventaire du Château de Nérac (1555)." *Bulletin des amis du Château de Pau* 12 (1962):11–16.

———. "En marge des vieux inventaires:De la garderobe d'Henri de Navarre aux Etats de Béarn de 1581." *Bulletin des amis de Château de Pau* 14 (1962):1–4.

———. "Mémoire des meubles que Madame (Catherine de Bourbon) a prins dont fault déscharger le concierge (1593)." *Bulletin de la société des sciences, lettres et arts de Pau* 3 (1959):11–19.

Bèze, Théodore de. *Histoire ecclésiastique des églises réformées au royaume de France.* 4 vols. Ed. by G. Baum and E. Gunitz. Paris, 1883–89.

Berger, Xivrey de and J. Gaudet, eds. *Recueil des lettres missives de Henri IV.* 9 vols. Paris, 1872–83.

Bordenave, Nicholas de. *Histoire de Béarn et Navarre, 1517 à 1572.* Ed. P. Raymond. Paris, 1873.

Boulenger, Jacques and Abel Le Franc, eds. *Comptes de Louise de Savoie et Marguerite d'Angoulême.* Paris: Champion, 1905.

Cazaux, Yves, ed. *Mémoires et autres écrits de Marguerite de Valois: la reine Margot.* 1628. Reprint. Paris: Mercure de France, 1986.

Chalenay, Louis, ed. *Vie de Jacques Esprinard, rochelais et journal de ses voyages au XVIe siècle.* Paris: S.E.V.P.E.N., 1957.

Documents du Minutier Central des notaires de Paris: Inventaire après décès (1483–1547). Tome I. Paris: Archives Nationales, 1982.

Dussienx, L. ed. *Lettres intimes d'Henri IV.* Paris, 1876.

Ferrière-Percy, H. de La, ed. *Lettres de Catherine de Médicis.* 10 vols. Paris: Imprimerie Nationale, 1888–1909.

Fontanon, A. de, ed. *Les Edicts et ordonnances des rois de France.* 4 vols. Paris, 1611.

Génin, F., ed. *Lettres de Marguerite d'Angoulême.* 2 vols. Paris, 1841–42.

Griselle, E., ed. *Etat de la maison du roi Louis XIII.* Paris: Paul Catin, 1912.

James, M. E., ed. *The Estate Accounts of the Earls of Numberland, 1562–1637.* Durham: Surtees Society, 1955.

Jourda, P., ed. *Correspondence de Marguerite d'Angoulême.* Paris: Champion, 1930.

Lamothe, A. de. "Marché passé entre le prince de Condé et le Sieur Dubyé." *Revue des sociétés savantes* 7 (1874):495–505.

Laprade, Jacques de. "Un inventaire de joyaux de la reine Catherine de Navarre (1517)." *Gazette de Beaux Arts* (May 1962):4–14.

———, ed. "Inventaire de la vaisselle que Monseigneur (Alain d'Albret) veut engaiger ou vendre ... pour recouvrir argent pour le bailler à Roy de Navarre pour lui aider à recouvrir son royaume." *Bulletin de la société des sciences, lettres et arts de Pau* (1961):83–87.

———. "Un inventaire des bijoux, joyaux, bibelots précieux de Marguerite d'Angoulême (1535)." *Bulletin des amis du Château de Pau* 13 (1962):3–18.

———. "Inventaire des habillemens de la Royne envoyez à Sa Majesté et delivrez à Me Jehan Daulphin son tailleur et vallet de chambre ... le XXVIe d'avril 1572." *Bulletin des amis du Château de Pau* 9 (1961):10–16.

———. "Un inventaire des tentures et des meubles transportés de Pau à Nérac en 1578." *Bibliothèque d'humanisme et Renaissance: Travaux et documents* 24 (1962):413–430.

Larroque, Tamizey de. "Inventaire des meubles du château de Nérac en 1598." *Recueil des travaux de la société d'agriculture, sciences et arts d'Agen* 11 (1872):1–28.

Le Blant, Robert. "Marché de viande et poisson pour Catherine de Bourbon." *Bulletin philologie et historiques (jusqu'à 1610) du comité des travaux historiques et scientifiques (année 1968, Actes du 93 Congrès national des Sociétés savantes)* (1971):126–41.

L'Estoile, Pierre de. *Mémoires-journaux, 1574–1661*. 4 vols. Paris: Tallandier, 1882.

Leschassier, J. "La Maladie de la France." [1602] In *Oeuvres*. Paris, 1649.

Mesmes, H. de. *Mémoires inédits de Henri de Mesmes, Seigneur de Roissy et de Maldssise*. Ed. E. Frémy. Paris: E. LeRoux, 1886.

Molinier, E., and F. Mazerotte, eds. *Inventaire des meubles du château de Pau, 1561–1562*. Paris: Société des Bibliophiles français, 1892.

Monluc, Blaise de. *Military Mémoires*. Edited by Ian Roy. London: Longman, 1972.

Ritter, R., ed. *Lettres et poésies de Catherine de Bourbon*. Paris: Champion, 1927.

Rochambeau, Marquis de. *Lettres d'Antoine de Bourbon et de Jehanne d'Albret*. Société de l'histoire de France. Paris: Librairie Renouard, 1877.

Roelker, Nancy Lyman, trans. and ed. *The Paris of Henry of Navarre as Seen by Pierre de l'Estoile: Selections from His Mémoires-journaux*. Cambridge, Harvard University Press, 1958.

Tableaux des anciennes mesures du Departement des Basses-Pyrénées comparées aux mesures républicaines. Paris, An VII.

Books

Appaduri, Arjun, ed. *The Social Life of Things: Commodities in Cultural Perspective*. Cambridge: Cambridge University Press, 1986.

Ariès, Philippe, and Georges Duby, eds. *Histoire de la vie privée*, vol. 3, *De la Renaissance aux Lumières*. Ed. Roger Chartier. Paris: Seuil, 1986.

Babelon, Jean-Pierre. *Henri IV*. Paris: Fayard, 1982.

Baulant, Micheline, and Jean Meuvret, eds. *Prix des céréales extraits de la mercuriale de Paris*. 2 vols. Paris: S.E.V.P.E.N., 1960–1962.

Baumgartner, Frederic J. *Henry II: King of France, 1547–1559*. Durham, N.C.: Duke University Press, 1988.

Beck, Leonard N. *Two Loaf-Givers: or a tour through the gastronomic libraries of Katherine Golden Bitting and Elizabeth Robins Pennell*. Washington, D. C.: Library of Congress, 1984.

Beik, William. *Absolutism and Society in Seventeenth-Century France: State Power and Provincial Aristocracy in Languedoc*. Cambridge: Cambridge University Press, 1985.

Bergin, Joseph. *Cardinal Richelieu: Power and the Pursuit of Wealth*. New Haven and London: Yale University Press, 1985.

Bitton, Davis. *The French Nobility in Crisis, 1560–1640*. Stanford: Stanford University Press, 1969.

Blanchet, J. Andrien. *Histoire monétaire du Béarn*. Paris, 1893.

Bloch, J. R. *L'Anoblissement en France au temps de François Ier*. Paris: Librairie Félix Alcan, 1934.

Bohanan, Donna. *Old and New Nobility in Aix*. Baton Rouge: Louisiana State University Press, 1992.

Bois, Guy. *The Crisis of Feudalism: Economy and Society in Eastern Normandy c. 1300–1500*. Cambridge: Cambridge University Press, 1984.

Bonney, Richard. *The King's Debts: Finance and Politics in France, 1589–1661*. Oxford: Clarendon Press, 1981.

Boucher, Jacqueline. *Société et mentalités autour de Henri III*. 4 vols. Lille: Champion, 1981.

Bouchet, Jean, and Guillaume Paradin. *La Révolte de la Gabelle en Guyenne et à Bordeaux en 1548*. Bordeaux: Atelier Aldo Monvzio, 1981.

Boutier, Jean, Alain Dewerpe, and Daniel Nordman. *Un tour de France royal: le voyage de Charles IX (1564–1566)*. Paris: Aubier-Montaigne, 1984.

Boutruche, Robert, director. *Histoire de Bordeaux*. 8 vols. Bordeaux: Fédération historique du sudouest, 1966.

———. *La Crise d'une société: Seigneurs et paysans du Bordelais pendant les Guerres de cent ans*. Paris, 1947.

Braudel, Fernand. *La Méditerranée et le monde méditerranéen à l'époque de Philippe II*. Paris: Armand Colin, 1949.

Bryant, Lawrence. *The King and the City in the Parisian Royal Entry Ceremony: Politics, Ritual, and Art in the Renaissance*. Geneva: Librairie Droz, 1986.

Buisseret, David. *Henri IV*. London: G. Allen & Unwin, 1984.

Champion, Pierre Honoré Jean Baptiste. *Catherine de Médicis présente à Charles IX son royaume*. Paris: Grasset, 1937.

Charbonnier, Pierre. *Guillaume de Murol: Un petit seigneur auvergnat au début du XVe siècle*. Clermont-Ferrand: Institut d'études du Massif central, 1973.

Chartier, Roger, ed. *De la Renaissance aux Lumières*. Vol. 3. *Histoire de la vie privée*. Eds. Philippe Ariés and Georges Duby. Paris: Seuil, 1986.

———. *The Cultural Uses of Print in Early Modern France*. Trans. Lydia G. Cochrane. Princeton, N.J.: Princeton University Press, 1987.

Chartier, Roger, Marie-Madeleine Compère, and Dominique Julia. *L'Education en France du XVIe au XVIIIe siècle*. Paris: Société d'édition enseignement supérieur, 1976.

Clark, Peter, ed. *The European Crisis of the 1590s: Essays in Comparative History*. London and Boston: G. Allen & Unwin, 1985.

Constant, Jean-Marie. *Nobles et paysans en Beauce aux XVIe et XVIIe siècles*. Lille: Champion, 1981.

Dartigue-Peyrou, Charles. *Jeanne d'Albret et le Béarn d'après les délibérations des Etats et les registres du Conseil Souverain, 1555–1572.* Mont-de-Marsan: Imprimerie Jean-Lacoste, 1934.

———. *La Vicomté de Béarn sous le règne d'Henri II d'Albret (1517–1555).* Paris: Les Belles Lettres, 1934.

Denholm-Young, N. *Seignorial Administration in England.* London: Barnes & Noble, 1937.

De Ruble, A. *Antoine de Bourbon et Jeanne d'Albret.* 4 vols. Paris: A. Labitte, 1881–86.

———. *Jeanne d'Albret et la guerre civile.* Paris: E. Paul et Guillemin, 1897.

———. *Le Mariage de Jeanne d'Albret.* Paris: A. Labitte, 1877.

———. *Mémoires et poésies de Jeanne d'Albret.* Paris: E. Paul, Huart et Guillemin, 1893.

Desgraves, Louis. *Etudes sur l'imprimerie dans le sud-ouest de la France aux XVe, XVIe et XVIIe siècles.* Amsterdam: Erasmus, 1968.

———. *Les Haultin, 1571-1623.* Geneva: Librairie Droz, 1960.

Desplat, Christian. *Navarrenx.* Pau: Société des sciences, lettres et arts de Pau et du Béarn, 1981.

———. *Peuples et élites du Béarn: Histoire d'une culture provinciale du XIVe siècle à 1789.* Pau: Editions du Hedas, 1980.

Dessert, Daniel. *Argent pouvoir, et société au Grand Siècle.* Paris: Fayard, 1984.

Devèze, Michel. *La vie de la forêt française au XVIe siècle.* 2 vols. Paris: S.E.V.P.E.N., 1961.

Dewald, Jonathan. *The Formation of a Provinicial Nobility: The Magistrates of the Parlement of Rouen, 1499–1610.* Princeton: Princeton University Press, 1980.

———. *Pont-St-Pierre, 1398–1789: Lordship, Community, and Capitalism in Early Modern France.* Berkeley: University of California Press, 1987.

Dontenwill, Serge. *Une seigneurie sous l'ancien régime: L'Etoile en Brionnais du XVIe au XVIIIe siècle, 1578–1778.* Roanne: Horvath, 1973.

Doucet, Roger. *L'état des finances de 1523.* Paris: Imprimerie Nationale, 1923.

———. *Les Institutions de la France au XVIe siècle.* Paris: A. and J. Picard, 1948.

Durand, Yves, ed. *Hommage à Roland Mousnier: Clientèles et fidélités en Europe à l'époque moderne.* Paris: Presses Universitaires de France, 1981.

Elias, Norbert. *Court Society.* Trans. Edmund Jephcott. New York: Pantheon Books, Basil Blackwell, 1983.

Elliott, J. H. *Imperial Spain, 1469–1716.* New York: Penguin, 1963.

Fairchilds, Cissie. *Domestic Enemies: Servants and Their Masters in Old Regime France.* Baltimore: Johns Hopkins University Press, 1984.

Febvre, Lucien, and Henri-Jean Martin. *L'apparition du Livre.* Paris: Michel, 1958.

Ferrière-Percy, H. de La. *Marguerite d'Angoulême, ses livres de dépenses, 1540–1549.* Paris, 1862.

Flandrin, Jean-Louis. *Families in Former Times: Kinship, Household, and Sexuality.* Trans. by Richard Southern. Cambridge: Cambridge University Press, 1979.

Foisil, Madeleine. *Le Sire de Gouberville: Un gentilhomme normand au XVIe siècle.* Paris: Aubier-Montaigne, 1981.

Forissier, Marc. *Nérac, ville royale et huguenote.* Nérac: Editions Albret, 1942.

Forster, Robert. *The House of Saulx-Tavanes: Versailles and Burgundy, 1700–1830.* Baltimore and London: Johns Hopkins University Press, 1971.

———. *The Nobility of Toulouse in the Eighteenth Century.* Baltimore: Johns Hopkins University Press, 1960.

Frêche, Georges and Geneviève Frêche. *Les Prix des grains, des vins, et des légumes à Toulouse, 1468–1868.* Paris: Presses Universitaires de France, 1967.

Furet, François, and Jacques Ozouf. *Lire et écrire: l'alphabétisation des Français de Calvin à Jules Ferry.* 2 vols. Paris: Editions de Minuit, 1977.

Garrisson, Janine. *Henry IV.* Paris: Editions de Seuil, 1984.

Garrisson-Estèbe, Janine. *Protestants du Midi, 1559–1598.* Toulouse: Privat, 1980.

———. *Tocsin pour un massacre: La saison de Saint-Barthelemy.* Paris: Le Centurion, 1968.

Giesey, Ralph E. *Cérémonial et puissance souveraine, France, XVe–XVIIIe siècles.* Paris: Armand Colin, 1987.

———. *The Royal Funeral Ceremony in Renaissance France.* Geneva: Librairie Droz, 1961.

Gison, Stephane Claude. *Contribution à l'histoire de l'impôt sous l'ancien régime: La révolte de la gabelle en Guyenne.* Paris, 1906.

Goldsmith, James Lowth. *Les Salers et les d'Escorailles, seigneurs de Haute-Auvergne, 1500–1789.* Trans. Jacques Buttin. Paris: Clermont-Ferrand, 1984.

Gouron, Marcel. *L'Amirauté de Guienne.* Paris: Librairie du Recueil Sirey, 1938.

Graham, Victor E. and W. McAllister Johnson. *The Royal Tour of France by Charles IX and Catherine de Medici: Festivals and Entries, 1564–1566.* Toronto: University of Toronto Press, 1978.

Greengrass, Mark. *France in the Age of Henry IV: The Struggle for Stability.* London and New York: Longman, 1984.

Gutton, Jean-Pierre. *Domestiques et serviteurs dans la France de l'Ancien Régime.* Paris: Aubier-Montaigne, 1981.

Hanley, Sarah. *The "Lit de Justice" of the Kings of France: Constitutional Ideology in Legend, Ritual and Discourse.* Princeton: Princeton University Press, 1983.

Harding, Robert. *Anatomy of a Power Elite: The Provincial Governors of Early Modern France.* New Haven and London: Yale University Press, 1978.

———. "Provincial Governors of Early Modern France: Anatomy of a Power Elite." Ph.D. dissertation, Yale University, 1974.

Heal, Felicity. *Hospitality in Early Modern England*. New York and Oxford: Clarendon Press of OUP, 1990.

Holt, Mack P. *The Duke of Anjou and the Politique Struggle during the Wars of Religion*. Cambridge and New York: Cambridge University Press, 1986.

———. "A Prince of the Blood in the French Wars of Religion: François de Valois, Duke of Alençon and of Anjou, 1555–1584." Ph.D. dissertation, Emory University, 1982.

Huizinga, Johan. *The Waning of the Middle Ages: A Study of the Forms of Life, Thought, and Art in France and the Netherlands in the Fourteenth and Fifteenth Centuries*. New York: Anchor Books, 1954.

Hunt, David. *Parents and Children in History: The Psychology of Family Life in Early Modern France*. New York: Basic Books, 1970.

Huppert, Georges. *Les bourgeois gentilshommes: An Essay on the Definition of Elites in Renaissance France*. Chicago and London: University of Chicago Press, 1977.

Jacquart, Jean. *La Crise rurale en l'Ile-de-France, 1550–1670*. Paris: A. Colin, 1974.

Jouanna, Arlette. *Le Devoir de révolte: la noblesse française et la gestation de l'état moderne, 1559–1661*. Paris: Fayard, 1989.

Jourda, P. *Marguerite d'Angoulême*. 2 vols. Paris: Champion, 1930.

Jung, Marc René. *Hercule dans la littérature française du XVIe siècle*. Geneva: Librairie Droz, 1966.

Kalas, Robert John. "Wealth, Place, and Power in Sixteenth-Century France: The Rise of the Selve and Noailles Families." Ph.D. dissertation, New York University, 1982.

Kent, F. William. *Household and Lineage in Renaissance Florence*. Princeton, N.J.: Princeton University Press, 1977.

Kettering, Sharon. *Patrons, Brokers, and Clients in Seventeenth-Century France*. Oxford: Oxford University Press, 1986.

Knecht, R. J. *Francis I*. Cambridge: Cambridge University Press, 1982.

———. *Francis I and Absolute Monarchy*. London: Historical Association, 1969.

Labatut, Jean-Pierre. *Les Ducs et pairs de France au XVIIe siècle*. Paris: Presses Universitaires de France, 1972.

La Borde, J. B. *La maison Lareu, d'Asson: Une nourrice d'Henry IV*. Tarbes, 1923.

Lagrèze, G. Bascle de. *Le château de Pau*. Paris: Didier, 1854.

———. *La Navarre française*. 2 vols. Paris, 1881–82.

Le Roy Ladurie, Emmanuel. *Les paysans de Languedoc*. 2 vols. Paris: S.E.V.P.E.N., 1966.

Littleton, A. C. *Accounting Evolution to 1900*. New York: Russell & Russell, 1966.

Luchaire, A. *Alain le Grand, sire d'Albret*. Paris: Hachette, 1877.

Major, J. Russell. *Representative Government in Early Modern France*. New Haven and London: Yale University Press, 1980.

———. *Representative Institutions in Renaissance France, 1421–1559*. Madison: University of Wisconsin Press, 1960.

Mandrou, Robert. *Introduction to Modern France, 1500–1640: An Essay in Historical Psychology*. Trans. R. E. Hallmark. New York: Edward Arnold, 1975.

Maza, Sarah C. *Servants and Masters in Eighteenth-Century France: The Uses of Loyalty*. Princeton: Princeton University Press, 1983.

Mennell, Stephen. *All Manners of Food: Eating and Taste in England and France from the Middle Ages to the Present*. New York and Oxford: Basil Blackwell, 1985.

Mercer, Eric. *Furniture, 700–1700*. London: Weidenfeld and Nicholson: Meredith Press, 1969.

Merle, Louis. *La Métairie et l'évolution de la Gâtine poitevine de la fin du Moyen Age à la Révolution*. Paris: S.E.V.P.E.N., 1958.

Mertes, Kate. *The English Noble Household, 1250–1600: Good Governance and Politic Rule*. Oxford and New York: Basil Blackwell, 1988.

Meyer, Paul. *Inventaire des livres de Henri II, roi de Navarre*. Romania, 1885.

Mignet, F. *La Rivalité de François Ier et de Charles-Quint*. 2 vols. Paris: Didier, 1875.

Mousnier, Roland. *L'Assassinat d'Henri IV: 4 mai 1610*. Paris: Gallinard, 1964.

———. *Les Hiérarchies sociales de 1450 à nos jours*. Paris: Presses Universitaires de France, 1969.

———. *Les Institutions de la France sous la monarchie absolue, 1598–1789*. 2 vols. Paris: Presses Universitaires de France, 1974.

———. *La Vénalité des offices sous Henri IV et Louis XIII*. Paris: Presses Universitaires de France, 1948.

Neuschel, Kristin B. *Word of Honor: Intepreting Noble Culture in Sixteenth-Century France*. Ithaca and London: Cornell University Press, 1989.

Nunn, Joan. *Fashion in Costume, 1200–1980*. New York: Schocken Books, 1984.

Poumarède, J. *Les Successions dans le Sud-Quest de la France au Moyen Age*. Paris: Presses Universitaires de France, 1972.

Powis, Jonathan. *Aristocracy*. Oxford and New York: Basil Blackwell, 1984.

Raymond, P., ed. *Inventaire-sommaire des archives départementales antérieures à 1790: Basses-Pyrénées*, sér. B. Paris, 1863.

Ritter, Raymond. *Le Château de Pau*. Paris, 1919.

———. *Catherine de Bourbon, 1559–1604: la soeur d'Henri IV*. Paris: J. Touzot, 1985.

———. *La petite Tignonville*. Paris: Delmas, 1945.

Roelker, Nancy Lyman. *Queen of Navarre: Jeanne d'Albret, 1528–1572*. Cambridge: Harvard University Press, 1968.

Romier, Lucien. *Les Origines politiques des guerres de réligion*. 2 vols. Paris: Perrin et cie, 1913–14.

Salefranque, Pierre de. *Histoire de l'hérésie de Béarn*. Ed. V. Dubaret. Pau: Massignac, 1929.

Salmon, John H. M. *Society in Crisis: France in the Sixteenth Century*. New York: St. Martin's Press, 1975.

Sawyer, Jeffrey. *Printed Poison: Pamphlet Propaganda, Faction Politics, and the Public Sphere in Early Seventeenth-Century France*. Berkeley: University of California Press, 1990.

Schalk, Ellery. *From Valor to Pedigree: Ideas of Nobility in France in the Sixteenth and Seventeenth Centuries*. Princeton: Princeton University Press, 1986.

Schama, Simon. *The Embarrassment of Riches: An Interpretation of Dutch Culture in The Golden Age*. New York: Alfred A. Knopf, 1988.

Schnapper, B. *Les Rentes au XVIe siècle*. Paris: S.E.V.P.E.N., 1957.

Soulice, L. *Catalogue de la Bibliothèque de la ville de Pau, histoire locale*. Pau: Imprimerie Véronèse, 1886.

Stone, Lawrence. *The Crisis of the Aristocracy, 1558–1641*. Oxford: Oxford University Press, 1965.

———. *Family and Fortune: Studies in Aristocratic Finance in the Sixteenth and Seventeenth Centuries*. Oxford: Clarendon Press, 1973.

———, ed. *Schooling and Society: Studies in the History of Education*. Baltimore: Johns Hopkins University Press, 1976.

Strong, Roy. *The Renaissance Garden in England*. London: Thames and Hudson, 1979.

Tollemar, A., ed. *Un sire de Gouberville, gentilhomme campagnard au Cotentin de 1553 à 1564*. Paris: Mouton, 1972.

Vaissière, Pierre de. *Gentilshommes campagnards de l'ancien régime*. Paris: Perrin, 1905.

Véniel, Béatrice. "Les marchands pouvoyeurs au XVIe siècle." Thèse, troisième cycle, Université de Paris IV, 1972.

Weary, William. "Royal Policy and Patronage in Renaissance France: The Monarchy and the House of La Trémoille." Ph.D. dissertation, Yale University, 1972.

Wheaton, Barbara Ketcham. *Savoring the Past: The French Kitchen and Table from 1300 to 1789*. Philadelphia: University of Pennsylvania Press, 1983.

Williams, H. Noel. *Henry II: His Court and Times*. New York: Methuen & Co. Ltd., 1910.

Wiley, W. L. *The Gentlemen of Renaissance France*. Cambridge: Harvard University Press, 1954.

Wolfe, Martin. *The Fiscal System of Renaissance France*. New Haven and London: Yale University Press, 1972.

Wood, James B. *The Nobility of the Election of Bayeux, 1463–1666: Continuity through Change.* Princeton: Princeton University Press, 1980.

Zeller, Gaston, *Les Institutions de la France au XVIe siècle.* Paris: Presses Universitaires de France, 1948.

Zupko, Ronald E. *French Weights and Measures before the Revolution: A dictionary of provincial and local units.* Bloomington: Indiana University Press, 1978.

Articles

Aymard, Maurice. "Pour l'histoire de l'alimentation: quelques remarques de méthode." *Annales: Economies, Sociétés, Civilisations* 30 (1975): 431–44.

Baulant, Micheline. "Prix et salaires à Paris au XVIe siècle. Sources et résultats." *Annales: Economies, Sociétés, Civilisations* 5 (1976): 954–95.

Bennassar, Bartolomé, and Joseph Goy. "Contributions à l'histoire de la consommation alimentaire du XIVe au XIXe siècle." *Annales: Economies, Sociétés, Civilisations* 30 (1975): 402–30.

Billançois, François. "La Crise de la noblesse européene (1550–1650): Une mise au point." *Revue d'histoire moderne et contemporaine* 23 (1976): 258–77.

Boucher, Jacqueline. "L'évolution de la maison du roi des derniers Valois aux premiers Bourbons." *XVIIe siècle* 34 (1982): 359–79.

Charbonnier, Pierre. "La Consommation des seigneurs auvergnats du XVe au XVIIIe siècles." *Annales: Economies, Sociétés, Civilisations* 30 (1975): 465–77.

Clark, Peter. "The Ownership of Books in England, 1560–1640: The Example of Some Kentish Townfold," in *Schooling and Society: Studies in the History of Education.* Ed. Lawrence Stone. Baltimore: Johns Hopkins University, 1976, 95–111.

Collins, James. "The Economic Role of Women in Seventeenth-Century France." *French Historical Studies* 16 (1989): 436–70.

Communay, A. "Madeleine de la Fargue, nourrice du roi Henry IV." *Etudes historiques et réligieuses du diocèse de Bayonne* (1903): 99–110.

Constant, Jean-Marie. "Gestion et revenus d'un grand domaine aux XVIe et XVIIe siècles d'après les comptes de la baronnie d'Auneau." *Revue d'histoire économique et sociale* 50 (1972): 165–202.

Couperie, François. "Enquêtes ouvertes, marchés de pourvoirie." *Annales: Economies, Sociétés, Civilisations* 11 (1964): 467–78.

Crouzet, Denis. "Recherches sur la crise de l'aristocratie en France au XVIe siècle: les dettes de la maison de Nevers." *Histoire, Economie et Société* 1 (1982): 7–50.

Davies, Joan. "Family Service and Family Strategies: The Household of Henri, duc de Montmorency, ca. 1590–1610." *Bulletin of the Society for Renaissance Studies* 3 (1985): 27–43.

Desgraves, Louis. "Répertoire des ouvrages de contreverse entre catholiques et protestants dans le Sud-Ouest, entre 1584–1630." *Annales du Midi* 79 (1964):153–87.

Dessert, Daniel. "L'Affaire Fouquet." *L'Histoire* 32 (1981):39–60.

Flay, C. Barrière. "Le capitaine Jean Le Comte: gouverneur du château et de la ville de Foix, 1584–1600." *Bulletin périodique de la société ariègeoise* 5 (1906):1–95.

Frêche, Georges. "Cinquante et une mercuriales du massif central (XVIe–XIXe siècle)." *Annales du Midi* 141 (1979):29–52.

Goldthwaite, Richard. "The Florentine Palace as Domestic Architecture." *The American Historical Review* 77 (1972):977–1012.

Greengrass, Mark. "Noble Affinities in Early Modern France: The Case of Henri I de Montmorency, Constable of France." *European History Quarterly* 16 (1986):275–311.

———. "Property and Politics in Sixteenth-Century France: The Landed Fortune of Constable Anne de Montmorency." *French History* 2 (1988):371–98.

Holt, Mack P. "Patterns of *Clientèle* and Economic Opportunity at Court during the Wars of Religion: The Household of François Duke of Anjou." *French Historical Studies* 13 (1984):305–22.

Hourmat, Pierre. "Henri de Navarre, gouverneur de Guyenne et la ville de Bayonne, 1576–1584." in *Henri de Navarre et le royaume de France, 1572–1598*. Pau: Éditions Marrimpouey, 1984.

Jago, Charles. "The 'Crisis of the Aristocracy' in Seventeenth-Century Castile." *Past and Present* 84 (1979):60–90.

Kalas, Robert. "The Selve Family in Limousin: Members of a New Elite in Early Modern France." *The Sixteenth Century Journal* 18 (1987):147–72.

Kent, F. William. "Courtly and Family Interest in the Building of Filippo Strozzi's Palace." *Renaissance Quarterly* 30 (1977):311–23.

Kettering, Sharon. "Clientage during the French Wars of Religion." *The Sixteenth Century Journal* 22 (1989):221–39.

———. "Giftgiving and Patronage in Early Modern France." *French History* 2 (1988):221–39.

———. "Patronage and Kinship in Early Modern France." *French Historical Studies* 16 (1989):408–35.

———. "Patronage and Politics during the Fronde." *French Historical Studies* 14 (1986):409–41.

———. "The Patronage Power of Early Modern France Noblewomen." *The Historical Journal* 32 (1989):817–41.

Kleinman, Ruth. "Social Dynamics at the French Court: The Household of Ann of Austria." *French Historical Studies* 16 (1990):517–35.

Lachiver, Marcel. "Prix des grain à Paris et à Meulan dans la seconde moitié du XVIe siècle (1573–1586)." *Annales: Economies, Sociétés, Civilisations* 36 (1971):140–50.

Lefebvre, Pierre. "Aspects de la 'fidèlité' en France au XVIIe siècle: le cas des agents des Princes de Condé." *Revue historique* 25 (1973):59–106.

Love, Ronald S. "All the King's Horsemen: The Equestrian Army of Henry IV, 1585-1598." *The Sixteenth Century Journal* 22 (1991):511–33.

Major, J. Russell. "The Crown and the Aristocracy in Renaissance France." *American Historical Review* 69 (1964):631–45.

———. "Noble Income, Inflation, and the Wars of Religion in France." *American Historical Review* 86 (1981):21–48.

Massie, J.-F. "Pierre de Sarrabaig: Le fils de la nourrice du prince Henri III de Navarre, ascension sociale d'une famille béarnaise." *Bulletin de la société des amis du château de Pau* n.s. 72 (1927):67–80.

Mousnier, Roland. "Les Concepts d'ordres, d'états, et de fidélité et de monarchie absolue en France de la fin du XVe siècle à la fin du XVIIIe siècle." *Revue historique* 147 (April-June 1972):289–312.

Muchembled, Robert. "Famille, amour et mariage: mentalités et comportements des nobles artésiens a l'époque de Philippe II." *Révue historique* 247 (1972):247–55.

Nadar, Helen. "Noble Income in Sixteenth-Century Castile: The Case of the Marquises de Mondéjar, 1480–1580." *Economic History Review* 2nd ser., 30 (1977):411–28.

Neuschel, Kristin. "Noble Households in the Sixteenth Century: Material Settings and Human Communities." *French Historical Studies* 15 (1988):595–622.

———. "The Picard Nobility in the Sixteenth Century: Anatomy and Power." *Proceedings of the Western Society for French History* 9 (1981):42–49.

Ourliac, P. "La Famille pyrénéenne au Moyen Age." In *Recueil d'études sociales publiées à la mémoire de F. Le Play*. Paris, 1956:257–63.

Perroy, Edouard. "Social Mobility among the French Noblesse in the Later Middle Ages." *Past and Present* 20 (1962):25–38.

Phelps-Brown, E. and Hopkins, Sheila V. "Wages and Prices: Evidence for Population Pressure in the Sixteenth Century." *Economica*, n.s. 24 (1957):289–306.

Raymond, P. "Extraits des registres de la Chambre des comptes de Pau (XVI XVIII siècles) d'après un manuscript appartenant au baron de Laussat." *Bulletin de la société des sciences, lettres, et arts de Pau* 1 (1872):124–256.

———. "Notes extraites de comptes de Jeanne d'Albret et de ses enfants, 1556–1608." *Revue d'Aquitaine et du Languedoc*, 11(1866):129–84; 12(1867):162–80, 411–24.

Reynolds-Cornell, Régine. "Reflets d'une époque: Les devises ou emblèmes chrestiennes de Georgette de Montenay." *Bibliothèque d'Humanisme et Renaissance* 48 (1986):373–86.

Ritter, Raymond. "Les jardins du château de Pau sous Henri IV." *Pyrénées* 37(1957):41–45.

Robert, Jean. "Les grande et petite écuries d'Henri III de Navarre." *Bulletin de la société des amis du Château de Pau*, n.s. 88 (1983):3–39.

Saint-Jacob, P. de. "Mutations économiques et sociales dans les campagnes bourguignonnes à la fin du XVIe siècle." *Etudes rurales* 1 (1961–62):34–39.

Salmon, J. H. M. "Storm over the Noblesse." *Journal of Modern History* 53 (1985):242–57.

Schalk, Ellery. "Clientage, Elites and Absolutism in Seventeenth-Century France." *French Historical Studies* 14 (1986):442–46.

Somme, Monique. "L'alimentation quotidienne à la cour de Bourgogne au milieu du XVe siècle." *Bulletin philologie et historique (jusqu'à 1610) du comité des travaux historiques et scientifiques* (1972)104–17.

Vedel, Jacques. "La consommation alimentaire dans le haut-Languedoc aux XVIIe et XVIIIe siècles." *Annales: Economies, Sociétés, Civilisations* 30 (1975):478–90.

Index

Accounts
  dominial, 9
  extraordinary, 168, 195-96
  of chateau remodeling, 183
  ordinary
    and eating patterns, 138
    and food expenditures, 144
    and household expenditures, 127-28
  organization of, 183
  and war, 195
Admiralty of Guyenne, 53-54, 61-64
Albret family
  biographies, xiii
  Chateau of Pau, 179-82
  chateaux, 178-87
  clientage connections, 220
  commission of books and phamplets by, 191-92
  duchy of, 35-36
  estate management of, 43
  finances of, 77, 179, 183-85, 217-18, 221
  fortunes of, 219
  and Haute-Navarre, 47
  household
    provisioning of, 127
    size of, 86-92, 94-95
    gifts, wages, pensions, 106-14
  lands of, 30-31, 46-48, 59-61
  and purveyorship compensations, 150-52
  and Religious Wars, 77
  power of, 187-92
  relations with purveyors, 150
  rights of, 56
  spending patterns of, 166-93
  use of economic trends, 220
Albret, Henri d'
  admiral/governor of Guyenne, 51-52, 54-56
  biographies of, xiii-xiv
  and Chateau of Pau, 180, 182
  at court, 46-48
  courtship of, 49
  death of, 61
  dominial revenues of, 1-43
  and Francis I, 47-52, 182

Albret, Henri d' (*continued*)
  as governor, 50
  grants to, 48-49
  household of, 86-88
  income of, 1
  in Italy, 49
  landholdings, 1-3, 5-7, 50
  leasing policies of, 9
  libraries of, 189-90
  luxury expenditures of, 167-68
  marriage of, 3, 48-50
  and the military, 50, 54
  and Navarre, 59-60
  officeholding of, 51-54
  prison escape of, 49
  privileges for Henry II, 59
  purveyor contracts, 146
  revenue sources of, 48-49. *See also* Offices
Albret, Jeanne d', 19, 60-62
  and Bearn, 93
  at court, 59-60
  death and funeral of, 203
  excommunication of, 92
  and Ferdinand of Aragon, 46-47
  finances of, 19
  household of, 89-92, 118-21
    and Huguenot leanings, 90-93
    Catholics in, 93
    finances in, 94-95
    size, 86-89, 94-95
  Huguenot supporter, 64, 90-94, 194-95
  lands of, 20
  luxury expenditures, 168-72
  marriage negotiations, 171
  marriage, 59, 61
  and military offices, 61
  patroness, 60-61
  and printing press, 191-92
  and purveyorship contracts, 147
  receipts, 61
  and Religious Wars, 196-203
Alienation of land, 30-31
Angoulême, Marguerite d', 87-88
  and Aragón, 47
  at court, 59
  courtship, 49
  economic concerns 58

239

Angoulême, Marguerite d' (*continued*)
    humanist, 190-91
    landholdings of, 3
    letters of, 88
    libraries of, 190-91
    marriage of, 48-50
Architecture, 182
Armagnac
    lessees in, 29
    management of, 9, 20-25
    nobles in, 29
    rebates in, 33
    and Religious Wars, 20-25
Architecture, 182
Art, artifacts, 189, 191-93
Auctions
    difficulties, 27
    of forestland, 38-39
    of leases, 11, 14-16
Auzere, Adrian, 215

Bandits, 39
Banquets, 138-40
Bearn
    Albrets as protectors of, 9, 93-94
    Blaise de Monluc in, 62-63
    Catholic Church in, 199
    estates, 7, 48-49, 70, 183-85, 197
    Huguenots in, 93-94
    printing press in, 191-92
    in Religious Wars, 197-98
    rents, 9, 200
    revenues from, 2
    safety, 9
Beaulieu, Edict of, 205
Bedchambers, 81-82, 91, 97
Bellay, Catherine du, 90-91
Bellenger, Simon, 216
Benefits
    for merchant-purveyors, 152
    of service, 102-5, 107
Bergerac, Treaty of, 208
Bible stories, 187-88
Bible, French translations of, 192
Biographies, xiii
Books, 189-92
Bordeaux, Parlement of, 52-53
Bordenave, Nicholas, 191-92
Bourbon, Antoine de, 61-62, 198
Bourbon, Catherine de, 69-76

Bourbon, Catherine de, (*continued*)
    finances of, 69-71, 172-73, 176-78
    gifts to, 75
    and Henri de Navarre, 71
    household, 100-1
    letters, 75
    marriagef, 121
    patronagef, 100-101
    pension, 75
    sale of offices by, 74
    and Selve family, 120-21
    territories controlled by, 70
Bread, 134
Bureaucrats, 84

Calvinism, 19-20, 37, 193. *See also* Huguenots
Campagnie d'ordonnance, 48
Capitalism, xiv, xv
Castles. *See* Chateaux
Catholic Church, 93, 197, 199, 204-7
Caution, 27-28
Ceremony, 83, 164-65
Chabot, Philippe, 53-54
Chambre des comptes
    chateau rebuilding, 184
    establishment, 5-6
    loans, 27
    at Nerac, 6
    at Pau, 5-6, 66-67, 180
    procedures of, xvii, 6
    research in, xvi-xviii
Chateau of Pau, 179-85, 197
Chateaux, 18, 178-85, 197
Children, 115-16, 119-21, 124
Choisné, Etienne, 153-55
Choisné, Jean, 153-55
Churches. *See* Calvinism; Catholic Church; Huguenot
Church lands, 208-10
Client. *See* Household; Service
Clientage connections, 220
Clothing, 166-78
    gifts of, 117
    of Navarrese, 175-76
    and social status, 166-67, 175
Commodities, 164-93
Compensation. *See* Wages
Conspicuous consumption, 164-65
Contracts, 127, 144-48, 150-57, 162-63

Contributions, 214
Court, 46-48, 105-6, 126
Credit and spending, 165
Crests, 188
"Crisis of the aristocracy" thesis, 43, 167-68, 219, xiv, xvi
Culinary conceits, 129-34. *See also* Food

d'Albret. *See* Albret
d'Angoulême. *See* Angoulême
De Bourbon. *See* Bourbon
De Navarre. *See* Navarre
DaGusan, Jean, 17-18
Debt
    of Albret family, 170, 198
    of Catherine de Bourbon, 177-78
    of Henri de Navarre, 204, 216-18
    of Henri III, 67
    payment of , 67, 201-3, 216-18
    in Religious Wars, 198, 201-3
Delicacies, 129-39, 156-57
Diplomacy, 212-13
Dominial revenues, 1-43
Donations. *See* Gifts; Patronage
Donjon, Chateau of Pau, 182
Dowries, 171
Drink. *See under* Food

Economics, 8
    and feast and food, 139-40
    and hospitality, 125-26
    and morality, 145
    and noble fortunes, 220
    and purveyorship contracts, 145
    and service benefits, 83, 102-5, 107
Edict of Beaulieu, 205
Education, 115-16, 200
Elizabeth I, Queen of England, 200
Employees, 84-89, 101. *See also* Servants
England, 200
Environment. *See* Forests
Estate management, 43
Excommunication, 92
Exemptions, 56-57, 59, 116
Expenditures. *See* Finances

Faget, Bernard, 17
Fairs, 57
Family advancement, 102-3, 115, 118-21
Fast and feast days, 136-38

Feasts., 138-40
Ferdinand of Aragon, 46-47
Fezenzaguet
    leasing in, 17 25, 29
    management of, 9-10
    and Religious Wars, 25
Fidelite, 107, 112, 123
Finances. *See also* Economics
    of Jeanne d'Albret, 94-95
    aristocratic, 165
    of Catherine de Bourbon, 173, 177-76
    conservatism, 126
    contributions, 214
    of estates
        artifact purchases, 192-93
        Bearn, 48-49, 183-85, 197
        chateau improvements, 179, 183-85, 193
        conspicuous consumption, 165
        food, 139-44, 162-63
        hospitality, 125-26
        household accounts, 83-84, 93-94, 98
        stables, 173-74
    extraordinary accounts, 164-93, 195-96
    of Henri de Navarre, 98
    of Huguenots, 194-218
    income from church lands, 210
    and land, 208, 216-17, 221-22
    loans, 172, 176, 200
    luxury, 164-93
    and marriage, 171
    and purveyors, 148, 152
    in Religious Wars, 31-32, 66-68, 77, 99-101, 195-96, 204-9, 213-17, 221-22
    royal, 66-68, 165
    restabilization attempts, 210-11
    superintendent of, 83, 87
Fish, 136-38
Fleix, Treaty of, 97, 210, 212
Foix, Catherine of, 47
Foix, Odet de, 50
Foix-Navarre-Albret. *See* Albret; Navarre
Food. *See also* Contracts; Meat; Prices;
    consumption, 83, 124-63
    drink, 27, 134-35, 157-62
    and social rank, 124, 134, 138-40
    economics of, 136, 139-44
    expenditures on, 162-63

Food (*continued*)
    fruit, 135-36, 156-57
    game, wild, 134
    importance of, 124, 138-39
    meat, 128-34
    prices, 148-49
    and religion, 136-38
    vegetables, 135-36, 157
Forests, 36-42. *See also* Timber
Francis I
    death of, 58
    and Henri d'Albret, 47-52, 182
    imprisonment, 49
    grants from, 50-51, 56-57
Furniture, 187-89

Gardens, of Pau, 184-87
Gender, and commodities, 173, 193
Gifts, 76-77
    of food, 124
    royal, 44-77. *See also* Patronage
    to servants, 107, 112-14, 117
Governor of Guyenne, 50, 56, 205-6
Governorships, 50, 62
Grain, 35-36
Grande écurie, 174
Grants, 48-49
Gratifications, 48-49
Grazing rights, 38
Guise family, 86-87
Guyenne
    admiralty of, 51-54, 61-64
    governorship of, 50, 56, 205-6

Hapsburgs, 55, 59-60
Haute-Navarre, 47
Hautlin, Jerome, 192
Hautlin, Pierre, 192
Henri II
    death of, 91
    grants by, 59-60
    king of France, 58
    and nobility, 88
Henri III, 66-67
Henri (IV) de Navarre, 95-98, 204, 216-18
    and Catherine de Bourbon, 69-71, 75
    and Chateau of Pau, 184
    debt of, 204
    as governor, 62-64, 153-55, 205-6
    and horses, 174

Henri (IV) de Navarre (*continued*)
    household, 95-98, 175-76
    as king, 216
    and military, 96-99, 212-14
    and pensions, 68-69, 71, 75
    finances of, 23, 173, 176, 194-95, 206-8, 210-14
    gardens of, 185, 187
    grande écurie of, 174
    international relations, 212-13
    lands of, 23, 210-11
    marriage of, 95, 171, 203
    petite écurie of, 174
    political power of, 185, 187
    religion, 95-98, 175-76218
Horses, 173-74
Hospitality, 125-26. *See also* Finances; Food
Holy League, 197, 204-5
Households
    of Jeanne d'Albret, 86-95, 118-21
    banquets, 138-40'
    of Catherine de Bourbon, 100-101
    ceremony, 83
    clothing, 175-76
    finances, 94-95
    food, 83, 124-63
    of Henri de Navarre, 95-98
    maintenance, management, 69-70, 78-79, 98
    and military, 79-80, 96-99
    linens, 157
    patronage in, 78-80
    provisioning, 127
    public vs. private aspects, 98
    purveyors in, 152
    records, 127
    size, 84-92, 94-95
    structure, 81-85
    Valois royal, 85-86
    wages, 83, 87, 93-97, 106-11
Huart, Pierre, 150, 152
Huguenots. *See also* Calvinism; Protestants
    in Bearn, 94-95
    and Catherine de Bourbon, 100-101
    church of, 199-200
    finances during war, 172, 195-96, 216-17
    and Foix-Navarre-Albrets, 64-65

Huguenots (*continued*)
general assembly, 215-16
and Henri de Navarre, 95-96
indoctrination, 90-91
and Jeanne d'Albret, 92-93
propaganda of, 192
religious reform, 199
and Religious Wars, 89, 211-12
Humanists, 190-91

Italy, 49
Izernay, Sieur d', 58-59, 87

Jewelry, 167, 172, 200

Kinship networks, 220
Kitchens, 81, 83

L'Ile Jourdain. *See* Armagnac
La Fons, Louis, 155
La Rochelle, 65
Lands
  church, 208-10, 214
  lease and sale, 202, 208-11, 216-17
  maintenance, 18
  and marriage agreements, 49-50
  and Religious Wars, 19-29, 31, 221-22
Langey, Madame de, 90-91
Lawsuits, 153, 155
Leases. *See* Rents
Letters, 69-70, 75, 88
Letters patent, 64-65
Libraries, 189-90
Lit de Melusine, 188
Loans, 172, 176, 200
Luxuries, 164 93

Maitres d'hotel. *See* Officers
Male spending, 173
Manuscripts, 189-90
Markets, 128-29, 147-49, 157, 159
Marriages
  and landholdings, 3
  in Mouceau family, 120-21
  negotiations, 17-171
  of Henri d'Albret, 48-50
  of Henri de Navarre, 95
Medici, Catherine de, 91-93
Merchants,157, 159. *See also* purveyors
Mesmes, Henri de, 173, 202, 204

Military. *See also* Religious Wars
  of Antoine de Bourbon, 61
  campaigns, 141
  duties and privileges of, 51-52
  expenditures of, 183-84, 211-14
  finances, 217
  of Henri d'Albret, 50, 54
  of Henri de Navarre, 96-99
  and households, 79-80, 88-89
  of Jeanne d'Albret, 61
  maneuvers, 54, 55-56
  officers, 48-56, 114
  outfitting, 173
  and Religious Wars, 205, 207-8
  wages, 214, 216
Mills, 35-36
Mocet, Henri, 152
Moissens, Henri d'Albret, sieur de, 114
Monceau family. *See also* Selve; Thignonville
  Cecile, 119-21
  Jeanne, 119-21
  Lancelot de, 118-19
Monluc, Blaise de, 44, 62-63, 89
Monnyer, Adam, 146
Montmorency, Anne de, 45, 59

Navarre
  Catholic church in, 199
  finances, 112-14, 217-18
  forest management in, 37
  possession disputed, 46-48, 59-61
Navies, 54-55
Nevers, Louis de Gonzague, duc de, 45
Nobility
  aspirations of, 179-80
  economics of, 126, 220
  and food, 124
  in household service, 81-83, 86, 88, 96-100, 102-5
  leases, 28-29
  marriages, 171
  and purveyors, 150
  Protestant, 65-66, 194-95, 217
  and Religious Wars, 66
  wages, 104-5
Noblesse oblige, 125-2

Odet de Foix, 50

Offices; officers, 44-77, 98, 101-23. *See also* Military; Patronage
  governorships, 50-51
  household, 81-82, 96-98, 105-6, 143-44, 147
  pensions for, 112
  in Religious Wars, 99-101

Pamphlets, 192
Paintings, portrait, 189
Palaces and gardens, 178-87
Paris, 149, 151
Parlements, 52-53, 63-65
Parties casuelles, 74-75
Patriarchy, 189
Patronage, 44-80, 94-99, 220, 112
Pau, xvi, 179-87, 197
Payments. *See also* Pensions; Wages, salaries
  in kind, 35
  to purveyors, 152-55
  of salaries, 51
  to soldiers, 214
Peace of Amboise, 197
Peace of Saint Germain, 201
Pensions, 76-77. *See also* Wages, salaries
  for Albret, 60, 112-16
  economic benefits, 57
  of Navarrese, 70, 97
  in Religious Wars, 66-67
  royal, 57-58, 68-71, 75, 89
Perigord, 9, 15-16, 18, 31
Petite écurie, 174
Political power, 185, 187
Portrait paintings, 189
Pouvre, Henri, 191
Power, 164, 185, 187
Prices
  food, 145-47, 149, 156-57, 159
  and purveyorship contracts, 146, 148-50
Printing presses, 191-92
Prisons, 18
Privilege. *See also* Exemptions
  and *noblesse oblige*, 125
  royal, 56-57, 59
Propaganda, 192
Property, 16-18. *See also* Chateaux; Land
Protestants, 19-20, 37, 65-66, 192-93. *See also* Calvinism; Huguenots

Public management, 98
Purveyors, 129, 134
  advancement of, 152
  and Albret fortunes, 162-63
  contracts, 127, 144-48, 150-57, 162-63
  duties, 147
  and food prices, 149
  and household service, 152
  and nobility, 150
  lawsuits of, 153, 155
  leaving service, 156
  payment of, 152-55
  role of, 145-46
  wages, 151-52

Regin, Claude, 93-94
Religious artifacts, 191-93
Religious Wars, 63, 89-98, 194-218
  exemptions, 116
  and Fezenzaguet, 25
  and finances, 66, 77, 99-101, 141, 168-70, 197, 209-12, 221
  and households, 80
  and La Rochelle, 65
  and leasing policies, 17-29
  and nobles, 66
  and Pau, 66-67
  and purveyors, 155-57
  and rebates, 32-33
  and rents, 23, 197
  taxes, 209
Rentier landlordship, 3, 5
Rents, 9, 11, 14-29, 31
  as alternative to timber harvesting, 39, 42
  on Albret domains, 3, 5, 15-16
  income from land, 71
  periods of, 11
  rates, 9, 11, 17, 29-30
  receipts, 23
  short term, 11, 17-18, 20, 23, 27, 29
  and Religious Wars, 19-29, 31, 197
Revenues. *See also* Rents
  collection, 207
  extraordinary, 71, 74
  from land, 202
  from timber harvests, 36-42
  payments in kind, 35
  royal, 7-8

Rights, 6-7, 38, 53, 56. *See also* Exemptions; Privileges

Saint Bartholomew's Day Massacre, 22, 96, 203-4
Salaries, *See under* Wages and salaries
Salic law, 47
Saulx-Travanes, Gaspard de, 45
Seigneuries, 6-7, 52-53, 56
Self-sufficiency, 126
Selve family, 118-21. *See also* Monceau; Thignonville
Selve, Marguerite de, 118-21
Servants, 87, 94, 96, 101, 115-16, 118-21
Service. *See also* Offices, officers; Purveyors
   benefits, 102-5, 118-21
   at court, 105-7
   household, 79-80, 101-2, 115
Ships, 54-55
Silverplate, 169-72
Social rank, 138-40
Social status, 106-7, 166-67, 178-87
Social stratification, 81, 134, 138, 140
Spain, 55
Squires, 82-83
Stables, 81-83, 173-74
Status, 85, 106-7, 164-93
Subsistence, 126

Tailors, 175-76
Tapestries, 187-89
Taxes, 116, 209
Tenants, 39
Terride, Baron of, 20
Thignonville family. *See also* Selve; Monceau
   Jean, 119
   Lancelot de Monceau, 118-19
Timber. *See also* Forests harvesting of, 37-39, 42
   sale of, 36-42
   transport of, 38, 42
Transportation, 82-83
Traveling expenses, 212
Treaties,
   Bergerac, 208
   Fleix, 67, 97, 210, 212

Urban development, 179-80

Valois monarchy, 55, 91-92
Valois, Marguerite de, 67
Venier, Imbert, 31
Vineyards, 161
Vingles, Jonah de, 191

Wages and salaries, 8, 99, 114, 117
   for governorships, 50
   household, 83, 87, 93-97, 106-11
   military, 214, 216
   payment of, 51
War
   financing, 216
   fortunes of, 55
   treasurers and commissioners, 214-15
Wars of Religion. *See* Religious Wars
Wealth, uses of, 221
Weddings, aristocratic, 171. *See also* Marriage
Wine, 134-35, 157-62

Other Titles Available in
SIXTEENTH CENTURY ESSAYS & STUDIES SERIES
NMSU LB 115 · Kirksville MO 63501-0828

Ardolino, Frank. **Kyd's Spanish Tragedy.** Vol. 29 of Sixteenth Century Essays & Studies. ISBN 0-940474-31-X., ... cloth $35.00

Brink, Jean R., Allison P. Coudert, Maryanne C. Horowitz, eds. **The Politics of Gender in Early Modern Europe.** Vol 12 of Sixteenth Century Essays & Studies, 168 pp. Index. ISBN 0-940474-12-3 .... cloth $35.00

Brink, Jean R., ed. **Privileging Gender in Early Modern England.** Vol. 23 of Sixteenth Century Essays & Studies, 250 pp. incl. Index. ISBN 0-940474-24-8... cloth $35.00

Brunelle, Gayle. **The New World Merchants of Rouen: 1559-1630.** Vol. 16 of Sixteenth Century Essays & Studies, 190 pp. Illus., Index. Bib. ISBN 0-940474-17-4 .... cloth $35.00

Burnett, Amy. **The Yoke of Christ: Martin Bucer and Christian Discipline.** Vol. 26 of Sixteenth Century Essays & Studies, approx. 250 pp. Index. Vol. 26 of Sixteenth Century Essays & Studies. ISBN 0-940474-28-X. .... cloth $35.00

Christensen, Carl C. **Princes and Propaganda: Electoral Saxon Art of the Reformation.** Vol. 20 of Sixteenth Century Essays & Studies, 149 pp. Index ISBN 0-940474-21-2. .... cloth $35.00

Coats, Catherine Randall. **Subverting the System: D'Aubigne and Calvinism.** Vol. 14 of Sixteenth Century Essays & Studies, 136 pp. Index. ISBN 0-940474-03-4... cloth $35.00

Dick, John A.R. & Anne Richardson, **Tyndale and the Law.** Vol. 25 of Sixteenth Century Essays & Studies, 114 pp. Index. ISBN 0-940474-24-8... cloth $35.00

Donnelly, John Patrick, Robert M. Kingdon, Marvin W. Anderson, eds. **A Bibliography of the Works of Peter Martyr Vermigli.** Vol. 13 of Sixteenth Century Essays & Studies, 136 pp. Index. ISBN 0-940474-14-X .... cloth $50.00

Fix, Andrew C., and Susan C. Karant-Nunn. **Germania Illustrata: Essays On Early Modern Germany Presented To Gerald Strauss.** Vol. 18 of Sixteenth Century Essays & Studies, 167 pp. Index. Bib. ISBN 0-940474-19-0 .... cloth $35.00

Friedman, Jerome. **Regnum, Religio et Ratio: Essays Presented to Robert M. Kingdon.** Vol 8 of Sixteenth Century Essays & Studies, 186 pp. Bib. ISBN 0-940474-08-5... Pbk only. $25.00

Geiger, Gail. **Filippino Lippi's Carafa Chapel: Renaissance Art in Rome.** Vol. 5 of Sixteenth Century Essays & Studies, 240 pp. 80 b&w Illus., Index. Bib. ISBN 0-940474-05-0 .... cloth $50.00

Graham, W. Fred, ed. **Later Calvinism: International Perspectives.** Vol. 22 of Sixteenth Century Essays & Studies, 564 pp. Index. ISBN 0-940474-23-0.. cloth $45.00

Hillerbrand, Hans J., ed. **Radical Tendencies in the Reformation: Divergent Perspectives.** Vol. 9 of Sixteenth Century Essays & Studies, 210 pp. Index. Bib. ISBN 0-940474-09-3.. Pbk $25.00

Lindberg, Carter, ed. **Piety, Politics, And Ethics: Reformation Studies in Honor Of George W. Forell.** Vol. 3 of Sixteenth Century Essays & Studies, 210 pp. Index. Bib. ISBN 0-940474-03-4 .... cloth $35.00

Loeschen, John R. **The Divine Community: Trinity, Church, and Ethics in Reformation Theologies.** Vol. 1 of Sixteenth Century Texts and Studies, 238 pp. Index., Bib. ISBN 0-940474-01-8.. cloth $35.00

Martin, A. Lynn. **Jesuit Accounts of Epidemic Disease in the Sixteenth Century.** Vol. 28 of Sixteenth Century Essays & Studies. ISBN 0-940474-30-1... cloth $35.00

Ryding, Erik S. **In Harmony Framed: Musical Humanism, Thomas Campion, And The Two Daniels.** Vol. 21 of Sixteenth Century Essays & Studies, 136 pp. Index ISBN 0-940474-22-0 .... cloth $35.00

Safley, Thomas Max. **Let No Man Put Asunder: The Control of Marriage in the German Southwest 1550-1600.** Vol. 2 of Sixteenth Century Essays & Studies, 210 pp. Index. ISBN 0-940474-02-6... cloth $35.00

Schilling, Heinz. **Civic Calvinism in Northwestern Germany and the Netherlands, 16th-19th Centuries.** Vol. 17 of Sixteenth Century Essays & Studies, 167 pp. Index. Bib. ISBN 0-940474-18-2 .... cloth $35.00

Schnucker, R.V., ed. **Calviniana: Ideas and Influence of Jean Calvin.** Vol. 10 of Sixteenth Century Essays & Studies 288 pp. Index. Bib. ISBN 0-940474-10-7.. cloth $35.00

Sessions, Kyle, and Philip Bebb, eds. **Pietas Et Societas: New Trends in Reformation Social History.** Vol. 4 of Sixteenth Century Essays & Studies, 240 pp. Index. ISBN 0-940474-04-0 .... cloth $35.00

Smeeton, Donald. **Lollard Themes in the Reformation Theology of William Tyndale.** Vol. 6 of Sixteenth Century Essays & Studies, 240 pp. Index. Bib. ISBN 0-940474-06-9... cloth $35.00

Spalding, James C., ed. **The Reformation of the Ecclesiastical Laws of England, 1552.** Vol. 19 of Sixteenth Century Essays & Studies, 274 pp. Illus. Index. ISBN 0-940474-20-4... cloth $35.00

Thorp, Malcolm R., and Arthur J. Slavin, eds. **Politics, Religion and Diplomacy in Early Modern Europe: Essays in Honor of DeLamar Jensen.** Vol. 27 of Sixteenth Century Essays & Studies. ISBN 0-940474-29-8. .... cloth $35.00

Tracy, James. **Luther and the Modern State of Germany.** Vol. 7of Sixteenth Century Essays & Studies, 108 pp. Index. ISBN 0-940474-07-7. .... cloth $35.00

Vermigli, Peter Martyr. **Early Writings: Creed, Scripture, Church,** ed. Joseph C. McLelland; tr. Mariano Di Gangi; intro. Philip McNair. *The Peter Martyr Library no. 1*. Vol.30 of Sixteenth Century Essays & Studies. ISBN 0-940474-32-8. .... cloth $35.00

Vermigli, Peter Martyr. **A Dialogue on the Two Natures in Christ,** ed. and tr. John Patrick Donnelly, S.J. *The Peter Martyr Library no. 2*. Vol. 31 of Sixteenth Century Essays & Studies. ISBN 0-940474-33-6. .... cloth $35.00

Williams, George Huntston. **The Radical Reformation. 3rd ed.**, enlarged and revised. Vol. 15 of Sixteenth Century Essays & Studies, 1,513 pp., updated Bib., 5 indexes ISBN 0-940474-15-9. .... cloth $125.00

HJ
1079
.E95
1993

38240s